FREAKS

FREAKS

Myths and Images of the Secret Self

LESLIE FIEDLER

ANCHOR BOOKS
DOUBLEDAY

New York   London   Toronto   Sydney   Auckland

An Anchor Book

PUBLISHED BY DOUBLEDAY

a division of Bantam Doubleday Dell Publishing Group, Inc.
1540 Broadway, New York, New York 10036

ANCHOR BOOKS, DOUBLEDAY, and the portrayal of an anchor
are trademarks of Doubleday, a division of Bantam Doubleday Dell
Publishing Group, Inc.

Freaks was originally published in hardcover by Simon & Schuster
in 1978. The Anchor Books edition is published
by arrangement with the author.

Library of Congress Cataloging-in-Publication Data

Fiedler, Leslie A.
  Freaks: myths and images of the secret self/Leslie Fiedler.
1st Anchor Books ed.
  p.   cm.
Originally published: New York : Simon and Schuster, © 1978.
Includes bibliographical references (p.   ) and index.
1. Abnormalities, Human—Social aspects. I. Title.
GT6730.F53   1993
573.8—dc20   93-6479
CIP

Acknowledgments

This book is a meditation, a history, and a continuing dialogue with the world. For the first, I needed stretches of time long and untroubled enough to permit exploration of my inner self; for the second, access to documents and pictures dated from 2800 B.C. to the administration of Jimmy Carter; and for the last, opportunities to address groups interested enough to hear me out and committed enough to respond helpfully.

Such time was provided me by the State University of New York at Buffalo, which freed me from teaching obligations for three summers, and by the Program in Twentieth Century Studies at the University of Wisconsin–Milwaukee, which granted me a three months' Fellowship in 1974. But especially I owe thanks to my wife, Sally Andersen Fiedler, who not merely endured but blessed my excursions into the dark places of my own psyche, and was there waiting when I returned.

The individual books, myths, manuscripts, paintings, and prints on which I have drawn for this illustrated mytho-history are specified in the text and bibliography. What remains to be said is that I would never have found them at all without the aid of the staffs of the Erie County Library, the Public Library of the City of New York, the libraries of my

7

own university, the University of Toronto, the University of Wisconsin–Milwaukee, and Marquette University. I am also indebted to the diligence and ingenuity of my research assistants, Larry Yep, John Hanson, Gary Gabriel, Nancy Walczyk, Paul Kugler, and Diana George.

It is hard to thank adequately those who have responded to my sometimes irreverent and eccentric interpretations of the meanings of Freaks and their relationship to the secret self, because they have been so many that they blur in my memory into a faceless, but not voiceless, audience. No one I have ever talked to about this study has failed to offer in return anecdotes, ranging from pertinent to irrelevant, opinions, ranging from sympathetic to hostile, or information, ranging from reliable to thoroughly undependable. I am particularly grateful to the Kyoto Seminars on American Literature and Professor Nobunao Matsuyama, who organized them; to the Tudor and Stuart Club at Johns Hopkins University and Frances Ferguson, who invited me to address them; to the Department of Psycho-Endocrinology at the Children's Hospital of Buffalo; to the Society for Arts, Religion, and Contemporary Culture and Betty Meyer, who arranged my appearance before them; to the Semester of the Arts at UCLA and Peter Clothier, its organizer. They provided me with much-needed occasions to talk out and rethink at various stages along the way what remained for so long a work-in-progress.

Finally, I want to express my gratitude to Tom Collins, in conversations with whom the idea for this book first emerged; to Anthony Burgess, who urged me to carry on with it when I was reluctant to begin; and to Joyce Troy, my secretary, who bore patiently with my visions and revisions, false starts and second thoughts, emendations and excisions—helping to establish order in what threatened continually to end in chaos.

LESLIE A. FIEDLER

Buffalo, New York
May, 1977

To my brother who has no brother
To all my brothers who have no brother

Contents

Introductory

We live at a moment when the name "Freaks" is being rejected by the kinds of physiologically deviant humans to whom it has traditionally been applied: Giants, Dwarfs, Siamese Twins, Hermaphrodites, Fat Ladies, and Living Skeletons. To them it seems a badge of shame, a reminder of their long exclusion and exploitation by other humans, who defining them thus have by the same token defined themselves as "normal." Like all demands on the part of the stigmatized for a change of name, this development expresses itself as a kind of politics. But it remains a politics without a program, unlike the analogous efforts of those once called "niggers" and "colored" to rebaptize themselves first "Negroes," then "blacks"; or of former "ladies" and "girls" to become "women"; or of ex-"faggots" and "dykes" to transform themselves into "gays."

There is, that is to say, no agreement among those traditionally called Freaks about what they would like for programatic reasons to be called now; only a resolve that it be *something else*. Those who

The Monster of Cracow. Sixteenth-century print.

still earn their living by exhibiting themselves in side shows apparently prefer to be known as "entertainers" and "performers," like
tightrope walkers and clowns. But larger numbers of "strange people" do not want to be considered performers or indeed anything
special or unique. They strive, therefore, to "pass," i.e., to become
assimilated into the world of "normals," either by means of chemotherapy, like certain Dwarfs and Giants, or difficult and dangerous
operations, like some Hermaphrodites or joined twins.

Meanwhile, the name Freak which they have abandoned is being claimed as an honorific title by the kind of physiologically normal but dissident young people who use hallucinogenic drugs and
are otherwise known as "hippies," "longhairs," and "heads." Such
young people—in an attempt perhaps to make clear that they have
chosen rather than merely endured their status as Freaks—speak of
"freaking out," and, indeed, urge others to emulate them by means
of drugs, music, diet, or the excitement of gathering in crowds. "Join
the United Mutations," reads the legend on the sleeve of the first
album of the Mothers of Invention. And such slogans suggest—as the
discontent of circus performers does not—that something has been
happening recently in the relations between Freaks and non-Freaks,

implying just such a radical alteration of consciousness as underlies the politics of black power or neo-feminism or gay liberation.

Some Freaks have been trying to shuffle off their invidious name for a long time—ever since January 6, 1898, at least, when, according to a publicity release used as advance ballyhoo throughout Europe, the members of a traveling troupe from the Barnum and Bailey Circus held a protest meeting in London. Called by Miss Annie Jones, the Bearded Lady, it was chaired by Sol Stone, the Human Adding Machine, and its minutes recorded with his feet by the Armless Wonder. But like most of their successors, they, too, were at a loss for an appropriate substitute for the "opprobious" name under which they had long suffered, and appealed to the public for possible alternatives. Some three hundred names were suggested, but none pleased the protesters, until the Bishop of Winchester urged that they be billed as "prodigies," and with near unanimity they concurred. In America, however, that name never caught on; and in any case, the whole affair may have been dreamed up by the Barnum and Bailey public relations staff. Yet this, too, would have been appropriate, since what Barnum called "humbug" is as intrinsic to "Freak shows" as pathos and wonder.

In his *Autobiography*, Barnum refers to human anomalies not as Freaks but as "curiosities," lumping them with other attractions which may seem to us of a quite different kind: the "Woolly Horse," for instance, a "genuine Mermaid," "Jumbo the Elephant," and Joice Heth, a black woman who claimed to be 161 years old and to have been the slave of George Washington's father. "Curiosity" is a typically Victorian word, memorialized in the title of Charles Dickens' most Freak-obsessed work, *The Old Curiosity Shop,* and reminding us that in that era the interest in Freaks had reached a high point. Indeed, Queen Victoria was quite as curious about Barnum's curious charges as was her favorite novelist. And in America the situation was much the same, with such eminent transatlantic Victorians as Abraham Lincoln and Mark Twain proving equally ready to take time off from a war or a book to receive and swap jokes with a Dwarf.

By the twentieth century, however, the reigning figures in politics had begun to break off the dialogue with Freaks which had lasted for millennia, surviving the fall of ancient empires, the emergence of modern nation-states, the invention of gunpowder and printing, and the extension of literacy and suffrage. Indeed, Victorian sentimentality and morality had already begun to undercut the possibility of continuing such a dialogue, even as Victorian curiosity was bringing it to a climax. And that surviving by-product of the era, Socialism, was eventually to spell its doom. The exhibition of Freaks was, for instance, forbidden by law in Hitler's "National Socialist" Germany, and is still prohibited in the Soviet Union.

Indeed, a sense of the Freak show as an unworthy survival of an unjust past spread everywhere in the early twentieth century, so that for a while it seemed as if those of us now living might well represent the last generations whose imaginations would be shaped by a live confrontation with nightmare distortions of the human body. But there has been a revival of the side show at carnivals and fairs which threatens to reverse the trend; though in the end it may prove merely a nostalgic and foredoomed effort, human curiosities having, for most Americans, passed inevitably from the platform and the pit to the screen, flesh becoming shadow. But the loss of the old confrontation in the flesh implies a trauma as irreparable as the one caused by the passage of the dialogue between King and Fool from the court to the stage: a trauma which is, in fact, a chief occasion for this book.

Perhaps, then, the very word "Freak" is as obsolescent as the Freak show itself, and I should be searching for some other term, less tarnished and offensive. God knows, there are plenty: oddities, malformations, abnormalities, anomalies, mutants, mistakes of nature, monsters, monstrosities, sports, "strange people," "very special people," and *phenomènes*. "Monsters" and "monstrosities" were until very recently the standard terms used in medical treatises on the subject, and "monster" is the oldest word in our tongue for human anomalies. But a quite recent book by Frederick Drimmer, who finds even "strange people" too reminiscent of outmoded prejudice, notes piously that "people may be different from everyone else but they don't enjoy being called monsters"; and goes on to observe that though "in circus sideshows they may jokingly refer to each other as 'freaks' . . . they don't relish it when anyone else applies that epithet to them." "Very special people" is his preferred alternative—a term so unfamiliar that he feels obliged to gloss it in his subtitle as

"Human Oddities." R. Toole Scott, on the other hand, though similarly motivated, uses as a heading in his splendid bibliography *Circus and Allied Arts* the French term *phenomènes*, presumably because no English word seems to him neutral or inoffensive enough.

For me, however, such euphemisms lack the resonance necessary to represent the sense of quasi-religious awe which we experience first and most strongly as children: face to face with fellow humans more marginal than the poorest sharecroppers or black convicts on a Mississippi chain gang. No wonder that novelists and poets have sought to evoke that aboriginal shudder—Carson McCullers, for instance, describing the feelings of Frankie, girl heroine of *The Member of the Wedding*, before the Half Man/Half Woman, "a morphodite and a miracle of science"; or Carl Sandburg, his own child-self confronting "a sad little shrimp of a Dwarf" and "Jo-Jo, the dogfaced boy, born 40 miles from land and 40 miles from sea."

"She was afraid of all the freaks," Mrs. McCullers says of Frankie, "for it seemed to her that they had looked at her in a secret way and tried to connect their eyes with hers, as though to say: *we know you. We are you!*" But Sandburg's key word is "bashful" rather than "afraid." "When you're bashful," he writes, "you have that feeling of eyes following you and boring through you. And there were at the sideshow these people, the freaks—and the business, the work of each one of them was to be looked at . . ." To

Dog-headed Man and Goose-headed Man. From *Monstrorum historia*, by Ulisse Aldrovandi (1642).

him, Freaks represent an absolute other, "mistakes God made," forced to exhibit themselves until death delivers them; whereas Carson McCullers finds them revelations of the secret self.

Yet both render the experience as a visual one, though of a very special kind—a kind which Marshall McLuhan defines in the course of attempting to define the mask. "The mask," he writes, "like the sideshow freak is not so much pictorial as participatory in its sensory appeal." But "participatory" suggests a link with the peep show and the blue movie as well: the sense of watching, unwilling but enthralled, the exposed obscenity of the self or the other. And only "Freaks," therefore, seems a dirty enough word to render the child's sense before the morphodite or Dog-faced Boy of seeing the final forbidden mystery: an experience repeated in adolescence when the cooch dancer removes her G-string and he glimpses for the first time what (as the talkers say) "you'll never see at home." And the sense of the pornographic implicit in all Freak shows is doubled in what has been called more grandly "The Show of Life," though carnival people refer to it as "pickled punks": a display of preserved fetuses in jars. This ultimate invasion of privacy, revealing what travesties of the human form even the normal among us are at two, three, or four months after conception, has sometimes outdrawn, though in the long run it has, of course, failed to replace, shows at which full-grown oddities have looked down out of living eyes to meet the living eyes of the audience.

That a much newer form of popular drama, the cinema, would attempt to capture and preserve the horror of such encounters was inevitable enough, though it was not until 1933 that Todd Browning (who a year before had brought *Dracula* to the screen) attempted to do so in a movie called quite simply *Freaks*. This book, in fact, represents a belated tribute to that great director and his truly astonishing film, since I can no longer disentangle my earliest memories of actual Freaks—encountered, I suppose, somewhere back of the boardwalk at Coney Island, the smell of fresh buttered corn and frying hot dogs in my nostrils—from the nightmare images he evoked. In the midst of the Great Depression, he gathered from circuses and side shows, carnivals and dime museums, scores of human anomalies to act out for an already terrified audience a terrifying fable of their condition and ours. And his movie has played and replayed itself in my troubled head so often that merely recalling it, I call up again not only its images, but the response of my then fifteen-year-old self.

That, despite its effect on me, it failed at the box office is hardly surprising, for it was bound to turn off an audience which thought of itself as already having troubles enough; and which, in any case, had no taste for either the kinky erotic thrills it boasted of giving or the quasi-religious awe it did not confess it evoked. We all firmly believed in those days that "science," which had failed to deliver us from poverty but was already providing us with weapons for the next Great War, had desacralized human monsters forever. Three decades later, however, Browning's *Freaks* was to be revived for a new audience capable of recognizing in the Bearded Lady, the Human Caterpillar, and the Dancing Pinhead, Slitzie, the last creatures capable of providing the thrill our forebears felt in the presence of an equivocal and sacred unity we have since learned to secularize and divide.

Moreover, within the last two or three years, it has been used as the prototype for an updated version called *Mutations,* in which a cast of natural monstrosities is supplemented by others produced in the laboratory—as if to make clear our current sense that science creates new terrors rather than neutralizes old ones. In the end, however, the manufactured Freaks of *Mutations,* in part because they are palpable and not very convincing illusions, move the audience to snicker in embarrassment and condescension instead of crying out in terror. Yet beneath the laughter some dim sense of the *sacer* survives, since the ridiculous and the monstrous are not really incompatible. Indeed, the very word "Freak" is an abbreviation for "freak of nature," a translation of the Latin *lusus naturae,* a term implying that a two-headed child or a Hermaphrodite is ludicrous as well as anomalous.

Even now, many normals laugh not just in the presence of unconvincing Freaks but of any Freaks at all, making traditional jokes at their expense. Some, like the weary quip "How's the air up there?" shouted at Giants by backwoods wits, can never have been very funny; while others, like the observation that marrying female Siamese Twins is at least a way of getting two wives and only a single mother-in-law, can still extract a sexist grin.

Not only the words of anonymous jokesters, however, testify to the amusement men have always found in Freaks. As early as the second century A.D., Pliny wrote smugly that "formerly hermaphrodites were regarded as ominous signs, but today they seem merely entertainments." And in the court records of seventeenth-century Spain, Dwarfs are referred to, along with Negroes and Fools, as *gente de placer*, amusements for the bored aristocracy. We know that in the midst of the Civil War, Abraham Lincoln suggested his cabinet members take time out to swap jests with a Midget called Commodore Nutt, an episode dwelt on in a recent TV show about his life. And only a little earlier, Queen Victoria and her entire retinue had bellowed at the comical encounter of her pet poodle and Nutt's fellow Dwarf and friend, General Tom Thumb. But the laughter of "normals" must always have been ambiguous and defensive, like the titters of a contemporary undergraduate audience at a horror show. If Freaks are, indeed, a joke played by a "Nature" as bored and as heartless as any small boy or feudal lordling, the joke is on *us!*

Indeed, the more archaic levels of our own minds suggest that perhaps such creatures not only are not bad jokes, much less products of random chemical changes in our genes, as we have more recently been persuaded to believe, but omens and portents—as the oldest word used to name them in our tongue indicates. "Monster" is as old as English itself, and remained the preferred name for Freaks from the time of Chaucer to that of Shakespeare and beyond. The etymology of the word is obscure; but whether it derives from *moneo*, meaning to warn, or *monstro*, meaning to show forth, the implication is the same: human abnormalities are the products not of a whim of nature but of the design of Providence.

In the ancient world, such signs were deciphered by experts in fetomancy (prophecy by means of fetuses) or teratoscopy (divination based on examination of abnormal births), as subtle in interpreting their meaning as those who read omens in the flight of birds or the entrails of sacrificed beasts. Indeed, the oldest surviving "document" dealing with monsters is a Babylonian lexicon of monsterology, inscribed on clay tablets which date from about 2800 B.C. All three traditional subclasses of monsters are represented in the tablets, *monstres par excès, monstres par défaut,* and *monstres doubles.*

The first always seem to portend ill ("When a woman gives birth to an infant who has six toes on each foot, the people of the world will be injured"). The second are more ambiguous—a child without a penis and nose, for instance, signifying that "the army of the king will be strong," but one without a penis and belly button indicating that there will be "ill will in the house." Similarly with the third— the birth of androgynes, for instance, bodes ill, while a janicepts baby is a good omen ("When a woman gives birth to an infant that has a head on the head . . . the good augury shall enter into the house"). The Romans, on the other hand, thought of all three classes as ill-omened.

And there were among them priestly executioners who dispatched monstrous children at birth by exposure or ritual sacrifice. Indeed, among all ancient peoples there have been such destroyers of malformed children. This history tells us, and the response we feel in the presence of Freaks confirms. But that was elsewhere or at least elsewhen, we assure ourselves. The most celebrated of joined twins, Chang and Eng, may have barely escaped such a fate not much over a century ago in Siam, but in America they became rich and famous. And though the mummy of a Dwarf, dug up out of the sands of Egypt quite recently, may have originally been killed with due rites and ceremonies as was fitting in his culture, we merely display his remains in a museum as is fitting in ours.

Even the ritualized murder of Freaks, however, seemed in ancient times to verge on sacrilege, and its incidence, therefore, was much lower than we might suppose. Sometimes, indeed, they were preserved and worshipped, as was clearly the case of a hideously distorted *shamanka* (female medicine woman) found in an underground cave in Czechoslovakia in the midst of ritual splendor 25,000 years after her interment. And even the Emperor Augustus, convinced that all Freaks, especially Midgets, possessed the Evil Eye, nonetheless had created for his court a gold statue with diamond eyes representing his pet Dwarf, Lucius.

So there never was in earlier times any total genocidal onslaught against Freaks like that launched by Hitler against Dwarfs in the name of modern "eugenics." And it is even likely that fewer monsters were denied a chance to live in older "priest-ridden" societies than in an AMA–controlled age like our own, in which "therapeutic abortions" are available to mothers expecting monstrous births, and infanticide is practiced under the name of "removal of life supports from non-viable major terata."

At any rate, the word "monster" retains much of the awe once felt in the presence of newborn malformations, and the word, therefore, along with its variant form, "monstrosity," has never disappeared from the working vocabulary of carnivals and side shows. Indeed, I can still replay in my head the spiel of a Freak show "talker," familiar to me since childhood. *Jo-Jo, the Dog-faced boy*, that ghost of a voice keeps saying, *the greatest an-thro-po-log-i-cal mon-ster-os-i-ty in captivity. Brought back at great expense from the jungles of Bary-zil. Walks like a boy. Barks like a dog. Crawls on his belly like a snake.* And at the drawled five syllables of *mon-ster-os-i-ty*, I feel my spine tingle and my heart leap as I relive the wonder of seeing for the first time my own most private nightmares on public display *out there.*

Why have I not used the word "monster," then, to describe those "unnatural" creatures whose natural history I am trying to write? In 1930, C. J. S. Thompson called a similar study *The Mystery and Lore of Monsters.* But over the more than four decades since its appearance, the term "monster" has been preempted to describe creations of artistic fantasy like Dracula, Mr. Hyde, the Wolf Man, King Kong, and the nameless metahuman of Mary Shelley's *Frankenstein.*

Around these imaginary creatures there has been created a cult, which, beginning as a parodic protest against the stuffy established churches, has assumed the status of a genuine religion, albeit one celebrated in the catacombs of contemporary pop culture, which is to say, in movie houses and underground comic books. It was there that characters created chiefly by Victorian writers of popular fiction were metamorphosed into demons and demigods by a congregation high on grass and sporting buttons which read DRACULA LIVES.

The classic films which they continue to watch and from which the iconography of the comics is derived were made, however, not in the late 1960s when certain physiological normals who called themselves Freaks took to the streets, but during the Great Depression; so that even now it is difficult to imagine Dr. Frankenstein's Monster except as he was played by Boris Karloff, his face stiff under pounds of makeup and the ends of bolts protruding from his shaven skull. Moreover, no matter how many times we have seen the gaunt and beclawed Dracula of Franz Murnau's earlier *Nosferatu* or Christopher Lee's later, more svelte version of the same character, the Vampire Voivode remains for most of us the pallid and black-cloaked villain acted by Bela Lugosi in Todd Browning's 1931 movie with which the Revival of Monsters began. But though Browning also redeemed Freaks for the movies, we must not confuse the two.*

Certainly the freaky young do not. Even stoned out of their minds at the latest horror show of some campus film series, or alone in their rooms watching the Fright Night feature on TV, they are aware that monsters are not "real" as Freaks are; i.e., their existence is not granted by a consensus which includes "straights" as well as "heads," the waking consciousness as well as the dreaming one. Whatever margin of ambivalence a particular viewer may feel toward such monsters, they are experienced in the main as other, alien, even hostile. If they project any experience of the self, it is of that self dissolving in the depths of a nightmare or a particularly bad "trip." They evoke in us chiefly fear and loathing, which we may, indeed, need as therapy or *askesis*, but from which we gladly awake.

To be sure, monsters have a mythological dimension like Freaks, and in this respect they are unlike the category of unfortunates whom early French teratologists called *mutilés:* the blind, deaf, dumb, lame, crippled, perhaps even hunchbacks and harelips, though these are marginal; along with amputees, paraplegics, and other victims of natural or man-made disasters. Children who are born legless or armless, their limbs amputated by a tangled umbilical cord, are sometimes hard to tell from true phocomelics, or seal-children, with vestigial hands and feet attached directly to the torso. But once identified, they are primarily felt as objects not of awe but of pity.

---

* Oddly enough, the street tradition of American blacks uses the term "Freaks" for a wide range of deviants, including the movie monsters; so that the "toast" called "The Freak's Ball" reaches its climax with the appearance of Frankenstein (i.e., the Monster): "He had a mismatched body with two left heels, / Long dick hangin' out like a four-yard reel . . ."

The true Freak, however, stirs both supernatural terror and natural sympathy, since, unlike the fabulous monsters, he is one of us, the human child of human parents, however altered by forces we do not quite understand into something mythic and mysterious, as no mere cripple ever is. Passing either on the street, we may be simultaneously tempted to avert our eyes and to stare; but in the latter case we feel no threat to those desperately maintained boundaries on which any definition of sanity ultimately depends. Only the true Freak challenges the conventional boundaries between male and female, sexed and sexless, animal and human, large and small, self and other, and consequently between reality and illusion, experience and fantasy, fact and myth.

To be sure, no actual Freak threatens all of these limits at once. Dwarfs and Giants, for instance, challenge primarily our sense of scale, Hermaphrodites our conviction that the world neatly divides into two sexes, and so on. In the sixteenth century, however, a kind of total monster called the "Monster of Ravenna" was conceived, in which men continued to believe for three centuries, just as they believed in six-legged calves or joined twins. Its picture, fixed and

The Monster of Ravenna.
From *Monstres et prodiges*,
by Ambroise Paré (1573).

unchanging, appeared in all the major tetratological works of the time, side by side with conventionalized engravings of actual monsters.

Of it, Ambroise Paré writes at the end of a chapter called "Examples of the Wrath of God": "Another proof. Just a little while after Pope Julius II sustained so many misfortunes in Italy and undertook the war against King Louis XII (1512), which was followed by a bloody battle fought near Ravenna, there was born in the same city a monster with a horn on its head, two wings and one foot like that of a bird of prey, an eye at the knee cap, and participating in the nature of male and female . . ." The accompanying illustration clarifies the last detail, showing the monster with budding female breasts and, just above the beginning of its single scaly leg, a rather infantile penis canted to the right to reveal the hairless vulva beside it. And Pierre Boaistuau (as translated by Edward Fenton in 1519) not only specifies that "it was double in kind, participating both of the man and woman," but adds that it had "in the stomach the figure of a *Greke* Y, and the form of a crosse."

Not content to leave this creature "so brutall and farre differing from humaine kinde" as a general symbol for the wrath of God, Boaistuau explains the horn as signifying pride and ambition, the wings lightness and inconstancy, the lack of arms want of good works, the eye in the knee too much love of worldly things, the "ramping foot" usury and covetousness, and the double sex "the sinnes of the *Sodomites*." The added ypsilon and the cross, he makes clear, are signs of salvation, indications of a way out of the calamity portended by so monstrous a birth.

To a modern eye, however, the composite creature seems not so much an allegory specially created by a vengeful but ultimately merciful God exasperated by Italian moneychangers and pederasts, as a quite human attempt to sum up in a single iconic form the essential nature of all Freaks. It is not only a *monstre par défaut*, lacking one leg and foot, but also a *monstre par excès*, possessing an oddly displaced third eye, as well as a supernumerary horn on its otherwise human head. And it is especially a *monstre double*, a multiple hybrid of bird and beast, beast and man, man and woman: a pictorial myth of the super-monster.

There has long been a debate in learned circles about which

came first: such grotesque fantasies, which were in due course identified with malformed humans who resembled them; or anomalous births, miscarriages and abortions, which bred nightmares, later transmogrified into deities or demons. Men have hewn out of rock and painted on the walls of caves freaklike figures ever since art began, and these have usually been considered idols or icons based on the human form but distorted for symbolic purposes. One of the most ancient and celebrated is the so-called Willendorf Venus, a barely iconic mass of petrified female flesh, traditionally interpreted as a fertility symbol.

A scholarly article which appeared in 1973, however, contends that it portrays with almost clinical accuracy a typical Freak: the victim of "diencephalendocrine obesity with parasymptomatic hypertonia, infertility and libido-reduction." Moreover, the author of the article goes on to argue, other monsters, long believed purely fantastic, may represent analogous attempts to represent anomalies found only in aborted fetuses. He cites as one example the Skia-

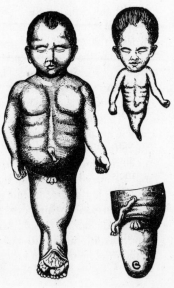

LEFT TOP: Sympus Monopus and LEFT BOTTOM: Skiapode.

RIGHT: Sirenoform infant. From *Anomalies and Curiosities of Medicine,* by George M. Gould and Walter L. Pyle (1896).

podes, creatures with a single foot large enough to use as a parasol, believed by Herodotus to be inhabitants of India, where—needless to say—they have never been found. And certainly the drawing of a mermaid-like fetus, or "Sirenoform symmelic miscarriage (*sympus monopus*)," which he reproduces strongly resembles the Renaissance engraving of the "imaginary" Indian monster which he prints alongside it.

Such evidence lends credence to the theory that the observation of human malformations preceded the creation of mythic monsters. We are given pause, however, by the fact that there exist certain long-lived fantasy creatures with *no* prototypes among actual Freaks, fetal or full-grown. Among them are those ostrich- or crane- or goose-necked men, sometimes bird-beaked as well, and occasionally bearded, whom medieval and Renaissance illustrations never tired of portraying. Most notable among them, perhaps, are the celebrated "men whose heads do grow between their shoulders," of whom Othello speaks to Desdemona. We have, indeed, testimony to the existence of such Blemmyae far more reliable than the words of a fictional character, since St. Augustine assures us that in his youth he had seen a "monstrum acephalon," which is to say, a headless monster, with his own eyes. And there are in the libraries of the Western world hundreds of illustrated texts in which we can still see them with ours.

What monsters men have needed to believe in they have created for themselves in words and pictures when they could not discover them in nature. And it is with that psychic need, then, that we should begin; seeking prototypes neither in history or anthropology, nor in embryology or teratology, but in depth psychology, which deals with our basic uncertainty about the limits of our bodies and our egos. More precisely, it is with the psychology of childhood that we must start, for in childhood such uncertainty is strongest and the distinction between the dreams it begets and the reality to which we wake hardest to maintain.

Not psychology textbooks, however, but children's literature, books written for boys and girls or usurped by them, provide the essential clues. Reading any of L. Frank Baum's Oz books, for instance, or James Barrie's *Peter Pan*, or *Alice in Wonderland*, or *Gulliver's Travels*, we cross in our imaginations a borderline which in childhood we could never be sure was there, entering a realm where precisely what qualifies us as normal on the one side identifies us as Freaks on the other. And after returning, we may experience for a little while the child's constant confusion about what really is freakish, what normal, on either side. For children the primary source of such confusion is scale, as Jonathan Swift and Lewis Carroll both make quite clear. And the living metaphors for the nightmare of relative size are Giants and Dwarfs, Fat Men, Fat Ladies, and Living Skeletons—by all odds the best-remembered, and sometimes even best-loved, of all Freaks.

Even before he has seen such side show Freaks or read about them, the child may have come to feel that compared to an adult, he is himself a Midget, while compared to a baby or his last year's self, he is a Giant. In his deep consciousness, he is forever growing bigger and smaller, depending on the context and the eye in which he sees himself reflected. "But am I really and truly big or small, or just right?" he continues to ask himself, even after he has ceased to grow—and begins, he may suspect, to shrink.

Scale is, however, not the only major identity problem with which children must contend. Born unhousebroken and half wild, dabbling in their own feces and popping into their mouths whatever unlikely object they can grab, they remain for a long time unsure—as the Alice books everywhere imply and Book IV of *Gulliver* explicitly states—whether they are beasts or men: little animals more like their pets than their parents. And the embodiments of the Freaks they feel themselves to be in this regard are the Wild Man of Borneo, Jo-Jo the Dog-faced Boy, or that quasi- or half-imaginary Freak, the "Geek," gobbling down live chickens and rats.

There is, in addition, the problem of child sexuality created by the bisexual, polymorphous, perverse nature of pre-pubescent children, and aggravated by the adult world's changing views of their sexual viability. Obviously, a child's notion of himself is derived from such views. How different, then, a young boy's attitude toward his own body in the heyday of Hellenistic pederasty, when his sexual ambiguity was considered erotically attractive, and that of a male child in, say, Victorian times, when he was deemed "innocent" until puberty and pointed from birth toward the achievement of exclusive male genitality. And how equally different a young girl's

TOP LEFT: Gulliver in the hands of a Brobdingnagian baby.
TOP RIGHT: Gulliver among the Brobdingnagian ladies.
BOTTOM LEFT: Gulliver bound by the Lilliputians.
BOTTOM RIGHT: Gulliver reviewing the Lilliputian parade.
Illustrations by Charles Brock for Jonathan Swift's *Gulliver's Travels* (1894).

attitude toward herself since Vladimir Nabokov's *Lolita* glorified the sexually aggressive "nymphet," and that of a twelve-year-old in the days when Lewis Carroll might, without suspicion of lubricity, ask her parents for permission to photograph her in the nude.

Yet whatever the sexual codes of his culture, pre-Freudian or post-Freudian, repressive or permissive, the child is bound to feel some monstrous discrepancy between his erotic nature and the role expectations of his era. And the incarnate symbols of his distress in this area are the sex Freaks: the Monorchid, the Eunuch, the girl without a vulva, the Hottentot Venus with labia halfway down her thighs, and especially the Hermaphrodite: Joseph-Josephine, Half Man/Half Woman.

Typically, however, children's books, being rooted not in the nightmares of sleep but in half-waking reveries, do not stop with this distress and confusion, but move on to a Happy Ending represented by waking up or growing up, or both. In Baum's *The Land of Oz*, for instance, the protagonist enters the scene as a boy but exits as a girl: a princess, in fact, restored to her throne once her true sex has been released from a witch's spell, i.e., once she has passed over the threshold of puberty. The Alice books, too, are about "growing up," though that process is not rendered in such explicit

RIGHT: Alice as Giant.
BELOW: Alice as Midget.
Illustrations by John Tenniel
in first edition of Lewis Carroll's *Alice in Wonderland*
(1865) and *Through the
Looking Glass* (1872).

sexual terms. For Lewis Carroll the process of female maturation implies learning to make oneself, rather than chance or circumstance, the arbiter of scale: learning to be just the right size for every occasion. Only then can a girl be "queened," and thus entering into full womanhood, distinguish the real from the make-believe, the human from the pseudo-human. What children's books tell us, finally, is that maturity involves the ability to believe the self normal, only the other a monster or Freak. Failing to attain such security, we are likely to end by not growing up at all, like Lemuel Gulliver, whom we leave at his story's end in a stall with beasts—his sole refuge from full adulthood, home, and the family.

But this was never the conscious point of the classic Freak show. A Victorian institution it is, like Victorian nonsense, intended to be finally therapeutic, cathartic, no matter what initial terror and insecurity it evokes. "*We* are the Freaks," the human oddities are supposed to reassure us, from their lofty perches. "Not you. Not *you!*" It is primarily to the actual children before them, along with what remains of the child in the hearts of their adult audience, that they speak. To this day circus people call such exhibitions "kid shows." Asked why, they say sometimes that the word "kid" means not child but put-on or send-up or hoax; or they may insist that it refers to those on display rather than those who have paid to see them, Freaks being notoriously—at least according to their exploiters—"just like children." But it is clearly actual boys and girls that the word intends, since no exhibitor can be unaware that the core of his audience is made up of children.

But the myth of monsters is twice-born in the psyche. Originating in the deep fears of childhood, it is reinforced in earliest adolescence by the young adult's awareness of his own sex and that of others. The young male finds that even after his whole body has ceased to grow and his scale vis-à-vis the rest of the world seems fixed once and for all, his penis disconcertingly continues to rise and fall, swell and shrink—at times an imperious giant, at others a timid dwarf. For girls at puberty, the growth of breasts is similarly traumatic. It is a rare young woman who in the crisis of adolescent shamefacedness does not feel herself either too flat-chested or too generously endowed, and in either case a Freak. So, too, burgeoning boys, in the locker room or at the urinal (and in an age of X-rated films, at the picture show as well), are moved to compare the size of their penises with those of others. And, of course, the whole body as well, at a point in life when one feels himself primarily a sex machine, is felt by both male and female as monstrously deficient or excessive, too tall, too short, too fat, too thin—still fixed in its freakishness though childhood has at long last been left behind.

Moreover, passing the line of puberty means for boys and girls alike the growth of hair around the genitals, more like animal fur than that on their heads; and for the boys, on face, chest, and belly as well. Both may have longed for the appearance of such signs of full maturity, but for both it stirs doubts about their place on the evolutionary scale. And when young women find what they are taught to regard as "excess hair" growing between their breasts, on the upper lips, in their armpits, or on their legs, they may doubt their full femininity as well as their full humanity. A whole industry, indeed, has grown up by exploiting this fear: advertising painless electrolysis, sure-fire depilatories, and dainty mini-razors for women eager to de-freakify themselves before a night of partying or a day on the beach.

Especially, however, it is at the sight, real or imagined, of each other's genitals that newly mature men and women endure traumas which reinforce the myths of monstrosity. It is the child's glimpse of his parents' huge and hairy genitals which perhaps lies at the origin of it all. Freud has argued that our basic sense of the "uncanny," which is to say, the monstrous, the freakish, arises from seeing for the first time the female genitals. But Freud's view is partial, since clearly the primordial model for our notions of the monstrous is each sex's early perception of the other's genitalia in adult form. A very young man looking at a vulva is likely to feel its possessor a *monstre par défaut*, while a very young woman looking at his penis may find him a *monstre par excès*. Or reflexively, he may feel himself a *monstre par excès*, she herself a *monstre par défaut*.

Finally, therefore, each sex tends to feel itself forever defined as freakish in relation to the other. And from our uneasiness at this, I suppose, arises the dream of androgyny. Through most of the course of Western history, however, that dream has been undercut by a profound fear of being unmanned or unwomaned, and by guilt for desiring such an event; so that actual Hermaphrodites seem to both sexes the most grotesque of all side show Freaks, a *monstre double* more terrifying than the fears it should presumably allay. Only very recently has our ambivalence in this regard begun to tilt toward the positive side, making the notion of "unisex" not just a useful come-on for barbers and clothes designers but the source of political slogans with wide appeal to the disaffected young, particularly the women among them. Still, as late as Fellini's *Satyricon* and Russ Meyer's *Beyond the Valley of the Dolls,* the image of a Hermaphrodite, naked or half-naked on the screen, continues to stir in the general audience a shudder of revulsion and fear, and a therapeutic titter.

It is, at any rate, the mythic monsters—those who, before they were exhibited at fairs and the courts of kings, already existed in

Two side show posters, Ringling Brothers Barnum and Bailey Circus, early twentieth century.
Circus World Museum, Baraboo, Wisconsin

fable and legend because they projected infantile or adolescent traumas—who most deeply move spectators to this very day. I myself, for instance, have recently made a pilgrimage to the Circus World Museum in Baraboo, Wisconsin, ". . . where circus history comes to life . . . 33 acres of displays, shows, demonstrations . . ." And there, in the midst of old circus wagons, a mechanical gorilla in a cage, a real, live tightrope walker, and a herd of performing elephants, I found the side show tent, where, fixed on a platform forever, stood the plaster images of representative Freaks. The sign before the entrance read "Congress of Strange People," a term which belongs to the twentieth century, and the statues inside were dressed, appropriately enough, in Victorian garb. But I was not surprised to discover that the choice of figures to occupy that limited space responded to our basic insecurities, the sort of primordial fears which I have been examining, about scale, sexuality, our status as more than beasts, and our tenuous individuality.

To represent the first—the child's oldest and deepest fear—were a Fat Lady, a Human Skeleton, a Giantess supporting on one hand a Dwarf, and the "Cardiff Giant," which was, of course, a notorious fraud. There was no Hermaphrodite to stand for the second fear, perhaps out of a sense that the Circus Museum was a family show; but a Bearded Lady did well enough. The third was doubly figured forth, in the form of Lionel the Lion-faced Man and Jo-Jo the Dog-faced Boy; while the fourth was embodied by Chang and Eng, the original "Siamese Twins," looking in formal nineteenth-century dress very respectable, and a little bored by the ligature to which they owed their fame and fortune.

Confronting them, I could feel the final horror evoked by Freaks stir to life: a kind of vertigo like that experienced by Narcissus when he beheld his image in the reflecting waters and plunged to his death. In joined twins the confusion of self and other, substance and shadow, ego and other, is more terrifyingly confounded than it is when the child first perceives face to face in the mirror an

OPPOSITE: TOP, Wax figures of Zip, Chang/Eng, Jo-Jo the Dog-faced Boy; CENTER, Snake Charmer, Giantess with Dwarf, Bearded Lady; BOTTOM, Living Skeleton, Fat Lady, Tattooed Woman. Contemporary publicity photographs. *Circus World Museum, Baraboo, Wisconsin*

image moving as he moves, though clearly in another world. In that case, at least, there are only two participants, the perceiver and the perceived; but standing before Siamese Twins, the beholder sees them looking not only at each other, but—both at once—at him. And for an instant it may seem to him that he is a third brother, bound to the pair before him by an invisible bond; so that the distinction between audience and exhibit, we and them, normal and Freak, is revealed as an illusion, desperately, perhaps even necessarily, defended, but untenable in the end.

PART ONE

1

Dwarfs: From Knoumhotpou to General Tom Thumb

Every child knows what a Dwarf is long before he has met one, and it therefore remains hard for all of us ever really to see one past the images first encountered in stories our mothers told us. "Once upon a time," we continue to hear in our adult heads, even as we stand at the side show, "there was a

Pygmy	Troll	Brownie
Dwarf	Leprechaun	Pixy
Elf	Midget	Gnome
Fairy	Sprite	Sylph
Fay	*Shi*	Lilliputian
Kobold	Pook	Munchkin
Goblin	Gremlin	Hobbit

The oldest of these names, Pygmy, is as old as the literary tradition of the West, being derived from a Greek word which means the distance from the elbow to the knuckles of a normal-sized man. But even it was entangled in legend from the start. How fitting, then, that when European explorers actually "discovered" dwarfed Negro tribes on the "Dark Continent" in the nineteenth century, they called them "Pygmies," though unlike their prototypes, they neither foil their bird adversaries by destroying their eggs nor clothe themselves only in their own long hair. They are, in fact, not notably different from any of their neighbors in the Niger Valley, except for size.

Yet at first they were remythologized rather than demythologized in film and fiction, so that for generations children have been exposed to images of diminutive black savages emerging from the jungle with blowguns in hand to surround parties of unwary white travelers. The myth to which we have assimilated the "Pygmies" is in fact the myth of the "primitive," born of modern imperialism and nineteenth-century racism, which is to say, early anthropology and popular evolutionary theory—as exemplified in Edgar Rice Burroughs' still beloved saga of Tarzan the Ape Man, who at one point is caught between warring "Minunian" or Pygmy tribes.

More recently, however, the revolt against nineteenth-century imperialism and the growth of African nationalism have undercut both ancient and modern mythology, leaving us with the unsolved mystery of *why* the Dwarf peoples of Africa, who medical studies indicate suffer from no lack of growth hormones, are so small. For years now medical authorities have been promising to send "a further" and presumably final "expedition to look into the matter by exploring the pygmies' metabolism."

But whatever the explanation, we are still confronted with the puzzling fact that Dwarfs are the only Freaks who exist not just as "sports" in a normal population, but as a whole tribe, a people, a nation. It is this, perhaps, which explains why we do not merely preserve their ancient names but continue to invent new ones. "Dwarf" and "Elf," for instance, belong to the Anglo-Saxon roots of our language, while "Fairy" and "Fay" came into use at the moment of its mating with French. But "Gnome" was created in the mid-seventeenth century by the alchemist Paracelsus. "Lilliputian" did not exist before its invention by Jonathan Swift in the early eighteenth century; and "Hobbit" was invented by J. R. R. Tolkien as

LEFT: A Good Elf. RIGHT: Thumbling. Illustrations by John D. Batten for *English Fairy Tales*, collected by Joseph Jacobs (1898).

late as 1937 as the name of a tribe of hairy-footed, diminutive, comfort-loving monsters, who captured the imaginations of many, including the freaked-out young of the fifties and sixties, predisposed in their favor by earlier exposure to the cartoons of Walt Disney and Baum's *The Wizard of Oz*. Even the word "Midget" dates back only to 1865, when it was coined as a diminutive of "midge," meaning fly or gnat, and tended to replace the more mythological "Fairy."

Dwarfs displayed in the taverns of Smithfield in the heyday of Bartholomew Fair were typically called such names as "Miss Morgan, the Windsor Fairy" or "Mrs. Dollie Dalton, the Little Fairy." And the mysterious suggestions implicit in such names became in the handbills a kind of popular poetry. "A living FAIRY, suppos'd to be a Hundred-and-Fifty years old, his face being no bigger than a child's of a month," one reads. Others, more eloquent, run: "The *Little-Woman*, NOT 3 foot high, and 30 years of Age . . . which is commonly called the *Fairy Queen*, she gives general satisfaction to all that sees her, by Diverting them with Dancing, being big with child . . ."; or "This is a Fairy Child, supposed to be born of *Hungarian* Parents, but chang'd in Nursing, Aged Nine Years and more; not exceeding a Foot and a-half high . . . You may see the whole Anatomy of its Body by setting it against the Sun. It never speaks.

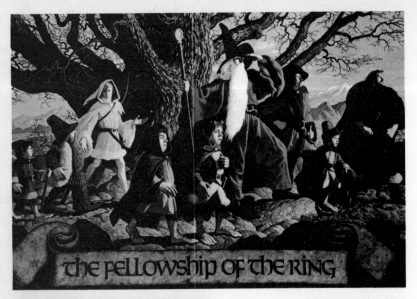

The Fellowship of the Ring

ABOVE: The Fellowship of the Ring, Hobbits, Elves, Dwarfs, and men. Illustration by the Brothers Hildebrandt for J. R. R. Tolkien's Trilogy of the Rings. (The Hobbit Calendar.)

From J. R. R. Tolkien Calendar, copyright 1976, published by George Allen & Unwin Ltd, an imprint of HarperCollins Publishers Limited, London.

LEFT: Orcs on the march. Illustration by Tim Kirk for J. R. R. Tolkien's *The Lord of the Rings*. (The Hobbit Calendar.)

Illustrations by Tim Kirk for his Master's Thesis project based on J. R. R. Tolkien's The Lord of the Rings, *reproduced in the 1975 J. R. R. Tolkien Calendar from Ballantine Books.*

It has no Teeth, but is the most voracious and hungry Creature in the World . . ."

Even when the hunger for the marvelous had abated, one of

Barnum's prize Midgets was still called the "Corsican Fairy." And Leopold Kahn, better known as Admiral Dot, was first billed as the "Eldorado Elf," though there seems to have been nothing elfin about that foul-mouthed and perpetually discontented performer. Though "Fairy" and "Elf" have disappeared, the even more archaic word "Dwarf" has continued in use, evoking fairy-tale associations in the minds of a generation which first met the seven companions of Snow White as Disney's Snuffy, Grumpy, Sneezy, Sleepy, Happy, Dopey, and Doc; and they blend into Tolkien's Dwalin, Balin, Kili, Dori, Hari, Ori, Doin, Gloin, Bifor, Bofur, Bombur, and Thorin, who in *The Hobbit* accompany Bilbo on his fantastic journey "There and Back."

Ironically, however, "Dwarf" is also the term by which doctors designate all undersized humans, and it was P. T. Barnum's preferred term as well. But in England and America we distinguish it from "Midget," using the former for little people long in the trunk, big in the head, short in the legs, and finally grotesque, and preserving the latter for those perfectly proportioned and beautiful. Indeed, though only English expresses it, there has always and everywhere existed the notion of the two Pygmy kinds, both thought of as living underground, either just below the surface of the earth or as deep into darkness as the deepest mine. But only Dwarfs have been consigned to the lowest depths, where they fuse into the figure of Pluto, the underworld rapist of the ancient Greeks, or are confused with the demons of popular Christianity. Even Tolkien, who tried sentimentally to redeem all little people, was compelled by tradition to note that Dwarfs are a "tough, thrawn race, holding a grudge, loving treasure—and for long, enemies of elves and men."

It was that tradition which Dickens evoked in *The Old Curiosity Shop*, in which the "goblin-like" Quilp represents the Dwarf as wicked lecher and persecutor of women, and the "fairy-like" little Nell the Midget as Elf-child. The extraordinary appeal of that novel is explained in part by the fact that thinking of diminutive humans in archetypal terms, we tend to identify them either with the very old or very young: monstrous parents who will not die, though they shrivel and shrink; or angelic children, fixed forever somewhere just short of puberty. Actual little people, however, have a disconcerting way of seeming both at once: old-young, young-old. And "Pin-

Quilp annoying his "little wife," mother-in-law, and female friends. Illustration by Phiz for Charles Dickens' *Old Curiosity Shop* (1841).

heads," those feeble-minded microcephalics, who for so many years remained favorite attractions at the side show, especially confound the confusion. Though not always true Dwarfs, they are likely to be well below average height, and their tiny pointed skulls, along with the innocent imbecility of their faces, lend them both a childlike and an archaic aspect.

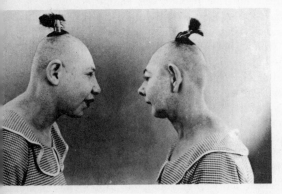

A pair of Pinheads. Contemporary publicity photograph.
Circus World Museum, Baraboo, Wisconsin

Sometimes, indeed, they have been presented as atavisms: vestiges of the childhood of the race, like Maximo and Bartola, a pair of half-mulatto, half-Indian "Birdheaded Dwarfs," who from 1851 to 1901 not only intrigued audiences at fairs and circuses but puzzled doctors and anthropologists. First presented as "child-idols" snatched from a nonexistent "Lost Aztec City of Iximaya," they remained entangled in a web of primitivizing fantasy worthy of Edgar Rice Burroughs, from which they were not completely extricated until the publication in 1968 of a study by the Mexican scholar Juan Comas. And "Aztec *children*" they remained in the popular imagination even after they had reached late middle age and were—though brother and sister—married to each other. (In name only, it would appear, since Maximo remained sexually a child until the end of his life.)

Nor did the notion of the microcephalic as archaic child die with them: Slitzie, a charming adult Pinhead whose mental age was three, was exhibited in the 1920s as "Maggie, the last of the Aztecs." It is, however, not as a surviving Aztec but a perpetual child that she is presented in Browning's *Freaks*, where she first appears playing innocently beside a stream with a couple of other beribboned microcephalics called Elvira and Jenny Lee Snow. When a horrified groundskeeper tries to run them out of his park lest they frighten real kids, their maternal guardian protests, "But they are just like children!"

Yet to an adult eye such "children" seem eternally at the point of withering into sudden and terrible senility, of passing from childhood to old age without ever having attained normal maturity. The achondroplastic Dwarf, however, appears to have been born old—like the villainous protagonist of Lagerkvist's *The Dwarf*, who says of himself: "The wrinkles make me look very old. I am not, but I have heard tell that we dwarfs are descended from a race older than that which now populates the world, and therefore we are old as soon as we are born." The true Midget, on the other hand, tends in fiction to die early, like Dickens' Nell.

Not only the terms "Dwarf" and "Midget," but all names used for men and women below normal height reflect our ambivalence toward the very young and the very old, our children and our parents. Brownie, Elf, and Pixy, for instance, cluster about the positive pole of our double response, while Gnome, Kobold, Troll, and Goblin tend toward the negative one; and others hang suspended between, until time and usage have sorted them out. Moreover, even such "scientific" terms as "achondroplastic" and "ateliotic" reinforce rather than dispel the ancient dualism.

As late as 1964, for example, Professor Maurice Patel, a member of the French Academy of Medicine, writing in a professional journal—though in a popular vein—distinguishes between what he calls "false dwarfs" and "true dwarfs, the ideal dwarf, the miniature man," comparing actual instances of the former with a fictional monster in a novel by Paul Bourget: "Nothing is missing . . . the huge head with its bulging forehead, giving an impression of malevolence; the smallness of the limbs, contrasting to the integrity of the trunk . . . and is this not the cause of their hatred for their neighbor, their voluntary isolation. They do not join together, they form no families." We are in the realm of mythology, and remain there as the doctor switches from fiction to painting. "In his painting, *Las Meniñas*," he continues, "Velásquez clearly wanted to show the contrast between the *nain pur* [pure dwarf] and the achondroplastic. In the former, the face is smiling, gracious; in the latter, the mouth, in the midst of the ravished cheeks, gives a sullen cast to the physiognomy . . . the victim of achondroplasia is a silent bear . . . The true *nain* loves family life; he forms unified groups with his own kind. They marry each other and seem quite content."

But Dr. Patel is finally obliged to grant that little people do not really fit into two mythological groups, since among "false dwarfs" there are to be found rachitics (victims of spinal osteomyelitis), thyroid or ovarian deficients, and hemimelics (with half limbs), as well as "classic" achondroplastics and "numerous varieties" of metaphysical dysostosis (rare developmental abnormality of the skeleton in which growth zones of tubular bones are expanded by deposits of cartilage). And the "pure dwarf" breaks into at least two categories: sexual and asexual ateliotics, the latter lacking gonadotropins, thyrotropins, and ACTH, the adrenocorticotropic hormone; while the former suffers only from "pinpointed thyroid deficiencies."

Some authorities would go even further in their onslaught against myth. "We're talking about forty different medical conditions," one of them insists. "The problem is in the formation of the bones. We can't document a biochemical abnormality in 85 per cent of the cases." Both Dwarfs and Midgets have, in short, been demoted from the status of symbolic figures, demonic and angelic, to that of patients, whose "cure" may well be in sight, once we have succeeded in stockpiling the appropriate growth hormones, "which can be obtained only from the pituitary of someone who has just died."

"If," says an article in volume 217 (1967) of the *Scientific American*, "sufficient amounts . . . could be administered to a sexual ateliotic during childhood, the outward manifestations of the condition should be completely correctible." Despite such boasts, however, the cure of Dwarfs has proceeded slowly and inconclusively. One can understand, therefore, why certain political and genetic reformers preferred wholesale euthanasia to retail chemo- or endocrine therapy. That was, at any rate, the way chosen by Adolf Hitler, when he sought to "purify" the German race by slating Midgets, along with Gypsies and Jews, for extermination in the gas chambers.

In earlier times the notion of "correcting" the condition of Dwarfs did not occur to their normal contemporaries, since they considered their condition an act of God. Nor did they typically advocate destroying them, since they were, in fact, classified as something different from real Freaks. In Gaspar Schott's *Physica curiosa*, for instance, published in 1662, they are categorized, with Giants and Fat Men and Women, as *mirabilia hominum*, human marvels, rather than *mirabilia monstrorum*, monstrous marvels. Not until the invention in the nineteenth century of teratology proper by Etienne and Isidore Geoffroy Saint-Hilaire did Dwarfs come to be lumped with monstrosities: creatures to be shuddered at and treated rather than, however ambivalently, adored. In ancient Egypt gods like Ptah and Bes were portrayed in the form of Dwarfs, and the High King on solemn occasions would mime their characteristics by "dancing the god." And even in later civilizations, which had removed them from their pantheons, Dwarfs were still sought after, made much of—"collected," in fact.

During Hellenistic times they were highly prized: displayed at feasts naked and bejeweled, or sent into the arena to fight each other, wild beasts, and "Amazons." Even after they had become buf-

The Dwarf god Bes. Ancient
Egyptian statuette.
The British Museum

foons and court pets in the late Middle Ages and Renaissance there
still clung to them an aura of the magical. It took the Victorian era
to complete the process of demythification by converting them into
public exhibits, subjects for medical study, and occasions for pity—
like orphans, abused animals, or the deserving poor. Nonetheless,
General Tom Thumb flourished at precisely that moment, pleasing
not only the popular audience but kings and queens and presidents
as well. He appeared before them, however, not as a denizen but as
a visitor, a kind of last ambassador of an "ancient race." Yet men
still continued to search the world for new Dwarfs, primarily to
please the taste of a large fickle public rather than a few great private collectors.

As late as the end of the sixteenth century King Sigismund-
Augustus of Poland had nine Dwarfs of his very own, and Catherine de' Medicis six; while a Roman cardinal called Vitelli was able
to assemble thirty-nine to serve at a special dinner. But within a
hundred years royal Dwarfs had begun to disappear from Western
Europe, the last official Dwarf at the court of France dying in 1662.

And the last Dwarf kept in any private residence in England belonged not to royalty but to the very rich and eccentric novelist William Beckford, whose Gothic romance *Vathek* is still read with pleasure.

As late as 1817, a visitor to his house, Fonthill Abbey, reported that "he was received by a dwarf . . . covered with gold and embroidery." It is hard to find reliable information about this Dwarf, whose name is variously given as Perro, Piero, and Pierrot, though his "owner" seems more often to have called him "Nanibus." "He is a Giaour and feeds upon toadstools," Beckford would tell the curious; and garbed him accordingly—feeling the need to create around himself a mock Gothic world in which a legendary monster was more at home than a "deformed and illfavored" Frenchman called Pierre Colas de Grailly. When misfortune forced Beckford into bankruptcy, the popular press found this was a fitting end for one who had "sheltered dwarfs."

Things proceeded at a somewhat slower pace in Russia, where in 1710 Peter the Great had no difficulty in gathering seventy Midgets of both sexes to help celebrate the marriage of his own favorite. But long before then the practice of manufacturing Dwarfs had ceased in the Occident. In the Orient, however, where trees and plants continue to be so distorted, babies were up until recent times similarly misshapen and shrunk. The practice is ancient in that part of the world, as is attested in Tale XXXI of P'u Sung Leng's *Strange Tales from a Chinese Studio:*

> In the reign of K'ang Hsi, there was a magician who carried about with him a wooden box, in which he had a dwarf not much more than a foot in height. When people gave him money he would open the box and bid the little creature come out. The dwarf would then sing a song and go in again. Arriving one day at Yeh, the magistrate there seized the box, and taking it into his *yamen* asked the dwarf whence he came. At first he dared not reply, but on being pressed told the magistrate everything. He said he belonged to a respectable family and that once when returning home from school he was stupefied by the magician, who gave him some drug which made his limbs shrink, and then took him about to exhibit to people. The magistrate was very angry, and had the magician beheaded, himself taking charge of the

dwarf. He was subsequently very anxious to get him cured, but unable to obtain the proper prescription.

And in attempting to explain rationally what the story renders as magic, a later nineteenth-century English translator quotes from a contemporary newspaper:

> "Young children are bought or stolen at a tender age and placed in a *ch'ing*, or vase with a narrow neck, and having in this case a movable bottom. In this receptacle the unfortunate little wretches are kept for years in a sitting posture, their heads outside being all the while carefully tended and fed . . . When the child has reached the age of twenty or over, he or she is taken away to some distant place and 'discovered' in the woods as a wild man or woman."—*China Mail*, May 15, 1878.

Even after rich collectors from the West no longer subsidized the actual shrinking and distortion of children, merchants in China and the Indies continued to counterfeit corpses of Dwarfs: drying small monkeys which had been first de-tailed and shaven of all hair except that on their skulls and chins.

Exactly how long a similar trade was plied in Europe is hard to say, though an offhand remark by Longinus in his famous essay *On the Sublime* suggests that it survived the coming of Christianity. Searching for a metaphor to express how the human spirit can be crushed, he writes, "Just as the cages (if what I hear is true) in which are kept the Pygmies, commonly called *nani*, not only hinder the growth of the creatures confined within them, but actually attenuate them . . . [even so] is all servitude . . . the cage of the soul."

The ancient Romans apparently also sought to produce stunted children by dietary deprivation, chiefly of "lime-salts," the lack of which was long thought to produce rickets. And though it is reported that most infants thus treated died, such practices were apparently considered economically viable. Similar procedures were being followed a millennium and a half later by a certain "poor man" and child peddler who, we learn, was accustomed to anoint the backs of his victims with a "triple mixture" of the fat of dormice, bats, and moles, in order to dry up their spinal marrow.

More humanitarian collectors of little men sought to mate male and female Dwarfs rather than deform the offspring of normal parents. But though such would-be breeders of Pygmies included distinguished noblewomen like Catherine de' Medicis, the Electress of Brandenburg, and Natalia, sister of Peter the Great, their experiments generally failed. Even when Dwarfs became pregnant, childbirth was difficult, requiring almost always a Caesarian section; and there is, of course, no absolute guarantee that two Dwarfs will produce another, or, indeed, that such offspring will long survive. Moreover, many types of Dwarfs are impotent, most notably the victims of Turner's Syndrome and the so-called asexual ateliotics, whose deformity is caused by pituitary malfunction.

One popular theory argues, indeed, that *all* Dwarfs are infertile, like the evil Dwarf of Pär Lagerkvist, who declares, "We dwarfs beget no young, we are sterile by virtue of our own nature. We have nothing to do with the perpetuation of life; we do not even desire it. We have no need to be fertile, for the human race itself produces its own dwarfs . . . Our race is perpetuated through them . . ." Another equally widespread conviction is that all Dwarfs are, though sterile perhaps, immensely concupiscent. And the popular press continues to feed that conviction with lurid accounts of their sexual exploits, particularly with full-sized human beings.

Not everyone everywhere has believed such "miscegenation" possible, and what may well be the most charming and witty poem about Dwarfs assumes its impossibility. Called "On the Marriage of the Dwarfs," it was written by the Restoration poet Edmund Waller to celebrate the wedding of "Gibson and Shepherd, each three feet ten inches in height. They were pages in the court, and Charles I gave away the female infinitesimal." The world being well stocked with normals, Waller observes, matches between them are constantly threatened by the appearance of possible new mates, but not so those of Dwarfs. "Design or chance make others wive," one of his couplets runs, "But Nature did this match contrive . . ." and he continues,

> To him the fairest nymphs do show
> Like moving mountains, topp'd with snow;
> And every man a Polypheme
> Does to his Galatea seem;

None may presume her faith to prove;
He proffers death that proffers love.

The match memorialized by Waller was as successful as he foresaw, Richard Gibson and Anne Shepherd living to the ages of sev-
enty-four and eighty-nine, and producing nine children, five of
whom survived. Moreover, they proved immune not only to connu-
bial boredom, but to the vicissitudes of politics as well. They survived three major revolutions, largely, it would appear, because
Richard, a talented painter of miniatures, was more changeable in
his allegiance to his patrons than to his wife—doing official portraits
of Charles I, Oliver Cromwell, James II, and William and Mary. But
in his notion of the sexual incompatibility of Dwarfs and normals,
Waller was wrong; since sexual relations are possible, at least between full-sized women and male Dwarfs, who are apparently as
well endowed sexually as their taller peers.

The evidence is more contradictory concerning the mating of
Lilliputian women and normal men. The film *Freaks*, for instance,
which deals centrally with the heartless victimization of a Midget
by a full-sized aerialist and her strongman lover, suggests that all
such marriages are foredoomed. Moreover, a 1963 novel by Herbert
Kubly, *The Whistling Zone*, recounts precisely such an event as
Waller foresees, the fucking to death of a Dwarf girl, "not quite human, having the size of a child and the look of an adult . . . like a
misplaced creature from outer space . . . dressed in white and
pink, like an oversized Christmas doll . . ."

In a popular and sensational compendium of medical lore published in 1898 by Drs. Pyle and Gould, however, there is a photograph of a Midget bride and her normal husband with a baby they
have presumably engendered. The editors attach no names to the
family group, assuring their readers instead that all three "were
exhibited some years since in the Eastern United States." Better
documented are cases of Dwarf males with "normal" brides, the best-
known being that of the Dutch Dwarf Wybrand Lolkes, who is typically shown in early nineteenth-century prints beside a lofty and
studiedly indifferent wife.

Another, more equivocal case is that of Matthew Buchinger, a
Freak widely exhibited in the early years of the reign of George II:

a phocomelic with flipperlike hands and feet attached directly to his body, he had learned to perform on the hautboy, bagpipe, dulcimer, and trumpet, to play cards and dice, write with a pen, juggle cups and balls, and "draw faces to the life." Moreover, a handbill of the time adds, "his playing at Skittles is most admirable . . . He likewise dances a Hornpipe in Highland Dress, as well as any man— without Legs." Finally, as the handbill does not inform us, he was married four times, fathering eleven children. And he was famous for having subdued the most recalcitrant and profligate of his wives by leaping into the air, knocking her to the ground with his head, and thrashing her with his flippers until she promised to be dutiful forever.

The most striking modern instance of a successful Galatea–Polyphemus alliance is that of Aurelio Tomaini, a Giant of 7 feet 4 inches, who weighed over three hundred pounds, and Jeanne, a Midget under three feet, weighing not more than eighty pounds. Not only did they thrive in show business, but after retirement ran a Sarasota motel still called the Giant's Motel, though he is long dead. In their case, however, they were both Freaks to begin with.

My own limited personal observation suggests that though Dwarfs occasionally achieve peaceful and enduring marriages with non-Dwarfs, such relations more typically conceal a desire to exploit the Freak partner either economically, as in Todd Browning's fictional case, or sexually, as in Victor Hugo's *L'Homme qui rit*, in which the man who laughs is not a Dwarf, but a Freak all the same, with a face surgically distorted into a permanent hideous grin. The declaration of "love" made to him by the sated voluptuary Lady Josiana strikes me as relevant to many Freak/non-Freak unions. "I love you not only because you are deformed," that lady declares, "but because you are low. I love monsters, and I love mountebanks. A lover despised, mocked, grotesque, hideous, exposed to laughter on that pillory called the stage, has an extraordinary attraction for me. It is a taste of the fruit of hell . . . I am in love with a nightmare. You are the incarnation of infernal mirth."

Hugo, who has a political point to make, sets this episode before the Revolution of 1789, but the sick yearning he portrays has survived the *ancien régime*. I myself once knew a freaked-out Freak student, an acid head as well as a Midget, who was, he explained, much in demand at the parties of his contemporaries, that latter-day aristocracy of the young. In the late sixties, which is to say, in the midst of yet one more "revolution," they would ask him to partici- pate in individual or group sex, sometimes heterosexual, sometimes homosexual, sometimes polymorphous perverse. But in every case, he insisted, he had sensed a need on the part of "normals" to create a scenario in which he was cast as the monstrous, the absolute other. Nor, I gather, was his case unique; even as I write these words, I am looking at a newspaper article about a French Dwarf, a notary pub- lic, who reports, "In 1970, I was sitting in a café and four English girls came in and sat at the next table. They soon made it clear that they wanted to sleep with a dwarf. When I told them I was a law official they got up and left in a hurry."

But perhaps his moral indignation (and mine) are beside the point, since in sex no one is immune to the allure of *otherness.* It is this which draws white to black, Gentile to Jew, urban type to coun- try bumpkin, old to young, and perhaps even—God save us all—men to women and women to men. Yet the alien, the other, with whom we seek to unite in love is preeminently represented by the Freak; and those societies, therefore, which have tried to socialize that eros may be healthier than those which treat monsters as erotic contra- band.

Certainly things were better for both Dwarfs and normals up through the eighteenth century, when the codes of gallantry did not completely exclude the most diminutive of adults (or, for that matter, children either) from the game of love, and "Count" Josef Boruwlaski could write a series of love letters to his fair, cruel, and full-sized Isalina, which, published in the latter years of his life, be- came a best-seller.

> October 17, ten at night
>   Cruel friend, what torments do you make me endure! What! eight full days have elapsed, and you have not deigned to answer me! Would it have been too hard for you to return me one line— to venture a single word by which the unhappy Joujou might be comforted? . . . Ah! dear friend, may you never experience tor- ture like mine! and, oh, pray make mine cease; let the tender and feeling Isalina cause no longer the misfortune of him whom she formerly called her dear
>
>   Joujou!

Count Josef Boruwlaski.
Anonymous portrait, eigh-
teenth century.
*By kind permission of the President
and Council of the Royal College of
Surgeons of England*

To be sure, he was dismissed out of hand by his jealous pa-
troness, the Countess Humieska, when Isalina yielded and married
him. And when he attempted thereafter to earn his living as a kind
of wandering minstrel, he was forced to endure what he called in
retrospect "the most cruel torments" at the hands of various admiring ladies, who taking him on their laps would fondle him as if he
were a pre-pubescent child. But worse was to come; for as age reduced his erotic appeal, he was compelled to exhibit himself in his
own house as a Freak rather than as an entertainer—at first for a
guinea a head, then five shillings, and finally a shilling. He insisted
on treating his paying audience as "friends" come to call, and to
maintain the illusion hired a butler who, showing them in or out,
would accept the going rate as a tip. At this point, too, the beloved
wife for whose sake he had endured banishment abandoned him,
setting him, the story has it, on a mantel, from which he screamed
helplessly as she disappeared out the front door.

In a sense, Boruwlaski's tragedy was to have lived too long, into Victorian times, when Freaks were prized more as curiosities and occasions for benefaction than as courtiers or erotic playthings. Or perhaps his mistake was to have moved from Poland to England, since by the time of his birth Puritanism had there struck a death blow to the erotic cult of the Dwarf, which, though momentarily and half-jokingly revived in the Regency, expired with the ascension to the throne of the most dour of queens. The Dwarfs' moment of supreme glory seems to have reached its peak in the reign of Charles I, at whose court Jeffery Hudson was presented to Queen Henrietta Maria baked in the crust of a cold pie.

Jeffery was a notable joker, whose crowning jest was "to make married men cuckolds without making them jealous and mothers of maids without letting the world know they had any gallants." Though only eighteen inches tall until his thirtieth year, he was a notably handsome man, as Van Dyck's painting of him and his beloved Queen attests. Jeffery is resplendent in satin and lace, and if there is a hint of mockery in the portrait, signified by the monkey on Jeffery's shoulder on whom the Queen's hand actually rests, it seems directed less at him than at Henrietta Maria, who had interceded for him at least once when his outsize courage had landed him in prison. Jeffery had shot dead from horseback a full-sized nobleman called Crofts, who had made snide remarks on his good fortune with the ladies, and had compounded the offense by appearing on the field of honor armed with (the record is not clear on this point) a child's gun or a syringe. Not gallantry but the fortunes of war finally destroyed Jeffery, who from his eleventh year had served as a courier to the ill-fated Stuarts. He was three times captured and held for ransom by pirates, on the last occasion enduring indignities (one can imagine the uses made of so childlike and charming a male on the Barbary Coast) which, he claimed, caused him to grow. He grew to the unlovely height of three foot nine, which forced him into retirement.

It is at this point that Sir Walter Scott portrays him in *Peveril of the Peak:* an aging and unfortunate courtier, still dressed in tattered scarlet velvet and lace, still boasting of his jests and gallantries, especially of the fifteen court ladies he let call him "Piccoluomini," "and on whome he had his amends . . . somewhere, and

Queen Henrietta Maria and Her Dwarf Jeffery Hudson, by Van Dyke
(c. 1635).
National Gallery of Art, Washington, D.C.

somehow or other—I *say* nothing if I had or no." For Scott, looking back from another age, the little warrior seems a burlesque figure. But Jeffery lived and died as a gentleman and defender of his Queen, important enough to be included in Fuller's *Worthies of England*. And he illustrates better perhaps than any other Dwarf the sense in which they, unlike other human oddities, belong to history rather than teratology.

Monstres par défaut they may be, but the lack which distinguishes them stirs only subliminal horror in the ordinary beholder. Sentimental onlookers want rather to kiss or cuddle creatures who remind them irresistibly of children and who combine, at their best, the wit of adults with the charm of a child. But not even wit and charm are necessary. Nicolas Ferry, universally known as Bébé, was not only feeble-minded but vicious: a drunken egomaniac who once, in a fit of envious rage, tried to push Boruwlaski into a fire. He

The Doll (Earle) Family. Contemporary publicity photograph.
Circus World Museum, Baraboo, Wisconisn

was, however, tiny enough (too small at birth even to suckle at a full-sized human breast) to have been treated like the spoiled child he seemed right up to the moment he died (in decrepit conditions) at age twenty-two.

A third contemporary Dwarf, the spy Richebourg, was able to pass as a baby and thus smuggle messages in and out of France on behalf of his aristocratic patrons during the Revolution of 1789. Once arrived in a friendly house, he would snatch his dispatch out from under his lace cape and light up a cigar. Though unaware, surely, of his notable predecessor, Harry Earles would play similar pranks on the movie lot where, during the 1920s, he was acting a Midget crook in infant drag in Todd Browning's *The Secret Three*. Greatest and most successful of all baby impersonators, however, was the twentieth-century Midget Franz Ebert, who looked so much more like an ideal toddler than any real infant that his picture was used for years on baby foods and baby powder.

Dwarfs have by no means been confined to playing baby roles. There is scarcely any career open to normal-size adults in which they have not distinguished themselves, and there are a few which only they could handle. Among the latter some are very old, and some as new as heavier-than-air travel. Ancient Arab "magicians," for instance, used them to manipulate from within "magic" chess pieces that presumably moved themselves. And anybody who has seen one or another of the "we're all in this together" war-effort films made during World War II realizes that Midgets can work inside the wings of bombers under construction where ordinary men and women do not fit.

In earlier times Dwarfs passed into positions of power in the world of normals by assuming the role of court jesters and Fools. Once granted the ear of a king, however, they proved capable of moving up from the status of mock commentator to that of real adviser. The Emperor Augustus, for example, is reported to have kept a Midget by his side for consultation on matters of state. And Bertholde, a Dwarf renowned for his wit, became in the late Middle Ages prime minister to the King of Lombardy. Since Church offices were also in the power of the court, Dwarfs were similarly elevated to high ecclesiastical positions, despite the injunction in Leviticus forbidding them to serve at the altar. Gregory of Tours was a Dwarf,

Owen Farrel, the Irish Dwarf.
Portrait taken from a paint-
ing, early eighteenth century.
*By kind permission of the President
and Council of the Royal College of
Surgeons of England*

as was a certain Godeau, whom Richelieu made Archbishop of
Grasse in 1672.

Indeed, when circumstance has cast them in such roles, Dwarfs
have proved themselves as capable of leading their people in battle
as any six-foot-tall king. Charles III, who ruled over Naples and
Sicily in the fourteenth century, was a Dwarf, as was Ladislas I of
Poland, referred to in the chronicles as the "Warrior Midget King."
Some would also list as Lilliputian monarchs Pepin the Short, Albert
the Grand, and even Attila the Hun, blood-thirstiest of all royal
killers. Not only is the record contradictory on this score, however,
but Attila reportedly kept a court Midget, the Moor Zercon, whom
he won in battle from a Roman general. And for me at least, it is difficult, though somehow titillating, to imagine a Dwarf ruler with a
pet Dwarf: a mid-sized achondroplastic, let us say, followed about
by a mini asexual ateliotic. Yet an old tradition describes the leader

Harvey Leach. From a contemporary print, eighteenth century.

of the Huns as "of low stature, broad and flat-breasted; his **head** greater than ordinary . . . and his eyes . . . continually rolling about."

In recent times the custom of keeping Dwarfs as jesters has disappeared almost entirely from the Western world. The last analogous situation about which I know anything involves not a king's court but the zany household of the late, great Hollywood comedian W. C. Fields, who was fond of surrounding himself with Giants, Pinheads, Midgets, and other grotesques. Among them was a "very small human being" whom Fields presumably hired to keep his martini glass full. It is he, perhaps, of whom it is told that when he proved dilatory or insolent, Fields would hide his false teeth until he swore to mend his ways.

By and large, Dwarfs no longer have a voice in the administration of public affairs, at least in the West. Alone among modern chiefs of state, Colonel Abdal Gamel Nasser kept by his side a Midget named Ahmed Salam, to whom he turned for advice at critical junctures. This seems fair enough in light of the Egyptian tradition dating back at least to the third or fourth century before Christ, when Knoumhotpou, a Dwarf whose mummy has been preserved, served as Keeper of the Royal Wardrobe.

But little people have long performed many other important roles in society, so they were not left unemployed when the doors of ministries and courts were closed against them. Dwarfs have distinguished themselves from earliest times in the arts, especially in literature. Aesop is the best-remembered among the ancients, but there was also the historian Procopius and Pheletos of Cos, a grammarian and poet so tiny that he had to weight himself down with stones lest the wind blow him away. Moreover, Dwarfs have served as consultants to scientists and philosophers as well as to kings, and sometimes after such apprenticeships have become scientists and philosophers in their own right, like Alypius of Alexandria, who was only seventeen and a half inches tall.

In ancient Greece doctors' assistants were customarily drawn from their ranks. And Tycho Brahe, the great pioneer of astronomy in the sixteenth century, depended on his Dwarf guru Zep not just for technical assistance but for access to the world of the occult. Always at home in the realm of magic, for which their mysterious dimensions seem somehow to suit them, it has proved easy for Dwarfs to make the transition from astrology to astronomy, alchemy to chemistry, and mesmerism to psychiatry. And less mysteriously, men and women of such stature find employment these days not only as chemical engineers and psychologists but as IBM operators and TV repairmen.

Less than one percent of people under four foot six may at present be engaged, as their official organizations like to inform us, in "show business," which is to say, in displaying themselves as Freaks. Yet it is as Freaks that most of us still imagine them, since we are likely to encounter them thus even today. If, on the one hand, the court buffoon has developed into the king's councillor, on the other, as entertainment has been democratized, he has turned first into the circus clown, then into the stage or tent show singer, the acrobat, mime, and parodist, and finally the actor.

The first stage in the democratizing of the court jester is preserved in the institution of the *bagonghi*, which distinguishes to this
day the Italian circus from all others. *Bagonghi* is not a proper name
but a generic one, borne by every Midget clown-acrobat who carries
on a tradition apparently begun by a certain Andrea Bernabé, who
was born in Faenza in 1850, in the commedia dell'arte. Like the
characters in the commedia, it is associated with a particular physical guise or "mask": in this case, that of the achondroplastic at his
most comic-hideous, with huge, lolling head, grotesque features,
and short, bowed legs. But it is, of course, a mask affixed from birth,
not one assumed and doffed as the night's entertainment begins and
ends; so that finally the role of the *bagonghi* is an equivocal one.

The *bagonghi* does not merely display his deformity, he per-
forms—leaping, juggling, jesting; and he needs, therefore, like any
other actor or clown, talent, devotion and long practice of his art.
But he also must be from the beginning monstrous and afflicted,
which is to say, pathetic. Indeed, there is a pop mythology dear to
Italian journalists which insists on seeing all *bagonghi* as victims of
their roles, super-Pagliacci. Did not Bernabé, that "complete and har-
monious human deformity," as the newspapers described him, break
his leg doing the *salto mortale* and end up peddling pencils in the
public squares; while among his successors one died young of alcoholism, another of overeating just before bed, and a third fell from
an excursion boat and was drowned. Or perhaps he leaped to his
death, since only a little earlier he had written in despair, "My
father was a poor farmer; would that everybody could be one. I
made a lot of dough, but it would be better if no one made his pile
like this."

Even when they are thought of as actors of dramatic roles
rather than exhibitions, Dwarfs have tended to be typecast, though
not so drastically perhaps as Siamese Twins or Bearded Ladies. To
be sure, they are not likely to be chosen to play Hamlet or King
Lear, Ophelia or Cleopatra, but I have no difficulty imagining a
Midget Richard III or Puck or even Iago. And in modern films as
well as stage plays they have in fact appeared in various roles. Harry
Earles, for instance, played bit parts in musicals before being cast
as a baby housebreaker and starring in Browning's *Freaks*. And he
ended as he began, singing and dancing along with his sisters, Tiny

and Daisy ("the midget Mae West"), in the Munchkin chorus line of *The Wizard of Oz*.

He was, however, never quite able to dissociate himself from the image of the side show Freak as the somewhat younger Dwarf actor Michael Dunne managed to do. We are likely to associate the latter not with the tent show but with such an ambitious movie as the one made from Katherine Anne Porter's *Ship of Fools;* though in his final film, which appeared in 1973 under the title *Mutations*—an odd adaptation, with s-f trimmings, of Browning's *Freaks*—he played the Dwarf manager of a side show, as many Midgets have been in reality. And with the filming of Nathanael West's *Day of the Locust*, Bill Barty, who played Abe Kusich, has emerged as Hollywood's leading Dwarf actor.

In the circus itself things have been changing for some time now. Or at least so an old-time "talker" and manager of Midgets like Nate Eagle asserts. He used to display his Lilliputian troupe in schools as well as circuses, where they helped him sell miniature Bibles; and when interviewing them for jobs he never asked their height or weight, only "What does your act consist of?" Even in mid-Victorian times, in fact, Barnum presented General Tom Thumb not as a monster but an actor. Indeed, on his triumphal return tour of England in 1857, Barnum reintroduced the most famous Midget of the modern world in the company of two famous actresses: the mother-daughter team who had won the hearts of America playing Topsy and Little Eva in *Uncle Tom's Cabin*. The boy born Charles Sherwood Stratton had become by that time as totally identified with his role as they with theirs, and the nature of that role is defined by his stage name.

"Tom Thumb," Barnum hoped, would evoke in his audience childhood memories of the old ballad "In Arthur's time, Tom Thumb did live," as well as fairy tales starring miniature Giant-killers like Hop-o'-my Thumb, Thumbling, and Thumbkin. The parodic title "General" was probably suggested by the first Midget ever commercially exhibited in America, "Major" Stevens; upping the rank makes the parody even clearer. And in Tom's case the device seemed especially apt, since from the first, the General's act included not only comic songs and repartee but mock impersonation of traditional and popular heroes, as well as ancient heroic sculpture. Indeed, his scale made it possible for him to mock the great of the normal world merely by miming them. Among his more successful travesties were Samson, Hercules, Frederick the Great, and Napoleon, whom he actually played once before the Duke of Wellington, surviving victor of the Battle of Waterloo.

If in one sense the General is the last jester to the crowned heads of Europe, in another he is something very new: a Connecticut Yankee in King Arthur's Court, fifty years before Mark Twain wrote the book which bears that title. And this too is apt, since Tom Thumb did come from and return to Connecticut, he and Barnum and Twain, in fact, all spending their last years in Bridgeport. From the start, Barnum had dressed Tom in clothes identical to his own, perhaps as a kind of joke on himself. But when they appeared before Queen Victoria in 1844, Tom aged seven and less than two feet, and Barnum thirty-four and six foot two, in matching knee breeches, white hose, and pumps, the script seems to have been written by the Twain of *Innocents Abroad*, itself still a quarter of a century in the future; and the joke is on someone else.

The delicious adventure began with Barnum posting before their London theater a placard reading "Closed this evening, General Tom Thumb being at Buckingham Palace by command of Her Majesty." And it ends with the little General, unable to back up fast enough to keep pace with Barnum as they withdraw from the Queen, turning every once in a while to run like hell. This unorthodox procedure apparently amused everyone but Victoria's poodle, who it enraged to such a degree that the General had to fight him off with his cane, "which," Barnum informs us, "renewed and increased the merriment of the royal party."

In between, the General had played the innocent to perfection, greeting everyone with a brash "Good evening, ladies and gentlemen!", assuring the Queen that her picture gallery was "first-rate," boasting to the Prince of Wales, who though only three was taller than he, "I feel as big as anybody." But the true climax was reached when, during his third visit, Tom, invited by the Queen to sing whatever song he pleased, complied by performing "Yankee Doodle." Apparently he thought of the song as a way of hinting at how much he desired a pony like that of the Prince of Wales, actually grimacing and pointing at that animal when he came to the line "riding

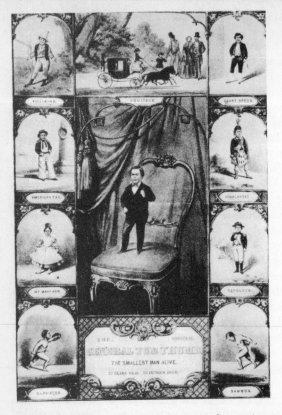

ABOVE: General Tom Thumb and his most famous impersonations. Lithograph by Currier & Ives.
BELOW: The wedding of General Tom Thumb and Lavinia Warren. From *Struggles and Triumphs: or The Life of P. T. Barnum*, by P. T. Barnum (1927).

on a pony." The court, however, took his choice for an audacious reference to the American Revolution.

He was, after all, still only a child. But he matured fast in the limelight, and by the time he had reached nine he was able to sum up his whole European tour for a clerical admirer (writing perhaps at the prompting of Barnum): "I have travelled fifty thousand miles, been before more crowned heads than any other Yankee living, except my friend Mr. Barnum, and have kissed nearly Two Millions of ladies, including the Queens of England, France, Belgium and Spain." If the style reminds us a little of Barnum at his most Horatio Algerish, at least it stops short of adding up the profits, as Barnum would have done had he been speaking for himself. It closes instead on that impresario's other characteristic note, self-congratulatory piety: "I read the Bible every day . . . I adore my Creator . . . He has given me a small body, but I believe He has not contracted my heart, nor brain, nor *soul* . . ."

General Tom Thumb lived for a long time after his early triumphs, becoming finally a portly, though still diminutive, citizen with a beard, faithful to his friend Barnum and his wife, Lavinia, a Midget of appropriate size whom he had won in a much-publicized struggle with Commodore Nutt, and had married in an even more publicized wedding at Grace Church in New York City. It seems, therefore, only fair that he be remembered with affection and esteem, a byword for and a symbol of Midgets at their best. Yet dissent has been registered against his popularity by Dwarfs as well as normals.

A notable example appeared very early in the French press. "Is there anything more humiliating for humanity . . ." wrote an anonymous defender of order and proportion, "than this success of a Midget who blots out in a moment our greatest men, this good fortune of a monster? for finally Tom Thumb is a monster . . . [whose] great talent consists in . . . kissing ladies . . . a million in England; and the English ladies are not disgusted! Tom Thumb does not seem deformed at first glance but his hair is coarse and thin . . . his nose practically non-existent, and his eyes bulging . . . and," the protest concludes, "some despot will doubtless buy him and make him his Fool. So be it!" Moreover, equally strong protests have been registered by Dwarfs, convinced that their status can never be normalized until the memory of show Midgets like Tom, whose image they find as offensive as blacks do his namesake in Harriet Beecher Stowe's much-maligned novel, have long been forgotten. The point, they insist, is not to submit to such images, but by subverting them to destigmatize themselves once and for all.

2

Dwarfs:
Changing the Image

To "change the image" of Dwarfs is no easy matter, since that image is rooted not just in mythology and popular culture but in high art as well. Long before Barnum, it had been fixed on canvas by Raphael, Mantegna, Bronzino, Velásquez, Carreño, Mora, Carpaccio, Van Dyck, Veronese, and Goya. Sometimes the Dwarfs in such paintings confront us head on, as they must have stared at the artist, in sullen resentment or real pleasure; sometimes they are caught at work or play. But always their scale is defined by contrast with normal children and adults, or with the animal pets who were their rivals, or simply with the vast spaces they inhabit but do not fit.

Velásquez, who was more obsessed by them, perhaps, than any other painter, managed in his famous *Las Meniñas* to include all three. It is the Infanta herself who occupies the center of his picture, but somehow the Dwarfs, off to one side, achondroplastic and ateliotic, male and female, steal the scene from her as well as from her kneeling maids and a mastiff, larger than any of them, who

Las Meniñas, by Velásquez (1656).
Museo del Prado, Madrid

seems straining to break out of the frame. Nor are they overwhelmed by the suggestions of other, vaster dimensions opening out from the crowded indoor scene: the painting within a painting on the farthest wall and the open door which frames a figure hesitating on the threshold.

But what is the tone of the picture, and, if it is permissible to ask, its intent, the intent of Velásquez's many portraits of Dwarfs? Is it merely the grotesque he seeks to evoke in the midst of courtly elegance? Is the final impact parodic? pathetic? ironic? Such questions were apparently on the mind of José Moreno Villa when in 1936 he published a study of Negro, Fool, and Dwarf "entertainers" at the Spanish court between 1563 and 1760. Moreno Villa is, however, a man of the twentieth century, his point of view influenced by a world which had come to see them as pitiable victims rather than laughable *gente de placer.*

Indeed, only a couple of years before he began to write, the first World Congress of Midgets had been organized in Budapest by little people determined to establish their full humanity against the stereotypes embodied in the paintings he was to describe. He tries to escape the limitations of his own historical consciousness, surmising that Dwarfs must have symbolized to the painters of the seventeenth century the mysterious and horrible. But he qualifies this with a suggestion that they may have served simply as foils to set off the grandeur and magnificence of their benefactors. He fails to deal, however, with what interests me more, namely, the painters' attitude toward the *use* of Freaks by those who were, after all, their users, too.

With which side did the court artists identify: with the dwarfed creatures on whose head some lord or lady typically rests a condescending hand in their pictures, or with those lords and ladies? No one has, as far as I know, asserted that they sided with the latter, though some art historians have argued that perhaps they identified with neither, merely rendering on command scenes both characteristic and picturesque. And some in recent years have insisted that paintings like *Las Meniñas* represent a covert protest on behalf of the unfortunates exploited to amuse the court.

A prowler in galleries and a thumber through art books like me, however, is given pause by the frequency with which Dwarfs are

Perkeo with Mandrill. German painting, early eighteenth century.
Fotogartner, Heidelberg

portrayed side by side with monkeys and dogs, sometimes quite viciously, as in the anonymous portrait of the hideous "Dwarf of Heidelberg," Perkeo, shown head to head with an even more hideous baboon. Apes have long been associated with, and sometimes even confused with, Pygmies, since at first Europeans thought of both of them as degenerate forms of humanity. Early legends in fact assign them a common origin, one claiming that both were made of the clay left over when God had finished molding woman around Adam's rib. More often, however, they were considered beast/human hybrids, produced when men coupled with the "lower animals" in defiance of God's law.

Moreover, the popular confusion of apes and Dwarfs was seconded by learning, Albertus Magnus, for instance, calling both *monstra* and *similitudo rationis hominae*, monsters and imitators of human reason. And when in the late Middle Ages the long-haired "monsters" we now call monkeys functioned as court pets side by side with Dwarfs, the old theories seemed confirmed. "That captive apes should be linked with court jesters," writes the art historian H. W. Janson, who has produced the definitive modern work on the subject, "is understandable enough; after all, the ape as domestic pet was the exact counterpart of the fool." But Fools and jesters, as we have noted but Janson does not make explicit, were often Freaks, particularly Dwarfs.

How tempting, then, for painters with satirical intent to show the ape and Dwarf together in a courtly context, even though they could scarcely portray the former without hearing in their inner ear the phrase *ars simia naturae*, "art is the ape of nature," which by Renaissance times was used by clerics and philosophers of all art, including portrait painting. Against such *vanitas* the Church deployed not only moral indignation but caricature, persuading the painters to turn their art on itself; so that from the late sixteenth century a satirical genre flourished in which monkeys are portrayed travestying all the ordinary occupations of men, including that of making portraits. Thereafter an artist could scarcely put an ape on canvas without being aware of himself as the ape of apes.

Only Edgar Allan Poe ever successfully subverted the iconography of ape and Dwarf, using it to satirize not the artist, but those who exploited both him and the court jester. In "Hop-Frog," Poe identifies with the abused Dwarf-Fool whose nickname gives the story its title, and who becomes finally a symbol for all alienated artists. The "apes" or "ourang-outangs" of the tale are the "normals" whom the Fool serves: the King and seven councillors, who begin mocking him and striking his Midget love, but end by foolishly collaborating in his "jest," disguising themselves with tar and feathers until they seem outwardly as subhuman as they have been inwardly from the start. At the close of the story, therefore, Hop-Frog is able to hang them all from a chandelier, high above their howling courtiers, who do not recognize them in the guise of apes; and there he burns them to "a fetid, blackened, hideous and indistinguishable mess."

1347.

ABOVE: *Magdalena Ruíz with Doña Isabel, Clara Eugenia and Monkey*, by Sánchez Coello, sixteenth century.
RIGHT: *The Dwarf Don Sebastián de Morra*, by Velásquez (c. 1648).
OPPOSITE LEFT: *The Dwarf Eugenia Martínez Vallejo* and
OPPOSITE RIGHT: *The Dwarf Eugenia Martínez Vallejo as Naked Bacchus* (c. 1680).
All paintings: Museo del Prado, Madrid

But apparently no artist using paints could identify so whole-heartedly with the jester-Fool. Instead, they sought to distance themselves from such lowly court entertainers by painting them in mock-mythological shapes, as, for instance, Carreño did in his portrait of a nude *enana* as Bacchus. His subject, Eugenia Martínez Vallejo, was more commonly known as La Monstrua, since she was not only dwarfed but feeble-minded and grotesquely fat. And the tendril of a vine which conceals her inappropriate sex underlines the mythological joke: a joke repeated in Bronzino's painting of a Midget Dionysus, whose model was Morgante, an Italian Dwarf almost as fat as the Monstress, though this time male at least.

Most daring of all such ironical devices was Dürer's rendering of a Dwarf Adam and Eve, in which the Freak travesty is extended to Holy Scripture itself. His jest verges on blasphemy; nor is it convincingly redeemed by the poet Giambattista Marino, who suggests in a verse commentary that not just the Mother and Father of mankind, but all of us since their original "breaking of the Law" have been, if not quite monsters, at least drastically diminished beings.

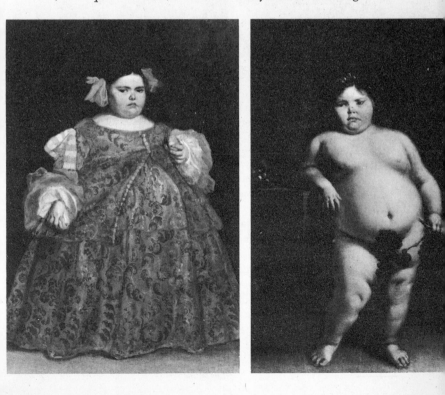

LEFT: *The Dwarf Don Juan of Austria,* by Velásquez (c. 1644).
Museo del Prado, Madrid
RIGHT: *The Dwarf of Cardinal de Granvelle,* by Antonis Mor (c. 1570).
Cliché des Musées Nationnaux

By and large, however, the painters of the sixteenth and seventeenth centuries emphasized the grotesqueness of Dwarfs by as-
sociating them with animals less ambiguous than the ape—chiefly
the dog. Long associated with the Devil, such beasts were a recognized symbol for sexuality and aggression, domesticated but unsubdued. Ladies coddled lap dogs even then, but the practice was
regarded by many as misguided or perverse. Popular mythology explained their affinity with a legend about how the Creator, having
somehow lost Adam's rib, created the second sex with the chopped-
off tail of a passing dog. In any event, not until Victorian times was
the housebroken wolf sentimentalized into "man's best friend." Until then, dogs were alternately fed and kicked by men, who, seeing

LEFT: Detail from *The Birth of Henry IV,* by *Eugène Déveria* (1827).
Cliché des Musées Nationnaux
RIGHT: *Dwarf and Dog,* by Karel van Mander III (c. 1650).
Statens Museum for Kunst, Copenhagen

them in sacred pictures crouched at the feet of the Virgin, understood that they represented everything which she, by virtue of her
immaculate conception and perpetual virginity, denied.

How then did the seventeenth century interpret their presence
in paintings of Dwarfs? And how shall we read them now? On the
most literal level, they are obviously there to establish scale. But for
that purpose, another human, a table, a chair, would do as well as a
hound or spaniel, who must therefore have represented something
more—something monstrous and comic at once. The device has been
used, in any case, almost as long as the art of portraiture has existed.
It is more likely that Renaissance painters reinvented the convention because they needed it, rather than that they consciously con-

LEFT AND RIGHT: *Las Meniñas,* two versions, by Picasso, Cannes (1957).
Picasso Museum, Barcelona

tinued an ancient tradition. Nonetheless, that tradition had been established in Egyptian tomb painting from the earliest period. A great noble called Ti, for instance, had painted on the walls of his sepulcher a Dwarf jester holding in his right hand a mock scepter and in his left a greyhound on a leash. Once reinvented, the conjunction of human and animal pets does not disappear from Western iconography but becomes eventually a stereotype which continues to influence at a level below full consciousness our attitudes toward Dwarfs and to possess the imagination of our greatest painters from Velásquez to Picasso (who did variations on Velásquez's *Las Meniñas* during the 1960s).

Even more influential are reworkings of that icon by popular book illustrators. Two of my own favorites are Phiz's rendering for Dickens' *The Old Curiosity Shop* of an encounter between the doggish Quilp ("a ghostly smile . . . constantly revealed the few discolored fangs that were scattered in his mouth, and gave him the aspect of a panting dog") and an actual chained dog, and an anony-

mous artist's portrayal of General Tom Thumb's fight with Queen
Victoria's poodle in Barnum's *Autobiography*. Neither illustrator, I
am sure, thought of himself as carrying on a tradition, since both
were paid only to keep faith with a given text. But, willy-nilly, they
reinforced attitudes toward Midgets, destined to live on after them
on posters, handbills, photographs sold to admiring fans—and especially the painted banners of Freak shows. No wonder the struggle
of the little people to free themselves from preconceptions has proved
so hard.

And no wonder some have come to think of artists and Dwarfs
as eternal enemies or polar opposites, though there have in fact been
Midget painters, like Matthew Buchinger, Richard Gibson, and
most notably that late nineteenth-century Freak, the quasi-Dwarf

General Tom Thumb battling
Queen Victoria's poodle.
From *Struggles and Tri-
umphs: or The Life of P. T.
Barnum*, by P. T. Barnum
(1927).

Quilp beating an angry dog.
Illustration by Phiz for
Charles Dickens' *Old Curi-
osity Shop* (1841).

Toulouse-Lautrec. Typically, however, when Midgets become painters, they move their normal-sized confreres to scorn. One of the most vicious portraits of such a Freak rival is the portrayal by Cézanne of Charles Lemperaire, the tone of which baffled and astonished me when I first encountered it hanging in the Jeu de Paume Museum in Paris. Cézanne's achondroplastic is rendered with a grotesqueness verging on caricature. But the tone is finally uncertain, so that even now I am unsure just what the painter's attitude was toward this alter ego, who was not only a Dwarf and a bad artist but, it seems clear, feeble-minded at least, if not a little mad.

Even when they did not practice the same art, Midgets have been regarded by painters as rivals. Certainly Robert Haydon so regarded General Tom Thumb, who was exhibiting himself in the Egyptian Hall in Piccadilly at the moment in 1844 when Haydon had just opened there with a show of his paintings. "Tom Thumb had 12,000 people last week," Haydon wrote in his diary. "B. R. Haydon, 135½ (the half a little girl) . . . Exquisite taste of the English people. They push, they fight, they scream, they faint, they cry help and murder!" But it was he who was crying help, really; for not long afterward he was found dead in his studio—having first cut his throat, then shot himself in the head.

It would be impossible to prove in a court of law the complicity of Tom Thumb in his death, though commentators ever since have suggested it. The coroner's jury which sat on the case declared Haydon insane. And his biographers add that he had been a manic-depressive for all of his adult life, alternating between periods of melancholy, in which he flirted with suicide, and spells of extreme elation, about one of which he himself wrote, "I have been like a man with air-balloons under his armpits and ether in his soul."

In 1844, moreover, Haydon had troubles enough to plunge a sane man into despair. He had recently emerged from a long term in debtor's prison, and his life-long feud with the Academy had grown more exacerbated, as it became clear that they would never permit him to decorate the Houses of Parliament. Once before, at least, he had saved himself from ruin with an exhibition in the Egyptian Hall. And when this time his magnificent canvas of Nero fiddling while Rome burned proved no match for Tom's travesties of ancient art and he ended up with a deficit of £11.8s.10d., he must have known it was all up with him.

It is, at any rate, too appropriate an encounter to dismiss as mere coincidence: the Dwarf's revenge on the artist for the centuries of indignity unforgettably described in Pär Lagerkvist's *The Dwarf*. Written in 1945, after its author had already won the Nobel Prize, that novel portrays its Dwarf protagonist as a moral monster: a symbol for the darkness in the human mind which undercuts our noblest endeavors; while its visionary painter represents life-enhancing impulses capable of redeeming what is basest in our lives. The Dwarf, of course, hates him on first sight, but is forced by him to pose in the nude, like Bronzino's Morgante. And remembering it afterward, he writes, "I stood there defenseless, naked, incapable of action, though I was foaming with rage."

Finally, Lagerkvist's sympathies are with the painter, whose curiosity to know the inner working of all things, even the most monstrous, is portrayed as eventuating not only in secular wisdom but in the creation of holy images. And his novel, therefore, I cannot help feeling as I read it again, must stir in any living Dwarf precisely the sense of impotent anger Lagerkvist attributes to his Midget Machiavel. Moreover, history was composing a strange commentary on Lagerkvist's fictional encounter even as he was setting it down. During the last years of World War II an "artist from Prague," known in the records only as Dina, was employed at the Auschwitz-Birkenau concentration camp to make drawings of the skulls, noses, and limbs of Dwarfs slated for execution in order to "purify" the German people. It is a final parody in which the comic is overwhelmed by horror.

And yet, I am driven to add that in retrospect the situation of Dwarfs vis-à-vis other Freaks seems not unrelievedly bad. Being, as it were, the Freaks *par excellence*, they have not merely suffered all the disabilities imposed on their kind, but have also enjoyed special privileges. Not only have they made it generally into the myths and fables, as well as the pantheons, of many nations, but they have also kept alive in the hearts of living believers the names of the magistrates and rulers who befriended them. Visitors to the Chinatowns of San Francisco and New York, for instance, often bring home with them grotesque images of the squat and smiling Fu Shen, god of happiness—unaware that the popular favor he enjoys rests in large part on his intervention on the behalf of Dwarfs when the Emperor Wu-Ti (A.D. 502–550) was drafting them into his service as jesters at a rate that threatened the extinction of their families. Moreover, though the names of no Hermaphrodites or joined twins or Armless and Legless Wonders have come down to us from classical times, ancient papyrus scrolls memorialize Knoumhotpou, and Pliny has recorded the dimensions of Canopas and Andromeda, favorites of the Empress Julia. And while history preserves the memory of the two-headed monster who played jester at the court of James V of Scotland only as "The Fool," anyone interested can discover that the Midget lady who attended Elizabeth I was called Mrs. Tomysen, and that the last surviving Dwarfs of Catherine de' Medicis were Merlin, Mandricart, Palavine, Radomont, and Majoski.

Even in the most grotesque paintings of Dwarfs and dogs, it is the Dwarf who has the last laugh, since the beast almost always remains anonymous, while his companion is known. Certainly no Freaks besides Midgets have been listed in such astonishing numbers among the great and near-great in Fuller's *Worthies*, the *Encyclopédie*, Walpole's *Anecdotes of Painting*, Redgrave's *Dictionary of Painters and Engravers*, the *Dictionary of National Biography*, and the *Dictionary of American Biography*. And surely no other category of anomalous humans is well documented enough to make possible such a *tour de force* of cataloguing as Walter de la Mare brings off in his *Memoirs of a Midget*.

On her twenty-first birthday, his heroine, a beautiful but diminutive English gentlewoman (later exhibited in a circus at the rate of "fifteen guineas for four nights hire" as "Signorina Donna Angelique, the Fairy Princess of Andalusia in Spain"), is presented with a seven-tiered birthday cake inscribed with the names of twenty-one eminent female Dwarfs. Actually de la Mare specifies only sixteen, cutting the list short with a cryptic "and the rest," perhaps because he feared boring the reader, perhaps because in reality he knew no more. But even sixteen—all genuine and attested—is impressive enough:

1. Lady Morgan (the Windsor Fairy)
2. Queen Elizabeth's Mrs. Tomysen
3. Empress Julia's Andromeda
4. Miss Bilby of Tilbury
5. Ann Rouse
6. "poor Ann Colby"

7. the Sicilian Mlle. Caroline Cramachi
8. Nanette Stocker (33 inches, 33 lbs. avoirdupois at 33 years of age)
9. "the blessed . . . Anastasia Borulawski [*sic*]"
10. Gaganini
11. "the gentle Miss Selby of Bath"
12. Alathea (the Guernsey Nymph)
13. Madama Teresi (the Corsican Fairy)
14. Mrs. Jekyll Skinner
15. "the appalling Nino"
16. Mrs. Anne Gibson (nee Shepherd)

Some of these are familiar to me, too, including the Windsor Fairy, Andromeda, Caroline Cramachi, whose skeleton is preserved in the British College of Surgeons, the Corsican Fairy, and Mrs. Anne Gibson, whose marriage to the Dwarf miniaturist Richard Gibson was celebrated by Waller. And Anastasia Boruwlaski is, of course, the sister of Josef Boruwlaski, who, though small enough to stand under his arm and once celebrated throughout Europe for her beauty, is now less well known than her brother, perhaps because she lived a retired life and died of smallpox at the age of eighteen. I am tempted to identify "the appalling Nino" as our old friend La Monstrua, but I can find nothing to confirm this. And I have, therefore, decided to include her in a list of five additional female infinitesimals, intended to bring the total up to the magic twenty-one. I have chosen three of my remaining four from among those born early enough to have been included in de la Mare's original group: a Dutch girl, Pauline Musters (Princess Pauline), the Mexican Midget Lucia Zarate, and, of course, Mercy Lavinia Warren Bump (or Bumpus), whose name Barnum abbreviated to Lavinia Warren for the sake of euphony.

The first is the shortest human who ever reached maturity, and the second—an emaciated ateliotic who weighed 4.7 pounds on her seventeenth birthday—the lightest; while the third rests beside Charles Sherwood Stratton (otherwise General Tom Thumb) under a headstone labeled simply "Wife." Lavinia Warren was an extraordinary woman, who began her career by teaching school at age thirteen (she stood on the desk to enforce discipline) and ended as

General Tom Thumb and
Lavinia Warren. Contempo-
rary publicity photograph.
Circus World Museum, Baraboo,
Wisconsin

OPPOSITE LEFT: Lucia Zarate,
Smallest Woman Who Ever
Lived. Contemporary pub-
licity photograph.

OPPOSITE RIGHT: Lia Graf.
The Midget who sat on J. P.
Morgan's lap. Contemporary
publicity photograph.
Both photos: Circus World Museum,
Baraboo, Wisconsin

a member of the Daughters of the American Revolution and the Order of the Eastern Star, as well as the author of one of the very few
autobiographies ever written by a Freak—still unpublished, alas. I
like to remember her best, however, in the presence of Abraham
Lincoln, who was struck by her resemblance to his much-maligned
and, for a man of his size, almost freakishly short wife.

Finally, taking advantage of the more than half a century that
has passed since the publication of *Memoirs of a Midget* in 1922, I
am nominating to fill the last blank on the cake Lia Graf, originally
called Schwartz, who was in June 1933 "a plump, well-proportioned
brunette" twenty-seven inches tall. At that time, "decked out in a
flowered blue satin dress and red straw hat," she was set suddenly
onto the lap of J. P. Morgan while he was testifying before the Sen-

ate Banking and Currency Committee. It was quite a change from the Ringling Brothers Barnum and Bailey Circus, where she was then appearing; and it remains unclear whether the stunt was dreamed up by one of their P.R. men or some liberal reporter eager to make the already legendarily vile financier look even worse.

If it was the latter, his strategy backfired badly, since Morgan ended up seeming for once avuncular and quite human. "Unusual and somewhat unpleasant," he said of the experience later; but taken unawares, he behaved less like the Bad Father to a nation than somebody's kindly grandfather. "I have a grandson bigger than you" was his first reported response. And his last—when news photographers urged Lia to take off her hat—was "Don't take it off, it's pretty." That his "granddaughter" turned out to be a grown-up female Dwarf merely heightened the pathos and comedy, as well as the oddly attenuated sexuality of the scene. In any case, J. P. Morgan had little to lose.

Not so Lia Graf. I doubt that the subsequent publicity could by itself have driven her out of show business and back to her native Germany, as sob-sister reporters have been insisting ever since. But it may have seemed to her a sign that the time had come to quit a career which she had perhaps never found congenial. Whatever the reason, she left the United States in 1935, despite the fact that Hitler was by then in control of her native land and she was half Jewish. Not only as a Jew but as a Dwarf, Lia Graf was doomed. In 1937, after all Freak shows were banned in Germany, she was arrested as a "useless person." Then in 1944 she was transported to Auschwitz, where it is possible that the infamous Dina from Prague (perhaps herself a Jew, trying thus to survive, like the Jewish doctor thanks to whose postwar account we know of her to begin with) made drawings of her head and nose to be dispatched to the Bureau of Race after she was dead. All we can be certain about is that she was never heard of again.

There are few cases as extreme as Lia's in the long history of dwarfdom; indeed, even in Hitler's Germany some Jewish Dwarfs escaped—like the celebrated Owitch family who survived and emigrated to Israel. Yet the fact that an event like Lia's death could occur even once casts new light on the situation of all Dwarfs everywhere and always: the vulnerability implicit in their special status and high visibility. And though from my point of view a future without Dwarfs—without Jeffery Hudsons or Richard Gibsons or Tom Thumbs or Lavinia Warrens—seems a future deprived by just so much of wonder and wit, I can understand their desire to "normalize" themselves, to escape the stereotyping which (at least in the minds of the most sensitive among them) has distorted their lives, predetermining their behavior in the actual world as well as their images in the eyes of normals. Erving Goffman in a study called *Stigma* discusses the way in which the stigmatized play up to such expectations, citing the case of "a dwarf who was a very pathetic example of this, indeed. She was very small, about four feet tall, and she was extremely well educated. In front of people, however, she was very careful not to be anything other than 'the dwarf,' and she played the part of the fool with the same mocking laughter and the same quick, funny movements that have been the characteristic of fools ever since the royal courts of the Middle Ages."

It was inevitable, therefore, that sooner or later such a desire would express itself politically, as it has beginning with the World Congress in Budapest, convened while Europe was preparing for World War II and just before Lia Graf was hauled off to jail. It seems apt enough that the first attempt on the part of Freaks to define themselves as an "oppressed minority" and to demand their full civil rights occurred in Central Europe, long the favorite hunting grounds for collectors of Freaks. Indeed, there are even now "authorities" who claim that so long as paprika remains the favorite seasoning in that region, mothers will continue to bear monsters. But it is even more apt that Dwarfs and Midgets, always in the forefront of human oddities, be the first to demand that they no longer be treated as less than human.

Some four decades have gone by since that demand was formulated, and it is hard to say how far we normals, upon whom the matter primarily depends, have moved toward meeting it. A good deal of piety on the subject has been expressed everywhere, but old terrors die hard, particularly when they are disguised as fables and jokes; and it seems improbable that anything can be radically altered until new myths have been created to replace the old. Meanwhile, certain token gestures have been made toward ensuring that Dwarfs and Midgets are not forever reminded of their disproportion to the life around them. In Gibsontown, Florida, for example, where circus people large and small spend their winters, a Midget-high counter has been built in the post office—a strange way to begin in the New World, especially in light of the fact that in the Old steps had been taken long before to accommodate their more critical needs. Or at least so I was assured by a Roman friend, who some twenty years ago showed me in his native city a *palazzo* that before World War I had served (he swore) as a whorehouse for Dwarfs.

Meanwhile, political and educational activity by Dwarfs for Dwarfs has continued—chiefly in Germany and the United States, where the Little People of America, Incorporated, has flourished, formulating and publicizing new demands. The first of these is implicit in the name of their organization, which contains what they take to be a non-mythological designation for themselves—or at least one free of the dangerous connotations of words like "Dwarf" or "Midget" or "Pygmy." Beyond this, they ask for drinking fountains, urinals, and telephones they can easily reach; cheap, ready-made clothes in their sizes; equal access to jobs now reserved for normals; special vocational training; and, especially, large-scale medical research into the causes and possible "cure" of dwarfism. More recently their German fellows have been asking for tax rebates or total remission of taxes to make up for the added expense of adjusting to a world scaled to the needs of larger others.

And even as I write this, I read in an Associated Press dispatch that in France, too, a successful jurist called Jean-Brisse Saint Macary, a 4 foot 5 inch achondroplastic who is also a "mountain climber and ace pistol shot," is planning to help the "10,000 French dwarfs" out of their misery by writing a candid account of his own anguish. "Then I will use my contacts," he goes on to say, "in government and the justice ministry to try to form an association of dwarfs duly recognized by the state." What encouraged him to the effort was, apparently, certain developments in the arts, in particular a recent Parisian adaptation of the opera *Turandot*, starring one woman and eighteen Dwarfs, which received popular acclaim.

In any case, I detect a certain note of defeatism in the most ebullient press releases of the much-longer-established LPA, as if even their own spokesmen can forget how limited a constituency the little people are. Individual Dwarfs may have been highly visible in the bad old days of their oppression, but as an organized group they fade into invisibility beside other stigmatized minorities like blacks, Indians, and Jews, or afflicted ones like heart disease victims, cancer cases, and sufferers from muscular dystrophy. Dwarfs fall, in fact, in their own self-consciousness, somewhere between the two categories; since, despite a literary tradition which regards them as an "ancient people" exiled among aliens, they tend to see themselves as patients needing help from chemotherapy or hormones. Whatever the total number of little people in the United States (and the numbers are difficult to determine), by the late 1960s, when the movement launched at the beginning of that decade seemed to have peaked under the leadership of a Texan called Lee Kitchens, a scant 750 had joined the organization. There were perhaps another thousand or fifteen hundred who could be thought of as sympathizers or fellow travelers, but most Dwarfs still continued to feel the call to organize as an invasion of privacy and a threat to whatever difficult individual adjustment they had made to the world around them. In any case, even if the perhaps tens of thousands of men and women under four foot ten had added their voices to those of the articulate two thousand, who would have heard them then above the voices of millions of students demanding peace and parity, more millions of blacks clamoring for political power, or the cries of the largest oppressed group of all, women.

Nonetheless, the LPA seems to have served the needs of a tiny minority within the small minority of Dwarfs—largely, it would appear, those closest to normal size, which is to say, somewhere just above four feet in height, and motivated by social rather than political aspirations. According to a study published in 1968 by a sociologist from Rutgers, only such personal motives could overcome the reluctance of most Midgets, strongly reinforced by their normal parents, to identify themselves as Freaks, and thus presumably cut themselves off forever from the larger community.

For some that identification produced the desired results. "I found a husband," one interviewee reported. "I have learned not to be afraid of other people because they are bigger," another told the interviewer. For some, however, it has worked quite the opposite way, proving only a muffed last chance, since their failure to make it socially in a sub-society of their peers deprived them of "their usual rationalizations about the impossibility of coping with a full-sized world." Yet no matter how modest their victories, how frequent their failures, or even how few of them have engaged in the enterprise at all, the little people will always be remembered as the first Freaks who attempted to demythologize themselves—or rather to remythologize themselves as an oppressed and stigmatized minority, rather than a collection of deviants from a desirable norm. After millennia of ghettoization, they have dared to dream of forging themselves into "the most cohesive class of people since the unification of the Jews."

Jew and Dwarf! How often that conjunction has occurred to me as I, a Jewish non-Dwarf, have pursued their history. Not only in the case of Lia Graf and Dina and the first sociologist to study their plight after organization, but in one particular vivid episode which I have until this point resisted writing down, though it continues to haunt me. In Josef Boruwlaski's account of his early years as a favorite of the Countess Humieska (the time was the middle of the eighteenth century, and he was perhaps fifteen or sixteen), he tells of an encounter with the "poor Jews" of eastern Poland, where in fact my own ancestors came from. Years had passed—years of exile and wandering—before he managed to write it all down, breaking off to express sympathy for the Jewish wretches who were whipped out of their hovels whenever the "sorry villages" through which they passed had no proper accommodations, so that he and his mistress, draping the filthy walls with tapestries, could find refuge from the cold.

Yet despite this disconcerting anecdote, the conjunction, the comparison, strikes me as apt. Looking back over their five thousand years of recorded history, it seems to me that the Dwarfs are, in a real sense, the Jews of the Freaks: the most favored, the most successful, the most conspicuous and articulate; but by the same token, the most feared and reviled, not only in gossip and the popular press, but in enduring works of art, the Great Books and Great Paintings of the West. They have been, in short, a "Chosen People," which is to say, a people with no choice; but they have begun, like the children of Israel, to choose at least to choose. How appropriate, then, that they, who began their escape from oppression via the back doors of the great courts of Europe and have prospered in show business in America, take the lead now in organizing for mutual defense, consciousness-raising, and social action.

If, like some Jews, some of them long to disappear into the "normal" world around them, even this seems to me finally fitting and proper. I would have hoped that they might limit their demands to equal opportunity and integration, so that when they cease to be "monsters" they will still be Dwarfs. And the fact that they call on medical science to make them like everyone else, moves me, therefore, to cry out in protest. But it is a protest which I know I really have no right to make—I who have stumbled through a world built to an alien scale only in earliest childhood and in occasional adult nightmares, from which I awake with the coming of dawn.

3

The Dream of Giants

Giants have moved through our dreams and stories ever since dreaming and storytelling began. Typically, they appear as the enemies of children, foredoomed perhaps, but awesome all the same. After a while, we know the happy ending that awaits the boy they threaten, but rereading such tales to our own children, we still tremble with Jack as he hears in hiding the terrible chant:

> *Fee Fie Foe Fum,*
> *I smell the blood of an Englishmun.*
> *Be he alive or be he dead,*
> *I'll grind his bones to make my bread.*

Not for a moment does it occur to us to put ourselves in the place of his overgrown foe, since in our deepest consciousness we remain forever little Jacks. Nor do we find it easier to identify even with the occasional Good Giants who find their way into children's stories, as

Fairy-tale Ogre with club. Illustration by John D. Batten for *English Fairy Tales*, collected by Joseph Jacobs (1898).

we tend to do with even the most malicious of Dwarfs. And this is natural enough, since there was a time when we were less than two feet tall and there will come one, if we live so long, when we will begin to shrink again. But only in the maddest euphoria of drugs do we imagine ourselves ten feet tall.

Even in more sophisticated fictions, therefore, Giants are portrayed as inimical others, appearing, for instance, not in Dante's Heaven or Purgatory but only in his Hell, where Ephialtes and Antaeus loom over his human-sized protagonists, like those shadowy creatures who towered over all of us in earliest childhood, stooping occasionally to pick us up in their great hands, though whether for good or ill we were never quite sure. By the time we ourselves become parents we have learned, perhaps, that our fathers are not always our enemies; but they were our first—and at some level they remain such to the end.

Perhaps it is different in other cultures. The Indians of North America tell themselves stories about immense but kindly protectors of men. And there are avuncular Good Giants in European literature as well, Rabelais' Gargantua and his son, for instance. But what their folk-prototypes were before he turned them into glutton-prankster-humanists with hearts of gold would be hard to say; and in any case, they exist in their newer form only for the learned. Even in present-day France the popular tradition speaks of a quite different Giant, a dark twin to Gargantua, called Isore; a ghost Giant, dead and entombed, though he demands still to be propitiated—apparently on the theory that even a dead father is a good father only when ritually appeased.

Moreover, the traditions which have most deeply influenced the post-Renaissance West—the Greek, the Hebrew, and the Norse—all represent human culture as beginning after a tribe of monstrous, patriarchal Giants has been killed off. And the tales about Giants which European and American kids most love still are symbolic accounts of such giganticides, suggesting that the enemy father must be cut down in his prime, either by an actual son or an appropriate surrogate, like Puss-in-Boots or the Little Tailor. Yet the boy cannot conquer by force, since that would mean to play the Giant's own game, but by cunning or wit or, for reasons that would have gladdened the heart of Freud, with the aid of the Giant's treacherous wife. So Jack triumphs over his cannibal enemy. So David slays Goliath, and Odysseus blinds and baffles Polyphemus.

True, Odysseus is a grizzled veteran with a grown son of his own when he meets his Giant; but to the Cyclops he seems "a puny good-for-nothing little runt." And so we remember him: naked, disarmed, and overmatched, a fit stand-in for the child. Disconcert-

Jack and the Giant. Illustration by John D. Batten for *English Fairy Tales*, collected by Joseph Jacobs (1898).

ingly, however, Homer's Giant does not die, for he has no soft-hearted mate to betray him, only wine to befuddle him. Yet the Odysseus story comes closer to the primal pattern than any later Greek story. None of Hercules' combats, for instance, recapitulates the archetypal struggle, not even that with Antaeus, whose mother, the sweet renewing Earth, is on the wrong side. Moreover, Hercules himself is a Giant, his seven feet or so dwarfed no doubt by the super-gigantic bulk of his adversaries—but, in any case, no Jack.

To find the mythic paradigm of our fairy tales, we have to return not just to the prehistory of the Greeks but, as it were, to pre-myth: to the bloody legend of the Titan Kronos-Saturn, who is not only, like Polyphemus and Jack's Giant, a cannibal, but—like the latter and unlike the former—is baffled by his own wife in his attempt to consume a normal-sized child. Moreover, Saturn is portrayed as being different from the son he tries to eat only in bulk, whereas Polyphemus is portrayed as a double monster, his single eye identifying him as a different kind of creature.

Similar attempts to distance or disguise the evil father-figure by making him scarcely human are to be found in the mythology of both the Greeks and the Hebrews. Geryon, for instance, another Giant victim of Hercules, possessed three heads, while the titanic brothers who assaulted Olympus—Briareus, Cottos, and Gyges—had fifty or a hundred arms. And though David's Goliath is freakish only in bulk, he is provided with a monstrous double, whom a double of David destroys. "And there was yet a battle in Gath," II Kings tells us, "where was a man of great stature, that had on every hand six fingers, and on every foot six toes, four and twenty in number. And when he defied Israel, Jonathan the son of Shimea, David's brother slew him."

When in the thirteenth century Dante reimagined Geryon as one of the minions of hell, he gave him a single head, but joined to that head (on the model of the fabulous Manticora, which also ate human flesh) a serpent's body ending in a scorpion's sting. And when the imminence of space travel set men to fantasizing new homes for Giants on still unexplored planets, Edgar Rice Burroughs populated Mars with creatures not only sixteen feet tall but green and six-armed as well.

Yet Goya, greatest of all European painters of Giants, portrayed them in the eighteenth century as different from us in bulk alone.

His canvases swarm with monstrous creatures, ranging from hunch-backed Dwarfs and phocomelics observed in the marketplace and the court to demons and grotesques bred of his own nightmares. His Giants, however, are distinguished by no deformity except their scale. Hundreds of feet tall, yet shadowy and weightless, they loom like shared hallucinations over battlefields, farms, and swarming cities. Typically, they are unidentifiable in history or myth, being neither the portraits of performing Freaks nor evocations of ancient fable. Called simply "Giant" or "Colossus" or "Fantastic Vision," they are clearly projections of private fears and guilts.

Only once did Goya draw on mythology, presumably because he had found in the myth of Kronos eating his young a vision of hor-ror which precisely matched his own. In his painting the scene is fixed forever at the moment when the head of the child-victim has just disappeared into the blood-dripping maw of the cannibal father. There is no hint of the eventual deliverance which the rest of the myth recounts, nor any suggestion of the events which have led up to the atrocity: no future and no past, only a static present of unen-durable pain. We have all been there in our troubled sleep, though none of us, perhaps, more vividly and obsessedly than Goya, whose final fate the scene uncannily prefigures: his skeleton lies in his tomb headless to this day—decapitated shortly after his death, no doubt by some psychopath inspired by this very painting. But standing before it or merely calling it to mind, we are tempted for an instant to believe that the Giant he dreamed and drew punished him for telling tales out of school, thus taking from us the consolation of the fake Happy Ending we have been tacking onto the nightmare for some three thousand years.

Whoever has stood long before Goya's painting does not readily forget it. Yet it did not fix for Giants, as the canvases of Velásquez and other court painters of the seventeenth century did for Dwarfs, an unchanging image through which we continue to perceive them. He has, indeed, few successors among the painters, since the colos-sal forms he portrays represent not living reality but archaic fantasy, for which literature and especially popular story provide a fitter me-dium. We think of Giants, moreover, as belonging to memories of our own childhood and the prehistory of the race: a past best repre-sented, perhaps, by the Black Forest of the Brothers Grimm.

But "Giant" is of Greek origin, like such other common names for the species as "Titan," "Colossus," and even "Ogre," which derives from Orcus, king of the underworld. And translating the German *Riese* so, we assimilate them—quite like the Hebrew Gibborim, Nephilim, Rephaim, Anakim, Emim, and Zamzummin, all called "giants" in the King James Version—to the gross and impious creatures who attacked Olympus. But in Greek tradition all Giants were brothers, begotten when the Earth was fertilized by the spilled seed of Uranus at the moment of his castration by his son Kronos, who in turn attempts to devour his sons, only to be deposed by Zeus, who escapes him. In myth what occurs simultaneously in dream is portrayed as happening sequentially in time—castration, cannibalism, rebellion; violence, revenge, guilt, and fear of counterrevenge—all somehow embodied in the nightmare conflict of gods and Giants and men. It is a universal fantasy, easily adaptable to new mythologies; medieval Christians, for instance, had little trouble identifying the Giants of Hellas who had stormed Olympus with those Old Testament "giants in the earth," begotten on the daughters of men by the fallen angels who had warred against Jehovah.

Certainly Dante finds no difficulty in making Nimrod, the "mighty hunter" and builder of the Tower of Babel, the leader of a band "of horrible giants whom Jove still threatens when he thunders." Hebrew and Greek, such colossal monsters stand together in the pit of Hell, equally vast and terrible and dumb. Essentially impotent, they can roar or babble but not speak sense, threaten but do no harm. They prefigure, in fact, Lucifer himself, whom Dante imagines as a Giant too, or rather a super-Giant, more than a third of a mile high. "I compare better with a giant," the Poet says, "than giants with his arms." Moreover, like certain of his mythological forebears, Lucifer has three heads, gnashing a sinner in each of his mouths: Brutus on the left, Cassius on the right, Judas in the center. But Brutus hangs eternally with "his head inside and his legs out," like the half-consumed son in Goya's painting, as myth, history, and nightmare come together to provide a symbol for utter damnation. "And now we must be on our way," says Dante's guide, Vergil, "for we have seen all."

But though Lucifer, which is to say, the primal fantasy of Oedipal guilt and punishment, lives forever, there are, Dante reassures us, no more actual "giants in the earth," since "Nature . . . has

Antaeus setting down Dante
and Vergil. Illustration by
Doré for Dante's *Divine
Comedy*. Nineteenth century.

given up the art of making such creatures" against which "mere men cannot defend." Not everyone, however, has been equally willing to grant that real Giants belong only to the past, certain late Renaissance authorities insisting, in fact, that there may be no region in which Pygmies are found but there are many countries where Giants live. The responsibility for a renewed faith in the existence of Giants belongs chiefly to Pigafetta, the chronicler of Magellan's voyages, who reported encountering in the Bay of San Julian at the tip of South America a group of natives so tall that the Spanish sailors reached only to their girdles. And for four centuries other explorers verified the account, estimating the height of the "Patagonians" at ten, eleven, or even twelve feet.

In recent years reliable investigators have finally laid the story to rest by actually measuring the Tehuelche Indians—as they are now less mythologically called—rather than estimating their stature in a first moment of wonder and euphoria. Their average height has turned out to be a modest 6 feet 4 inches, which makes them a little shorter than the African Watusi, who cannot, however, qualify as the race of the legendary Giants either. Some commentators still insist that the Patagonians may well have shrunk during the half a millennium since their discovery, as presumably all mankind has been shrinking since the moment of creation.

The authors of Genesis seem to have believed so in any case, as did Homer, who reports that in his time it took a platoon to lift a rock which a few generations before a single man could have handled with ease. And Pliny concurred, writing in his *Natural History* that "stature on the whole is becoming smaller daily . . . as the conflagration that is the crisis toward which the age is now verging is exhausting the fertility of the semen." In the eighteenth century, Christian scholars worked out the precise rate of our diminution, proving to each other's satisfaction that Adam had been nearly 124 feet in height, Noah twenty-seven, Abraham twenty, and Moses only thirteen. Clearly, they argued, if the coming of Christ had not miraculously stopped the process, we would all have eventually disappeared.

But such arguments from faith no longer prevail, and more recent investigations have revealed that certain fossilized bones, long taken as proof of such arguments, are the remains of mastodons and dinosaurs rather than men. The oldest genuine human or hominid fossils indicate, in fact, that our remotest ancestors were smaller rather than larger than we. Peking man, for instance, who dates back two million years, seems to have measured considerably under five feet, while a recently discovered skeleton in Ethiopia, which predates him by a million years, could have been not much more than three feet in height. Once *Homo sapiens* evolved, his height apparently remained constant until only a century or two ago, when our species, contrary to folk belief, began to grow rather than diminish.

How shocked we are still when we discover in the museums of Europe coats of mail too small to fit a present-day twelve-year-old. It would not have taken much of a man, we find ourselves thinking, to have passed as a Colossus among the puny warriors who originally wore them. And conversely, it takes a very large one to seem gigantic to a living generation of Americans, not only bigger than their parents and grandparents but aware that modern medicine and diet are creating generations who will grow bigger, as well as mature earlier, run faster, jump higher, and live longer, than they. Moreover, the sense of human scale is altered as week after week we watch creatures, who in another age we would have considered outsized monsters, hurtling into each other on the football field or trying to outleap each other on the basketball court.

Since the days of ancient Rome at least, men of extraordinary dimensions have been displayed in the arena, on the track, and in the ring, but until quite recently they were regarded not as models but as Freaks. I remember, for instance, the heavyweight boxer Primo Carnera, a mere six foot seven or eight, perhaps, but an acromegalic, clumsy and dumbly menacing as an Ogre, so that the crowds cheered for his smaller, more human opponents to bring him down. I saw him in the flesh toward the end of his career, when, his coordination completely gone, he barnstormed the country as a free-

The Colossus, by Goya
(1808).
Museo del Prado, Madrid

for-all wrestler, shaking off his dwarfish opponents on the way to inevitable defeat. I was with my son, then only five or six, who cheered with the rest when the Giant was finally pinned, but wept when we encountered him in the corridors afterward, battered and bleeding and blind-drunk—but somehow all the huger, like poor Polyphemus himself. God knows what guilt or self-reproach moved the small boy by my side; or maybe, like me, he was moved by the demythification of a dream.

Not just Carnera, I must have begun to realize even then, but all Giants are on the verge of ceasing to be perceived as monsters and wonders, becoming, if they are under seven foot six and can move with agility, mere athletes, a season's heroes. Even those who approach eight feet—and can therefore do little more than stand up and let themselves be seen—are experienced as mere performers, rather than an actual embodiment of mythic terror. How few, in any

Saturn Devouring His Children, by Goya (1821–23).
Museo del Prado, Madrid

Fantastic Vision, by Goya (1821–23).
Museo del Prado, Madrid

case, have topped the eight-foot mark: fewer than ten in all the world, it would appear, since reliable records have been kept. No wonder then that, on some level below reason, we continue to wish that somewhere in time lapsed or space unexplored there existed or might exist whole tribes who would dwarf us as adults, even as our parents did when we were kids.

Such a hope can lead to a kind of madness, the insane pursuit (and sometimes even the manufacture) of clues to prove the unprovable. In the early twentieth century, for instance, a reputable anthropologist insisted that the occasional Giants born to normal parents represent the emergence of recessive traits inherited from a race of Giants with whom *Homo sapiens* must have mated before recorded history began. And well into our own time, there have been mystical interpretations of ancient texts purporting to prove that the Old Testament "sons of God," who mating with the daughters of man produced "giants of the earth," were alien adepts come to visit and enlighten us, from the sun, perhaps, or other stars.

The most plausible of all such studies is Louis Charpentier's *Les Géants et le mystère des origines,* which appeared in 1969. Charpentier argues on the basis of myth, folklore, and archeology that the people traditionally known in Europe as *gigantes* must have been representatives of an old, highly developed civilization, scandalously misrepresented by the much smaller barbarians of the Mediterranean Basin, who first learned from them, then destroyed and vilified them. Builders of Stonehenge and those other megalithic structures so mysteriously scattered from England to Easter Island, they were —once more according to Charpentier—refugees from sunken Atlantis. And, he concludes, "This race who initiated and dominated through their knowledge, and who constituted the first aristocracy, were certainly very tall. They were the 'giants' . . ." Such a theory, however, undercuts the popular Giant-killer mythology even as it asserts the reality of the big people, turning them from the dull-witted enemies of littler but brighter humans into their intellectual superiors and maligned beneficiaries.

Other recent essays bred of similar gigantomania manage to preserve the archetypal image of the Ogre by sacrificing plausibility and compounding ancient mythology with modern fantasy. The most fascinating of such accounts is Polly Jay Lee's *Giant: A Pictorial History of the Human Colossus,* which appeared a year after the Charpentier book and contains scarcely a statement free of careless error or paranoic distortion. It is an untidy volume, which deals among other matters with the lives of contemporary show Giants, but it exists chiefly to propound the thesis that there has existed from very early times a humanoid subspecies, gigantic in stature, which survives on the margins of our civilization.

Called variously Kung-lu, Tok, and Gin-Sing, that species turns out to be nothing more than our old friends of the Sunday supplements, the yeti or Abominable Snowmen, known in America, where they have recently been made the subject of a popular film, as the "Big Feet." According to Miss Lee, they are—under whatever name— the descendants of the *Gigantopithecus blacki,* a skeleton of which was dug up not many decades ago in Java. But as the very name indicates, even the discoverer of that species, Ralph von Koenigwald, classified it as ape rather than man or hominid, knowing that our own remotest ancestors were notably smaller than ourselves. But everything is grist for the mill of the obsessed, bent on proving in the teeth of all evidence that Jack's cannibalistic Giant had an actual prototype.

Similar compulsive needs seem to have underlain the exaggerations of Magellan's crew about the size of their Giants, who in any case did not offer to eat them, but stood about docilely with their arms outstretched so that the smaller Europeans could walk under them in wonder. And some similar hunger to believe the unbelievable survives in our willingness, even eagerness, to be lied to about the occasional Giants we encounter at side shows and circuses, not only unmythologically sweet-natured but never quite tall enough to suit our mythological needs.

We do not ever, of course, experience the size of others—even in the normal range—in terms of meters or inches, but only relative to our own size, so that inevitably we exaggerate one way or the other. In the case of Giants, however, our errors go in one direction only, since we tend to assimilate them to the colossal beings of dream and story, who surpassed the nine-foot limit that experience indicates is as tall as a man can grow. Did not Gabbaras, a present from the Emperor of Arabia to the Roman emperor Claudius, stand 9 feet 5 inches high? And was not the Jew Eliezar, sent to Caesar by the King of Persia, fully ten?

Beyond nine feet, the not very efficient adjustment we have made to gravity since getting up on our hind legs fails. It was just short of this height, for instance, that the legs of the tallest man in recorded history, Robert Wadlow, betrayed him. Yet we ask to be deceived in this regard, and there are always promoters willing to oblige. It is instructive to consult the tables in the *Guinness Book of World Records,* which lists side by side the claimed versus the actual dimensions of the most famous show Giants. Indeed—as far as I can discover—in no recorded instance has any Giant, except possibly Wadlow, told the truth about his height even to his exhibitor; and that exhibitor, of course, has never been tempted to tell the truth to the audience.

Barnum, who had strict standards in such matters, declined to show any Giant under seven and a half feet or any Giantess under seven. But Giants who fell short of those limits seem to have had no compunction about lying to him and padding their shoes to prove it. No wonder that once in full regalia—with high-heeled boots and lofty shakos or sombreros or wigs—and mounted on cunningly concealed platforms, they came to share with their audiences the belief that they were in fact taller than any other human. To the naïve, stagecraft is not illusion but magic, and at the side show everyone "talkers" and performers as well as the "marks," become children, permitted not merely to hear but participate in a fairy tale.

Once in a great while, to be sure, there will appear among the onlookers someone who, though he has not yet learned to think of himself as a Giant, will realize that he is taller than the fabulous creature he has come to see. So Jack Earle once wandered into the Barnum and Bailey Circus in El Paso, Texas, to gawk at Jim Tarver, who was in fact three or four inches shorter than he. But the illusion survived, though the actors changed, when he replaced Tarver and became the "real," i.e., the reigning, "Tallest Man in the World." Even when ballyhoo has become history, the "truth" about such

LEFT: Jack Earle, Giant poet. Contemporary publicity photograph.
Circus World Museum, Baraboo, Wisconsin

RIGHT: Skeleton of Byrne, "The Irish Giant." From *Anomalies and Curiosities of Medicine*, by George M. Gould and Walter L. Pyle (1896).

matters is hard to determine. Two hundred years after his death, for instance, we do not know for sure the height of the Irish Giant Patrick Cotter. His gravestone asserts that he was 8 feet 3 inches, while the plate on his coffin reads 8 feet 1 inch, and a reliable modern biographer reports that he was only 7 feet 7 inches.

Such disagreements about measurements seem minor compared to the problems of identity which plague us not only in Cotter's case but in that of other once renowned Giants, many of whom seem mythologically interchangeable. There were, for instance, three major contenders for the title of *"the* Irish Giant" over a period of fifty years, Cotter, James Byrne, and Cornelius McGrath; and if we extend our time span a little, as many as a dozen minor contenders, one of them actually black. Cotter and Byrne, moreover, both called themselves "O'Brien," after the legendary Brian Boru, first king of Ireland. But the *Guinness Book of World Records* attributes the royal name only to Cotter, and the *Dictionary of National Biography* records his boast that he possessed "in his person and appearance all the similitude of that great and grand potentate."

Disconcertingly, however, a doctor who examined him during his lifetime reported that Cotter had an "uncommonly low forehead" and "large joints," and that finally he was "a weak and unreflecting person" verging on "extreme imbecility." Nor does he stand alone in this regard. McGrath, too, was reported by a neutral witness to be "clumsy made" and to talk "boyish and simple." Indeed, nineteenth-century writers tended to consider that most Giants were, like Cotter and McGrath, slow-witted and short-lived. "Giants are almost always characterized by mental and bodily weakness," concludes Edward J. Wood, whose *Giants and Dwarfs* appeared in 1868 but remains a major source book. And Dr. Paul Moreau in his *Fous et bouffons*, a "physiological, psychological and historical study" published in 1885, concurs, quoting to back up his views the co-inventor of scientific teratology, Isidore Geoffroy Saint-Hilaire, who classified Giants as "inactive, energyless, slow in their movements . . . in a word, weak in body as well as intelligence."

Twentieth-century experts grant that many Giants are dull in spirit and sluggish in body, but attribute this to pituitary or gonadal defects or "hypoplasia [underdevelopment or atrophy] of the thymus," and point out that only "pathological" Giants show such weaknesses. "True" or "genetic" Giants can compete mentally and physically with the acutest of normals, though they are not the colossal monsters we dream, seldom exceeding seven foot six, and *never* reaching eight feet, much less nine. It is the former whom we encounter at the side show—their hands, feet, lower jaws, and noses growing thicker with the years, until they resemble storybook pictures of Ogres. Yet no matter how like such storybook creatures they appear, they totally lack their legendary ferocity, being in fact the gentlest of Freaks. When not actually feeble-minded, they tend to be melancholy and hypochondriac, and with good reason, since they move through their brief lives crippled by the tug of gravity, which dooms their bodies sooner or later to buckle and break.

The medical records of Giants taller than eight feet are particularly appalling. John F. Carroll, for instance, may have reached 8 feet 7½ inches, but his height could not be accurately measured during the last fifteen years of his life because kyphoscoliosis, a kind of two-dimensional spinal curvature, had reduced it by nearly a foot. And John William Rogan, a Tennessee black who approached eight foot six, had to be measured sitting down, since adhesions had made his hips and knees unbendable. Similarly, the German Giant Constantine ended his life quite unmeasurable since both his legs turned gangrenous and had to be amputated. Moreover, Carroll lived to be only thirty-seven, Rogan thirty-four, and Constantine thirty.

Finally, Robert Wadlow of Alton, Illinois, the tallest of them all, died on July 15, 1940, at age twenty-two of "cellulitis of the feet aggravated by a poorly fitted brace." Apparently a man of normal intelligence and clearly one of great dignity (he refused to be shown in anything except his ordinary street clothes), he lived all his life in pain and terror. Only death stopped his inexorable growth, which pushed his relatively tiny head ever farther from his gross but fragile extremities, until he could no longer feel what was happening to them. At age ten, he stood 6 feet 5 inches and weighed 210 pounds; at thirteen, he was 7 feet 1¾ inches and 255 pounds; at sixteen, 7 feet 10 inches and nearly 400 pounds; on his twenty-first birthday, 8 feet 11 1/10 inches and 491 pounds. At this point his abused feet and legs were beginning to give way, so that at the time of his death a year and a half later he was using a cane and wearing braces in order to walk. But those braces finally betrayed him, rubbing one leg raw

LEFT: Chang Yu-sing, the Chinese Giant. Contemporary publicity photograph.
RIGHT: Robert Wadlow, Tallest Man Who Ever Lived. Contemporary publicity photograph.
Both photos: Circus World Museum, Baraboo, Wisconsin

until an infection set in, of which he remained unaware (the pain was nearly three yards from his brain) until it had spread to his whole body. Rushed to a hospital in Michigan, he arrived too late for any cure.

It is not only quasi-mythological monsters stranded in the twentieth century like Wadlow who have endured such suffering. From the moment they leave folklore and enter history, Giants have, ironically, bafflingly (how hard it is for us to sympathize with them!), played the role of victims rather than victimizers. Before they became side show attractions, they were used chiefly as soldiers—parade ground attractions placed conspicuously in the front ranks —and porters, lofty enough to impress visitors at the gates of kings.

It was chiefly in Germany and Russia that they were recruited as the former and in England that they served as the latter; but in both roles, they were more slaves than voluntary employees, and therefore abject behind their façade of grandeur.

Frederick I of Prussia was particularly unscrupulous in his methods of impressment, shanghaiing anyone seven foot or over he could find and kidnapping women of appropriate size to couple with them and produce a second generation. Hearing, for instance, of an outsize carpenter called Zimmerman, Frederick sent an agent to him to commission the building of a coffin large enough to fit someone just his size. It was, the agent explained, for a recently dead soldier too large for any standard box. When the job was done, he expressed doubt about whether even the huge coffin Zimmerman had produced would be adequate, asking him to stretch out in it himself to make sure. Once his dull-witted victim was safely inside, the recruiter nailed the lid shut and shipped him off by carriage to Potsdam, where he arrived dead of suffocation. But that scarcely mattered, since even the bones of a Giant were enough to please the ruler, apparently as proud of the seven-foot-one skeleton in his closet as of the eight-foot-three living Scotsman who was the tallest of his elite corps.

Such early uses, however, seem not to have outlived their inventors. Frederick II, it turned out, wanted fighting soldiers rather than display Freaks, and so turned over his father's surviving Giants to his wife as a ceremonial bodyguard. And Catherine the Great, though titillated at first by the notion that immense stature might mean great sexual prowess, seems to have been rapidly disillusioned —or at least, she quite quickly switched from human Giants to stallions, actually dying in an attempt to consummate such a union, when the harness by which her partner was suspended broke. There were, of course, units oi especially tall men in the armies of various countries well into the twentieth century, but these consisted of strapping six-footers rather than "true Giants," which is to say, sluggish pituitary monsters approaching eight feet.

Gigantic porters, on the other hand, served the royalty of England from the reign of Elizabeth I to the time of the Prince Regent, when "Big Sam" was almost as well known as plump George or his plumper mistress. The three most famous, however—King James's

Walter Parsons, Charles I's William Evans, and Cromwell's notorious Daniel—belong to the seventeenth century, since in the eighteenth the more glamorous show Giants from Ireland captured popular fancy. In any case, the fates of the former tended to be melancholy. Evans, for instance, though (or, perhaps, because) he was knock-kneed, splay-footed, and lame, was on occasion forced to dance before Charles's courtiers, who would howl with laughter when at the climax of the anti-masque he pulled from his pocket the handsome and agile Dwarf Jeffery Hudson, as if to emphasize his own grossness and ineptitude.

Daniel, on the other hand, went religiously mad, as befitted his master, preaching through barred windows to amused throngs after he had been confined to Bedlam. He had admirers to the end, including Nell Gwyn, who gave him a Bible, and an anonymous lady, who cried out to his mockers that Festus had thought St. Paul mad, too. There are those who write of him still as a true prophet scorned, reminding us that reportedly he had predicted the major disasters of his time: the Great Fire, the Great Plague, and the restoration of the Stuarts to the English throne. But whatever his gifts, he made his final appearance in the madhouse, a double attraction in the days when Bedlam rivaled the "monster" show at Smithfield as a prime site for a Sunday outing.

Two of the three "Irish Giants" who replaced the porters in English esteem when the fashion changed fared no better. Cornelius McGrath, the eldest of the lot, died at twenty-four of an "intermittent fever," which left him toward the end "miserably pale and sallow," his "pulse quick," and his legs swollen; while his most eminent successor, James Byrne, reached only twenty-two, expiring, according to the old accounts, of "excessive drinking" and melancholia brought on by the robbery of his life savings of nearly eight hundred pounds. Patrick Cotter, who vied with Byrne for the royal name of O'Brien, reached the old age for a Giant of forty-six, though like the others he was weak and fragile throughout his whole career. Nonetheless, he seems to have been uncustomarily jolly as well as long-lived, and is remembered for such good-humored pranks as lighting his pipe from street gaslamps and kissing girls foolish (or wise) enough to lean out of garret windows as he passed by. Better endowed sexually than most Giants, he delighted the pun-loving

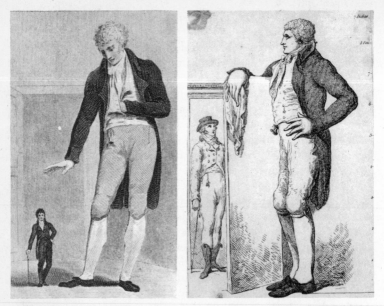

ABOVE LEFT: Patrick O'Brien (The Irish Giant) and Josef Boruwlaski. Early nineteenth century.
By kind permission of the President and Council of the Royal College of Surgeons of England
ABOVE RIGHT: Patrick O'Brien (The Irish Giant I). Early nineteenth century.
BELOW LEFT: Patrick O'Brien (The Irish Giant II). Early nineteenth century.
BELOW RIGHT:
Patrick O'Brien (The Irish Giant III). Early nineteenth century.

journalists of his time by marrying a lady called Cave, or as they preferred to put it, "The Giant's Cave."

Yet he too died haunted by fear of the fate suffered by so many of his freakish peers, ripped from their graves by "resurrection men" in the pay of doctors eager, in the first flush of medical experimentation, to lay hands on any human anomaly. The strange status of dissection at the moment, privately applauded but publicly forbidden, had turned grave robbery into a profitable occupation and Giants into high-priced commodities. The developing science of anatomy had, in short, made it possible by the mid-eighteenth century to exploit Freaks in a new way, so that even death no longer guaranteed them a final delivery from their indignities. To be sure, the Emperor Augustus had a vast hall decorated with the bones of "Giants" (probably the fossil remains of mammoths and dinosaurs rather than men), but he collected them with neither the diligence nor the self-righteousness of English doctors in the Age of Reason, who contracted for their bodies while they were still living, either with them or their exhibitors.

Cotter was resolved that his remains would molder into dust like those of ordinary men, and he arranged to be buried in a lead coffin in a grave hewn twelve feet down into solid rock. "He had a great dread of his body being taken up after his death," a nineteenth-century report tells us, "and gave particular directions for securing it in the grave. It was protected by iron bars, and arched over carefully with brickwork." Small wonder that he was troubled on this score, since earlier the corpse of Cornelius McGrath had not only been stolen by the students of Trinity College on the day it was to have been waked, but later dissected by their teachers, convinced perhaps that they were thus turning an undergraduate prank into a contribution to science. Or maybe they hoped by examining his bones, which are preserved to this day in the museum at Trinity, to determine whether his extraordinary growth had really been produced, as some still assert, by forced feeding of "mucilaginous foods" on the part of Dr. Berkeley, the Bishop of Cloyne; or whether, as others claim, the good bishop had only been trying by diet to alleviate the rheumatic pains which had vexed McGrath at sixteen.

But it is James Byrne, the other "O'Brien," who suffered most at the hands of the surgeons. A simple and habitually drunken peasant, made a celebrity by the mere accident of size, he was hounded all his life by doctors, who as he lay dying surrounded his house, in the simile of a contemporary journalist, "as Greenland harpooners would an enormous whale." He was first pursued by the most notorious sexologist of his age, a kind of proto–Wilhelm Reich called James Graham, determined to prove the virtues of his much-advertised "Celestial" or "Royal Patagonian Bed" on the "largest living male in England." Draped in blue satin and surrounded by six Ionic columns, it would produce, Dr. Graham boasted, when set to oscillating in time to music and radiating electric currents, a "superior ecstasy . . . never before thought of in this world." Moreover, he assured those willing to pay the required one-hundred-guinea fee, even "the barren must become fruitful when they are so thoroughly agitated in the delights of love." But despite the offer of a free night in "The Temple of Health and Hymen," Byrne turned Dr. Graham down flat, being, it would appear, impotent; or as he preferred to put it, "a perfect stranger to the rites of the Goddess Venus."

John Hunter, however, was not so easily turned aside. The most extraordinary surgeon of his time, he inspired a generation of physicians with a series of lecture demonstrations, for which he reportedly had to prime himself with liberal doses of laudanum. Since he wrote only with great difficulty, never having learned to spell or punctuate properly, and read with equal pain, Hunter was forced to function almost exclusively in the laboratory and the operating theater. There he learned and taught most of what he knew—experimenting on his own body (he once deliberately infected himself with syphilis), on dying animals brought to him from the menagerie of the Tower, and on corpses stolen for him by his faithful troupe of body snatchers. He was also a collector of macabre "curiosities," keeping live beasts caged in his garden, whose ornamental pool was ringed with human skulls; suspending from the ceiling of his entry hall the skeleton of a whale; as well as preserving, classifying, and displaying biological anomalies and rarities in the largest private museum in England.

In the case of Byrne, Hunter's scientific interests and his taste for the grotesque coincided, so that he resolved to have his body at all costs, setting on his trail the most notorious resurrection man in his employ. Scared half out of his scant wits by that malign presence, who sat patiently at each of his shows, like a living *memento mori*

ABOVE: Barnum's representative checking a Giant to verify his claimed height. From *Struggles and Triumphs: or The Life of P. T. Barnum,* by P. T. Barnum (1927).
RIGHT: Ella Ewing, the saintly Giantess. Contemporary publicity photograph.
Both illustrations: Circus World Museum, Baraboo, Wisconsin

among the merely curious onlookers, Byrne made careful plans. He provided himself with a leaden coffin, and a group of presumably loyal Irish boatmen pledged to row it out to sea once his corpse had been sealed into it and sink it too deep for recovery even by the medical students who were preparing a diving bell for this purpose.

But Hunter suborned Byrne's fellow countrymen, who submerged the coffin containing only the Giant's clothes and transported his naked body to the doctor's laboratory. Within minutes Hunter had chopped his remains into pieces and boiled away the flesh from the bones in his infamous kettle. Both kettle and bones (the latter turned brown by intense heat) can still be seen in the Hunterian Museum of the Royal College of Surgeons in London; the cauldron was briefly removed in 1895 to be shown to a gathering of doctors, assembled to honor the memory of "the father of British surgery." Moreover, if one looks closely at the portrait of John Hunter done by Sir Joshua Reynolds, he can make out the thighbone of Byrne on the wall behind him: shadowy token of a relationship as tragic in its own way as that of Tom Thumb and Robert Haydon in its. Indeed, even as there is a legendary enmity between Dwarfs and painters, so is there one between Giants and doctors; though in the latter case, it is the Freak who goes down to defeat.

4

Supermen and Superwomen:
The Terror Behind the Dream

Unlike Dwarfs, Giants survive for us primarily not in literature or on canvas, but in the dusty display cases of medical museums. Cotter reputedly kept a journal, which "a whim of the moment induced him to commit to flames"; and some two hundred years later, the ill-fated Jack Earle is said to have written a volume of poems called "Long Shadows," which I have never been able to find. And there is a brief autobiography published in 1865 by "Chang, the Tall Man of Fychow. In Height the Nearest to the Heavens of all other Men." But it is written (or, I suppose, ghost-written) in a pseudo-Oriental style so palpably fraudulent that it gives no real sense of his plight.

Thomas Wolfe, it is true, liked to think of himself as a Giant, especially after he had moved to New York in the mid-1930s to live among what he thought of as dwarfish Jews. But his attempt at describing how an overgrown alien feels in a world of smaller men is undercut by the fact that he was not much over six and a half feet tall. There is, in any case, no equivalent in any European language to Poe's "Hop-Frog," Lagerkvist's *The Dwarf,* or de la Mare's *Memoirs of a Midget:* no deeply moving fiction about a Giant who is, for good or ill, a man as well as a myth.

Oversizes appear in Dickens' *The Old Curiosity Shop,* but only as comic peripheral figures in a set piece that has, all the same, long haunted my imagination:

> . . . Why I remember the time when old Maunders as had three-and-twenty wans— I remember the time when old Maunders had in his cottage in Spa Fields in the winter time, when the season was over, eight male and female dwarfs setting down to dinner ever day, who was waited on by eight old giants in green coats, red smalls, blue cotton stockings, and high-lows: and there was one dwarf as had grown quite elderly and vicious who whenever his giant wasn't quick enough to please him, used to stick pins in his legs, not being able to reach up any higher.

Old Giants waiting on Dwarfs. Illustration by Phiz for Charles Dickens' *Old Curiosity Shop* (1841).

However brilliant, that scene is already a stereotype by the time of Dickens: one more version of an anti-myth of Giants invented as men grew uncomfortably aware of the discrepancy between their pitiful actuality and their horrendous legend. The oldest version, which purports to be history, describes a great assembly of Dwarfs and Giants convened in the seventeenth century at which the Dwarfs so "teased and tormented" the Giants that the latter "complained with tears in their eyes of their diminutive persecutors . . . and as a consequence sentinels had to be stationed in the building to protect the big creatures from the little." More clearly apocryphal is the often repeated story of the Austrian Giant Aymon and his Midget opponent Hans. Inspired in the eighteenth century by two medieval wooden statues preserved in the Castle of Ambras in the Tyrol, one of an eleven-foot Giant, the other of a three-foot Dwarf, it persists in two versions, the first wholly comic, the second ending in pathos. According to the first, the Dwarf was the aggressor from the start, threatening—absurdly—to strike the Giant across his face. But while the Giant was doubled up in laughter the Dwarf managed to untie his shoelaces, and when he bent to tie them, delivered the impossible blow.

The second begins with the Giant teasing the Dwarf about his size, until, enraged beyond endurance, the Dwarf calls on their master, the Archduke Ferdinand, to toss his glove onto the floor and order the Giant to retrieve it. Once that gross creature has kneeled, the Dwarf, in hiding behind the duke's chair, darts out and slaps him on the cheek. The whole court howls, and the Giant, shamed, withdraws to his chamber, from which he never emerges—dying of inconsolable grief. It is, symptomatically, the comic version which has survived, as the passage in Dickens makes clear. For there is something essentially ridiculous about a Giant defeated not even by a true Jack, but by a creature to whom Jack would have seemed gigantic.

Giants and Dwarfs have in fact almost always been treated as comic enemies, except by showmen who exhibited both and for publicity purposes sought to portray them as friends. But they distributed in vain prints of Patrick Cotter conversing with Boruwlaski in the eighteenth century, or photographs of Jack Earle with Harry

Doll perched on his shoulder in the twentieth. Insofar as we remember such portrayals at all, we remember them not as representatives of an improbable alliance between traditionally inimical Freaks but rather of the limits of human scale.

Certainly, I found the statue of Anna Swann, the Nova Scotia Giantess forever holding up Admiral Dot in the Baraboo World Circus Museum, no more moving than the personifications of Large and Small in a child's primer. Yet I know that in real life Anna Swann had been one of the most pathetic as well as pious of all modern Giants. There is, however, something inescapably comic in the notion of so huge a body kneeling to pray—just as there is in trying to imagine her playing, as she did, Lady Macbeth knee-deep in "normals," or being hauled out by mechanical hoist from the burning timbers of Barnum's American Museum. Not that I do not believe in her pain or terror or religious devotion or her right to play whatever role she chose on stage or off; merely that I am helplessly aware of how her size must have travestied whatever she attempted.

Only the grim anticlimax to the domestic idyll with which she ended her life seems to me to escape absurdity. Though apparently too large for marital bliss, Anna found a husband not much smaller than herself and built for them both—and, she hoped, their family to come—a suburban house scaled to their size. But the first baby she conceived was born dead, and when the second came to full term she endured some forty hours of labor which ended in paralysis of her abdominal muscles with the child's head barely emerging. Delivered by dint of hauling and tugging on the part of normal-sized attendants, it turned out to be a boy thirty inches long weighing twenty-four pounds. He survived for only one day and is buried beneath a stone inscribed simply "Babe." It was the end of childbearing for Anna, who died less than ten years later and lies in a grave surmounted by a marble statue of a woman in Greek robes. Life-size, which is to say, the size of an ordinary human rather than a Giantess, it bears the inscription "I shall be satisfied when I awake, with thy likeness." Anna had clearly not been satisfied with her own.

Attempting to retell her story, I am baffled by the fact that, like earlier accounts, mine does not transcend the appeal of a newspaper "human interest" article. Nor do any of the surviving photographs of her and her husband or the tomb of their lost child suggest the true terror of her plight. Yet the photographer's lens has succeeded better in capturing a real sense of what it means to be a Giant in a Lilliputian world than words on the page—but only when the camera is directed at the Giant standing side by side with his normal parents. Even the straightforward studio picture of Robert Wadlow and his father in the *Guinness Book of World Records* compels a shudder in anyone aware that mythologically the Giant represents the Bad Father, the dwarfish Giant-killer the rebellious son. Why then does Wadlow junior tower over his begetter, his face fixed in so conventional a smile? And why does each of them avoid the eyes of the other? If the photographer feels anything but awe at the size of the overgrown boy, his picture does not confess it—as Diane Arbus does, for instance, in her famous portrait called "Jewish Giant in the Bronx."

Her subject is Eddie Carmel—claimed height 9 feet ⅝ inch, real height 7 feet 7 inches—and his small-normal parents; but both her title and treatment strip the Barnum and Bailey show Giant, who lived from 1938 to 1972, of all identity except his Jewishness. And precisely this gives an added *frisson* to the picture, since in legend Giants are the most *goyish* of all Freaks—typified by the monstrous Goliath sent against the frail champion of the Jews, the boy-man David. Yet to compound the irony, American-born children of East European immigrants *do* customarily tower over their parents, though not to so exaggerated a degree. We first fully realize the horror and shame implicit in that fact when we confront Miss Arbus' portrait of a show Giant at home, his head bowed as if to mitigate the difference between him and his dwarfed parents, yet his sheer bulk threatening to bring down the walls of their tiny apartment.

But not for long, we somehow know, since like all Giants—perhaps more than others—such monstrous sons are foredoomed. Both Wadlow and Carmel, however, though destined to die early, are already young adults before the camera fixes their image forever. And by virtue of that fact they do not haunt me as I am haunted by the Prodigy of Willingham, an eighteenth-century Giant who never matured and of whom no picture survives. He exists for us now in words only: a report to the Royal Society of a certain "T. Dawkes Surgeon," and an inscription on his tombstone which reads:

Stop Traveller,
And *wondering*, know,
Here buried lie the *Remains* of
THOMAS,
The Son of *Thomas*, and *Margaret*
HALL,
Who,
Not *One* Year Old,
Had the Signs of MANHOOD:
Not *Three*,
Was almost *Four* Feet high:
Endued with Uncommon Strength,
A just Proportion of *Parts*,
And a STUPENDOUS VOICE:
Before *Six*,
Died,
As it were, of an ADVANCED AGE.
He was born in this Village Oct. XXXIth,
MDCCXLI, and in the same,
Departed this Life, Sept. iiid,
MDCCXLVII.

What the epitaph does not make quite clear is that Thomas had stopped growing several months before his premature death, showing in fact signs of advanced senility: a withered skin, bald patches on his head, and a scraggly beard like that of an old woman. Nor does it fully indicate the perturbation of his parents and their friends (to which we owe the intervention of Dr. Dawkes) at the fact that at age two and a half his limp penis measured $3\frac{3}{10}$ inches in length and $2\frac{7}{10}$ inches in circumference, and "the *Lanugo*, upon the *Pubes*, was as *long*, and as *thick*, and as *crisp*, as that of an *adult Person*." It was apparently his giant sex more than anything else which intrigued his fellow villagers, terrifying the little girls who used to tease him until he would "run after them with his *Penis* in his hand, and if he overtook them, to *piss* on them." Certain soldiers billeted in the neighborhood, on the other hand, amused themselves by plying him "with *Wine*, and other *inebriating* Liquors," and one, according to Dawkes, "did, by a certain Artifice, procure so strong an Erection, as threw the Boy into such an Ecstacy; that had not the *Father* intervened, they all believed he would have emitted."

Hercules and the Pygmies, by Dosso Dossi. Early sixteenth century.
Landesmuseum Johanneum Graz, Alte Galerie

Thomas not only died before attaining full gianthood, but his rate of growth had slowed so drastically that Dawkes had a vision of him as the opposite kind of Freak to what he had at first seemed. "For four Feet six inches, and a trifle more," the doctor comments, "which was his utmost perpendicular Altitude two months before he died, is but an insignificant Stature for a *Man*, who if with no better, should grow very *fat*, would give the Spectators of him, the natural Idea of a *Dwarf*. How strangely, how insensibly does Admiration infatuate us, and intoxicate our Reason." What is involved, however, is not so much a matter of "infatuation" as of the relativity of human stature, and especially its relationship to maturation and aging; so that once in the course of history, at least, there appeared a "prodigy" whom normals could consider both a Giant and a Dwarf.

Thomas Hall was, moreover, a Strong Man, able at age five "to take up and throw from him with much facility a blacksmith's hammer which weighed seventeen pounds." Nor is he unprecedented in this regard. History records the existence of other Dwarf Strong Men and Fat Midgets, one of whom, a perfectly globular young female of astonishing bulk for her size, looks out at us from the pages of Gould and Pyle's *Anomalies and Curiosities of Medicine*, where she is given no name, though elsewhere she is identified as Carrie Akers. And there have been, of course, monsters of obesity and paragons of strength among those of normal height. On the level of legend and dream, however, the Strong Man, the Fat Man, and the Giant tend to coalesce into a single mythological figure, colossal in all dimensions and irresistible in strength; and from time to time such Super-Giants have actually lived among us.

There looms, for instance, on the border between myth and history the immense hulk of the Emperor Maximus, who could wear his wife's bracelet as a wedding ring, and was reputedly between eight and nine feet tall. His weight is not a matter of record, but we do know that, like many other great overweights, he suffered from bulimia, a pathological compulsion to stuff himself—consuming four pounds of flesh and drinking six gallons of wine a day. But this seems moderate compared with the diet of the Alexandrian Arpocas, who (if the chroniclers can be believed) consumed at one sitting in the year A.D. 354 a boar, a hen, one hundred eggs, one hundred stone-pine kernels, a suckling pig, a bundle of hay, broken glass, hobnails, broom twigs, and four tablecloths—then claimed he was still hungry. Maximus ran, in any case, as much to muscle as to fat, being able to knock out the teeth of a horse with a single blow or to break its leg with a single kick.

More recently, similar combinations of strength, corpulence, and height have been found not only in American professional football players but among heavyweight weight lifters, particularly the Russians, and most strikingly of all among Japanese Sumo wrestlers. Selected in early childhood and force-fed on a high-protein seafood stew called *chanko-rigori*, these artificially bred Freaks have reached astonishing proportions, the tallest apparently having been a certain Ozawa, who wrestled in the early nineteenth century and reached 7 feet 3 inches, and the heaviest a contestant of the 1920s called Dewagatake, who weighed 420 pounds though he was only 6 feet 5 inches.

Any Giant over eight feet, of course, approaches record weight, though he may not look in his photographs particularly stout. Robert Wadlow, for instance, tipped the scales at over 480 pounds when he was still only 8 feet 8 inches. And though most Giants are, as we have observed, weak and sickly, "patients as well as monsters," a few have been remarkably strong, like King James's porter Walter Parsons, who began life as a blacksmith, and used to hang his hecklers from a hook in the castle wall, after having picked them up between thumb and forefinger. Some Fat Men, too, have possessed great strength; Daniel Lambert, the most famous of them all, at age nineteen lifted five hundred pounds.

Most ordinary Strong Men, however, have been neither monstrously tall nor fat, keeping alive the hope still exploited in the ads of pulp magazines that a "ninety-pound weakling" can, through scientific body building, grow strong enough to revenge himself or his girl on the naturally well muscled bullies of the world. The exploitation of such hopes achieved fame and fortune for their inventors, some of whom, like Charles Atlas or Sandow, became household names from the late nineteenth to the mid-twentieth century.

In any case, though super-strength may depend to a degree on natural endowment, it is neither apparent at birth nor forever unchangeable. The abnormally strong, therefore, even when they decide to become performers, cannot really be classified with other "Freaks" since they are able, if so inclined, to pass in the world of normals. Perhaps the most notable example of such a change of role was Giovanni Battista Belzoni, an Italian immigrant to Victorian England, who first achieved success as a Strong Man and borderline Giant (he seems to have been just under seven feet tall) but, dissociating himself from fair and theater, ended as an eminent Egyptologist.

To Charles Dickens he seemed a model for aspiring young men of lower-class origin, second only to Dick Whittington in mythic appeal. Dickens, who remembered Belzoni from his early days with Astley's Circus, sought to emphasize the long way he had come, writing, "The once starving mountebank became one of the most illustrious men in Europe!—an encouraging example to those, who have not only sound heads to project, but stout hearts to execute." But Belzoni himself tried to hush up his youthful career as a Freak and performer after he had established himself as an amateur archeologist and had won the gratitude of the English public by donating to the British Museum artifacts he had looted from the tombs of ancient Egypt. Recent scholars, who find his true history more fas-

LEFT: Sandow the Strong Man. From *Anomalies and Curiosities of Medicine,* by George M. Gould and Walter L. Pyle (1896).
RIGHT: Belzoni, the Patagonian Samson. Contemporary newspaper cut.

cinating than scandalous, have begun to remind us again of the years when, as the "Patagonian Samson," Belzoni set audiences to cheering by (once more according to Dickens) carrying twelve men on his head and shoulders, "while Madame in the costume of a Cupid, stood at the top . . . and waved a tiny crimson flag."

His pretentious stage name not only concealed his unglamorous origins as a poor Italian immigrant, but also evoked the mythological antecedents of both Giants and Strong Men. "Patagonian" refers to the colossal Indians allegedly discovered by Magellan's crew, and to sustain that image Belzoni typically appeared crowned with plumes; while "Samson" brings to mind that biblical scene dear to makers of spectacular films, in which the hero of Israel brings down the temple of the Philistines. Thinking of "Samson" we are likely to recall his Greek counterpart, Hercules, whose name has also been traditionally assumed by circus Strong Men. Only Atlas, who bore the world on his shoulders, has been evoked in descriptions of circus and fairgrounds Strong Men as often as the pair of berserkers doomed by a fatal weakness for women, but divinely appointed to deliver their people from monstrous or alien oppressors.

Oddly enough, in light of the antifeminist implications of these mythic names, both "Samson" and "Hercules" have been bestowed as titles of honor on Strong Women as well. At the time of the American Revolution, for instance, there appeared in the street fairs of Italy a woman called "Sansona" (the feminine form of Sansone, or Samson), and billed as a "Lady-Hercules," whose advance publicity announced that she would "bear on her breast a boulder weighing 8,000 pounds and walk barefoot on red-hot irons." And to this very day the counter-legend of the Amazonian woman persists in the popular imagination, figured forth just before World War II in the comic book heroine Wonder Woman, and currently reembodied as the "Bionic Woman"—a hybrid, like her male counterpart the "Six Million Dollar Man," of human flesh and advanced technology.

The Samson-Hercules archetype was reborn, after their names were remembered only in textbooks and European imperialism had opened up new worlds for super-heroes to conquer, as the supermale Tarzan the Terrible, the Indomitable, the Lord of the Jungle. A less equivocal figure than his two mythic predecessors, less dangerous as an ally, less susceptible to deceit, less stupid perhaps, his story does not end like theirs in death, but in immortality. Even he, however, was by no means the last of the avatars of phallic strength; at the very heart of the mid-twentieth-century urban landscape of telephone booths, skyscrapers, and subway tunnels the Strong Man deliverer reappeared yet again in the guise of Superman and Captain Marvel: those dream alter egos of the bespectacled reporter Clark Kent and the crippled newsboy Billy Batson, whose magical transformation is brought about by speaking the magic word SHA-ZAM, an acronym representing in three of its six letters the mythological prototypes of ancient Greece.

There has always been, I suppose, in the minds of many a disturbing sense of the discrepancy between such superhuman champions and the circus Strong Men, who in some sense embody them, yet perform trivial (and often faked) feats like tearing a telephone book in half, breaking chains, or lifting dumbbells. Perhaps, we are likely to surmise, these dime-a-dozen "Hercules" are nothing more than the neighborhood bully grown old and bitter. But only in films like Todd Browning's *Freaks* and Federico Fellini's *La Strada* are Strong Men presented as actual villains, enemies of their weaker confreres in carnival and side show. When Fellini's Strong Man ends up howling in inarticulate anguish on a lonely beach, and Browning's winds up in the mud beneath a circus wagon, a knife through his heart, we rejoice at the defeat of those who have illegitimately assumed the mythic guise of Hercules.

Like the Strongs, the Fats also seem different from other Freaks, since they, too, begin not with an irreversible fate, but a tendency, a possibility of attaining monstrous size, which they can fight or feed or merely endure. There are notable cases on record of side show Fat People who have, as it were, repented and been saved, returning to the world of normals, like some old alcoholic who has taken the cure or, indeed, some overblown businessman or housewife, working out with exercise machines, whirlpool baths, or diets.

The two most celebrated cases of shrinking Fats, however, were prodigies of stoutness to whom the ordinary 250-pound Weight Watcher would represent the "After" to which they aspired. William J. Cobb, who wrestled professionally under the name "Happy Humphrey," but apparently was not, dieted himself down from 802 to 232 between 1962 and 1965. And his achievement is matched by that of Mrs. Celesta Geyer, who published an account of her diminution in 1968 entitled *Diet or Die* and subtitled *How I Lost Four Hundred Pounds*. A circus performer, scared by her failing health, she achieved her major weight loss in fourteen months in 1950 and 1951, during which she went from 553 pounds to 152; but she apparently had become as addicted to shrinking as she had been to bloating (and in any event, what else did she have to do, having slimmed herself out of a career), so that by the time her book appeared she weighed only 110.

Oddly enough, in a country where dieting is a favorite occupation of the overfed and books on the subject sell madly, Mrs. Geyer's book did not do well. Its failure can be explained, perhaps, by the fact that there were so few others who could really identify with her super-plight. Or, perhaps, even those of us who long most desperately to be thin wish that there would continue to exist out there models—preferably dimpled and jolly and manifestly content—of the generous possibilities we have denied ourselves in pursuit of long life or perfect health. "Fat people have been featured on all important midways," a standard book on carnivals informs us. "They are the most popular of all human freaks of nature with the show-going public"—a public which, as the account does not say, continues to count calories and pop amphetamines even as it stares and, at some unconfessed level, envies corpulent Freaks.

But ambivalence toward both the freakishly obese and obesity itself as a kind of freakishness is by no means new. Deep in the mythology of the West abides the figure of Silenus—his great naked belly bouncing before him as he straddles an ass in the train of Dionysus—totally drunk, half asleep, manifestly happy. And his progeny have been many, from Friar Tuck to Falstaff to Santa Claus himself. Not for nothing was the Fat Man a symbol of carnival in those medieval pageants in which the Lean Man represented Lent. In cultures, or classes within cultures, whose codes are notably repressive and strict, fatness has, therefore, tended to be feared; but in more permissive and relaxed communities and castes, it is respected and honored. In either case, however, the Fat Man is assumed to be jolly. "Laugh and grow fat," the old saying has it; and who, whatever his attitude toward excessive laughter may be, does not believe it. A malign or dour human being who weighs more than three hundred pounds seems a contradiction in terms.

The subject is summed up with all of its contradictions in the first essay of a compendium of scientific nonsense called *Curiosities of Medical Experience,* published in 1839 by J. G. Milligan, M.D., M.A., "Resident Physician of the Middlesex Pauper Lunatic Asylum at Harwell." Dr. Milligan begins his essay on "Obesity" by informing us that "The ancients held fat people in sovereign contempt"; then goes on to explain that the Gentoos, who "enter their dwellings by a hole in the roof," consider as excommunicated offenders "anyone too fat to get through." And he brings the case for the prosecution to its climax by adding that certain medieval humanists considered obesity the outward and visible sign of the inward and invisible "indolence and apathy . . . and laxity of fibre" characteristic of decadent clerics during that period. But however reluctantly, he is compelled to modify his indictment, noting that in China "this calamity is considered a blessing," since intellectual endowment is believed in the Celestial Kingdom to exist in proportion to physical bulk; and that the Gordii "raised the fattest among them to the throne."

There have been, in fact, many rulers in the Western world who have been notable for their corpulence. These range from the almost immovable Dionysus, the Tyrant of Heraclea, who had needles inserted in his chairbacks to prevent his falling asleep while sitting and thus suffocating himself, to the lively Ptolemy VII, son of Alexander the Great, who when drunk would, forgetting his gross bulk, execute wild dances on top of his couch. More recent examples include William the Conqueror, Charles le Gros, Henry I, King of Navarre, Alphonse II, King of Portugal, Frederick I, King of Württemburg, and Louis XVIII. There has also been one remarkably fat Pope, Leo X, and at least one corpulent saint, Thomas Aquinas, called for a long time "The Dumb Ox of Sicily," who despite his 300-odd pounds, managed to levitate in his cell.

Small wonder, then, that in Renaissance Europe, where greatness of rank was so often associated with hugeness of girth, overweights were not made court pets like Dwarfs, hunchbacks, and Africans. It was not, in fact, until the eighteenth century that they

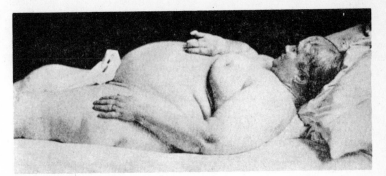

A case of adiposis dolorosa. From *Anomalies and Curiosities of Medicine,* by George M. Gould and Walter L. Pyle (1896).

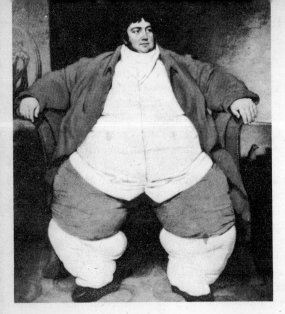

Daniel Lambert, the Jolly
Gaoler of Leicester.
Painting by Benjamin
Marshall.
Early nineteenth century.

began to come into their own as show Freaks for the popular audience. English audiences seem to have prized them especially, and
certainly the three most famous Fat Men of the age were born in
England: John Love, a 364-pound bookseller, Edward Bright of Mal-
den, a 616-pound tallow chandler, and Daniel Lambert, "the genial
and dignified keeper of Leicester Gaol," whose top weight was 739
pounds.

A contemporary witness describes Lambert as "a stupendous
mass of flesh, for his thighs are so covered by his belly that nothing
but his knees are to be seen, while the flesh of his legs, which resemble pillows, projects in such a manner as to nearly bury his feet."
And we learn more specifically that he measured 3 yards 4 inches
around the belly, 1 yard 1 inch around the leg; and that his coffin,
which was four feet across, took ten strong men to carry.

Lambert was apparently loved by all, though it was hard for
contemporary journalists to resist making puns at his expense. The
newspaper account, for instance, which describes his death in 1809
of "fatty degeneration of the heart," falls into the trap, noting that
"he had reached the acme of mortal hugeness." And there is a similar

play on words in the inscription on his tombstone: "In remembrance of that prodigy of nature, Daniel Lambert, a native of Leicester, who was possessed of an excellent and convivial mind, and in personal greatness he had no competitor . . ." It is an epitaph which has been much reprinted, but even those who have never seen it are likely to know of Daniel from the description of him in Pierce Egan's *Sporting Anecdotes*, or at least from the reproductions of his formidable bulk on tavern signs everywhere in England. His name, moreover, has passed into the language as a synonym for great size; Herbert Spencer, for instance, refers in his *Study of Sociology* to a contemporary scholar as "a Daniel Lambert of learning," and George Meredith in *One of Our Conquerors* speaks of London as the "Daniel Lambert of cities."

Most famous of Fat Men though he may be, Daniel Lambert is by no means the heaviest who ever lived. *Guinness* lists ten who surpassed 800 pounds, including Johnny Alee, who may have reached 1,132, and Michael Walker, who is reputed to have peaked at 1,187. But Robert Earle Hughes (born not very long after Robert Wadlow and on the same fertile Illinois soil) holds the record as "the heaviest medically weighed human" at 1,069 pounds. Like Wadlow, he did not live very long, dying at age thirty-two of what began as a simple case of measles but ended with his losing the use of his legs and developing uremia. Nor is his history untypical of the Fats in general. Lambert had reached only thirty-nine before being carried off by "fatty degeneration," and Alee fell through the floor of his cabin at thirty-four, dying of a heart attack while suspended by his armpits and screaming for help.

Yet we do not remember them like the Giants, as melancholy victims; in large part because they do not seem to think of themselves that way, having been as brainwashed as the rest of us into believing that laughter and obesity go hand in hand. Faced by the camera, at any rate, they guffaw, giggle, and slap their quivering thighs like the very embodiments of zest and joy—not only "witty in themselves, but the occasion of wit in others." That is why the males among them are called names like "Happy Jack," while the females tend to be known as "Dolly Dimples," "Baby Ruth," or "Jolly Irene." Indeed, though not immune to real sorrow, circus Fat Ladies have apparently proved as cheerful and amiable in private as they

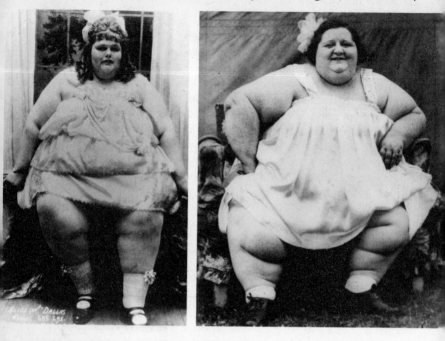

are presented as being in public. Baby Ruth Pontico, for instance, who weighed eight hundred pounds and choked to death when her nurses could not turn her over to clear her lungs after a simple oper-ation, was known as the "Fairy Godmother" to her fellow workers, to whom she displayed only her unfailing good nature.

A notable exception to all of this was Carrie Akers, who seems to have been noted for her bad temper. But she was, as we have already noticed, a Dwarf as well as a Fat Lady, and was well on the way to becoming a Bearded Lady, too, when she decided to retire from show business—which seems cause enough for the behavior which earned her the name "Quarrelsome Carrie." More typical, however, are the nicknames bestowed on Celesta Geyer, who was called first "Jolly Dolly," then "Dolly Dimples," but was also billed as the "It Girl" of Fat Ladies and "The World's Most Beautiful Fat Lady."

OPPOSITE LEFT: Alice from
Dallas. Contemporary pub-
licity photograph.
*Circus World Museum, Baraboo,
Wisconsin*

OPPOSITE RIGHT: Baby Ruth
Pontico. Contemporary publicity photograph.
*Theatre and Music Collection, Mu-
seum of the City of New York*

Carrie Akers, the fat Dwarf.
From *Anomalies and Curiosities of Medicine,* by George
M. Gould and Walter L. Pyle
(1896).

Even in the United States, where skinny women are accounted
especially attractive, she—and her sisters in size—had no difficulty
finding admirers, lovers, and husbands. Statistics tell us that women
plump to the point of being globular, though they may have only a
third as good a chance of getting into college as their skinny sisters,
have a much better chance of getting and staying married. All of us
have memories of having once been cuddled against the buxom
breast and folded into the ample arms of a warm, soft Giantess,
whose bulk—to our 8-pound, 21-inch infant selves—must have seemed
as mountainous as any 600-pound Fat Lady to our adult selves.
And to rediscover in our later loves the superabundance of female
flesh which we remember from our first is surely a satisfaction we
all project in dreams, though we may be unwilling to confess it once
we are awake.

Fat Ladies are, in short, the most erotically appealing of all

Freaks, with the possible exception of male Dwarfs. Indeed, societies less puritanical than our own, whose taste for skinny women
represents, perhaps, a vestigial fear of the flesh, have had no difficulty in acknowledging the fact, confessed in Victorian Tale only
in such jests as Sydney Smith's, who called the marriage of a friend
to a fat lady polygamous, on the grounds that she was capacious
enough to satisfy "the whole parish." In most times and places, particularly among the less educated classes, men have frankly adored
female obesity, like those Stone Age sculptors who created the
"Willendorf Venus"; so that only a genteel European traveler could
in our own century be astonished to discover that the "Venus" of a
Middle Eastern village weighed 637 pounds.

Such news had already reached England in 1896, when the
egregious doctors Pyle and Gould were titillating their readers with
accounts of how, in order to make them marriageable, "the Jewesses
of Tunis . . . when scarcely ten years old are subjected to systematic treatment by confinement in narrow, dark rooms, where
they are fed on farinaceous foods and the flesh of young puppies
until they are almost a shapeless mass of fat," while "Moorish women
reach with astonishing rapidity the desired *embonpoint* on a diet of
dates and a peculiar sort of meal." That the custom of prenuptial
fattening has not entirely disappeared from North Africa even now
is attested in *The Sheltering Sky*, a fairly recent novel by Paul
Bowles, whose underfed European heroine is stuffed with bananas
to make her substantial enough for sexual use by her North African
captor.

Moreover, at the very center of European culture, which is to
say, in breast-oriented, Madonna-ridden Italy, one can find a similar
attitude toward opulent female flesh. Ancient Roman matrons may
have half-starved their daughters before marriage, but their contempt for corpulence can only have been an upper-class aberration
—a deliberate protest, perhaps, against the proletarian cult of the
Adipose Venus. That cult survives to this day, in a land where certain villages each year crown a "Miss Fatty" and all classes throng
to the films of Federico Fellini, in which typically a young boy is
sexually initiated by a grossly fat female. In 8½ and *Satyricon* he
presents us with alternative versions of such an overblown Venus,
white and black; but his most revealing treatment of the subject

is to be found in *Amarcord*, in which a youth just past puberty almost dies of guilt and shame after having buried his face in the monstrous breasts of a tobacconist's clerk, a larger-than-life symbol for the taboo mother and the desired whore rolled into one.

No wonder, then, that *La Piazza*, a study of Italian street shows and fairs, reserves more than two-thirds of the space it devotes to Freaks to a discussion of the Fats and Thins, and that the Fat Ladies get most of those pages. "Those representatives of the gentle sex with particularly exuberant proportions and floridity," the author calls them, boasting that the most exuberant and florid of all have been Italians; and he quotes extensively from the handbills advertising their charms. "The beauty and sculptured proportions of Mlle. Thérésa," the most fulsome runs, "have more than once inspired the artists of Florence and all of Italy . . . colossal, gigantic, extraordinary, the most beautiful woman in the Universe . . . worthy of the chisel of Midas [*sic*] . . ."

He is considerably less enthusiastic about Fat Men, who, considered by the Italian audience less attractive than their sisters, "are rarely exhibited in our fairs." But it turns out that the "Human Elephant" was advertised as extravagantly as any Fat Lady. "Admire!" his flyer reads. "But above all, beware. Be on guard against EC-STACY, because he is truly beautiful!" Moreover, as we have already noticed, in some places (most notably England) where there has never been a true cult of the fat woman, the eighteenth century saw the development of a cult of the fat man (by which, I am convinced, Winston Churchill, that wiliest as well as most Falstaffian of all politicians, was able to profit at the polls in our own century).

Even Thin Men have had some vogue in England, as well as in America and France. It is quite another matter, the author of *La Piazza* assures us, in Italy, where they have tended to be universally scorned ("a certification of Italian good taste"), apparently because eros reigns in the side show as elsewhere, and skinniness is felt to be anaphrodisiac. He scarcely troubles to name any female Living Skeletons, though he does list the most famous of their male opposite numbers, despite the fact they were never "heroes of the street fairs," and details at some length the career of the most celebrated, Claude Seurat. Born in 1798, Seurat was exhibited far and wide for many years, dieting frantically all the while, it would appear, to

keep himself down to freakish weight, and to avoid romantic entan-
glements. Love not merely "seemed to him alien to his condition,"
but (he claimed to have learned from reading fiction) dangerous
to everyone, no matter how fat or thin. And his position seems finally
appropriate to his condition, since—despite frequent reports in the
popular press of marriages between Fat Ladies and skeletal males,
and the titillating possibilities of imagining them in bed together—
lifelong celibacy better suits the mythological meaning of the Living
Skeleton than wedded bliss. Most reported marriages of Fats and
Thins turn out, in fact, to have been fraudulent inventions of public
relations men; though in 1924 Pete Robinson, who weighed only 58
pounds, did actually marry Bunny Smith, who weighed 467.

Yet there is a kind of justification for the attempt to make of
such infrequent occurrences a typical legend, since excessive fatness
seems somehow archetypally female, and monstrous skinniness
male. Indeed, even now certain Mediterranean couples, particularly
among the working classes, tend to follow that pattern: the plump
bride growing heavier with the years, the lean groom ever thinner.
Finally, however, emaciated victims of muscular dystrophy or hy-
pophysia cachexia or anorexia nervosa like Seurat or Robinson signify Thanatos rather than Eros, death rather than love—as, indeed,
their most characteristic show names make evident: the Living Skeleton, the Skeleton Dude, the Shadow.

Though they are usually grouped with the Fats in studies of
human oddities, they are not true size or scale Freaks, challenging
conventional notions about growing up or growing down. Rather,
they call into question the distinction between the living and the
dead. Even in the world of the circus and the dime museum, therefore, they are associated not with Giants or Dwarfs or even Fats,
but with quite other show Freaks, sometimes genuine but much
more often faked, like the Ossified Man, the Petrified Man, or that
palpable but terrifying hoax (wherever it was exhibited, nurses
were in attendance and the more sensitive in the audience duly
fainted), the Headless Woman, who had presumably been decapitated in an auto accident but was kept alive by mechanical means.

The eerie nature of such brothers and sisters to the Living
Dead, the Zombie, the Ghost, the Vampire, even Frankenstein's artificially enlivened Creature, associates them more with monsters than

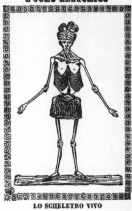

L'UOMO ANATOMICO

LO SCHELETRO VIVO

Freaks. And for that reason, perhaps, they have appealed to the literary imagination, particularly that of certain death-obsessed female Southern Gothicists like Carson McCullers and Eudora Welty, who seek to evoke the supernatural, or to suggest the possibility of a grim sort of survival after death. Standing before such side show exhibits, however—or even looking at their pictures in books—I find myself recalling not Miss Welty's "Petrified Man" but that oddly comic walking pile of old bones evoked in Robert Frost's poem "The Witch of Coos":

> If the bones liked the attic, let them have it.
> Let them stay in the attic. When they sometimes
> Come down the stairs at night and stand perplexed . . .
> Brushing their chalky skull with chalky fingers,
> With sounds like the dry rattling of a shutter,
> That's when I sit up in the dark to say . . .

There is, to be sure, something erotic as well as thanatic in these lines, since the skeleton is that of a dead lover. But what his restless dry bones signify is love lost or denied, and resurrected only as fear and guilt. The Fat Lady, however, signifies the very opposite of this: eros without guilt or limit or satiety or exhaustion. In light of which, it seems somehow right that the earliest icon of a Freak that has survived into our world be of such a phenomenon. Such reflections, however, take us into another realm: that of the sex Freaks and the myths through which we perceive them.

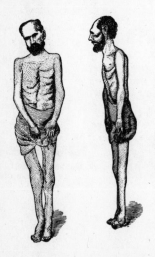

The Ossified Man. From *Anomalies and Curiosities of Medicine,* by George M. Gould and Walter L. Pyle (1896).

5

Beauty and the Beast: The Eros of Ugliness

All Freaks are perceived to one degree or another as erotic. Indeed, abnormality arouses in some "normal" beholders a temptation to go beyond looking to *knowing* in the full carnal sense the ultimate other. That desire is itself felt as freaky, however, since it implies not only a longing for degradation but a dream of breeching the last taboo against miscegenation. Once more the depraved aristocratic seducer of Victor Hugo's *The Man Who Laughs* speaks to the point:

> Am I a goddess? Amphritrite gave herself to the Cyclops "Flucti-voma Amphitrite." Am I a fairy? Urgele gave herself to Bugryx, a winged man with eight webbed hands. Am I a princess? Marie Stuart had Rizzio. Three beauties, three monsters . . . I act like a queen. Who was Thordope but a queen who loved Pteh, a man with a crocodile's head? She erected the third pyramid in his honour. Penthesilea loved the centaur who is now the star called Sagitarrius. And who do you think of Anne of Austria? Mazarin

Titania in love with the ass-headed Bottom. Illustration by Henry Fuseli for Shakespeare's *A Midsummer Night's Dream*. Engraved by P. Simon. Executed for John Boydell's Shakespeare Gallery. Late eighteenth century.

was ugly enough . . . Now you are not only ugly, but hideous. Ugliness is insignificant, deformity is grand. Ugliness is a devil's grin behind beauty; deformity is akin to sublimity.

The myth is that of Beauty and the Beast. Yet even deeper than the identification of the Freak with some creature lower on the evolutionary scale than man is the perception of him as something dumber and by the same token more potent than any beast: the *animal avidum generandi*, as Aristotle calls the pudenda of women, the beast greedy for generation; or rather, since the fairy-tale Beauty is typically female and the Beast male, the phallus, the lover as *nothing but phallus*.

There are, moreover, explicit sex Freaks: males with extraordinarily long penises, for instance (the longest on record measured just over fourteen inches), extraordinarily small ones, none at all, or—especially, perhaps—more than one. Whole ethnic groups have been

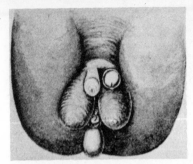

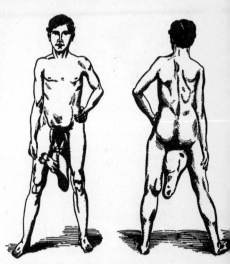

ABOVE: Double penis.
RIGHT: Jean Baptista dos
Santos, the "Di-phallic Man."
Both illustrations from
*Anomalies and Curiosities of
Medicine,* by George M.
Gould and Walter L. Pyle
(1896).

designated as freakish in this regard, like black Americans, who in
the street lore of whites are all credited with being monstrously
"hung." There are also legendary accounts of males with a bone in
their penises, the so-called missing rib of Adam; but in real life, such
a condition exists only as a pathological state called "priapism," immensely painful and ending in total impotence.

A third testicle, too (if, indeed, such cases actually exist), has
been considered worthy of being recorded, along with their total
absence. Ball-less men have, however, been so often artificially produced to provide innocuous guards for harems or male sopranos for
church choirs that anorchids do not stir much interest. And very
little, indeed, has been made in the annals of teratology of those
with extra-large or small balls, while even monorchids, those with
only one descended and visible, get no more than passing notice.
Since ovaries are invisible and vulvas and vaginas concealed, we
have to turn to medical textbooks for any extended discussion of
their abnormalities, which belong to the realm of pathology rather
than myth; though schoolboys up to the first half of this century believed that the pudenda of Chinese women were "slanty" like their
eyes.

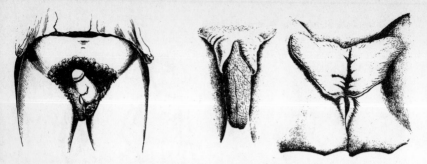

LEFT: Phalliform clitoris.
RIGHT: Enlarged labia of a Hottentot woman. Both illustrations from *Anomalies and Curiosities of Medicine,* by George M. Gould and Walter L. Pyle (1896).

Enlarged clitorises, however, have been subjects for popular attention ever since ancient times, when—if the Roman annalists can be believed—women thus endowed, the so-called *tribades* and *subigatrices,* used to practice with normal women vices *contra natura.* Perhaps the most extended account of the subject is to be found in Gould and Pyle's *Anomalies and Curiosities of Medicine.* Quoting such authorities as "Bartholinus, Schenk, Hellwig, Rhodius, Riolanus and Zacchias," that long-time best-seller tells us of "a clitoris as long as a little finger," "one which measured seven inches," another (the product, we are assured, of excessive masturbation) unmeasured but "enormous" and accompanied by "warts about the anus," and finally one "which resembled the neck of a goose and was 12 inches long." Its catalogue of marvels also includes cases of ossified clitorises, and even a bifid one, which is to say, a split or double organ.

I know of no instance, however, in which such anomalous women have been shown at fairs or side shows, and of only one in which a man with an extraordinarily large penis has been put on public display, that "Indian with his great tool," cryptically referred to in Shakespeare's last play, *Henry VIII.* When I was a boy of twelve or thirteen, however, I met a man with a twelve-inch prick, quite willing to show it to anyone willing to put up fifty cents and to listen to an account of all the trouble it had caused him in marriage and out.

An apparent exception to the almost universal taboo against the public exhibition of female sexual anomalies, however, was the "Hottentot Venus," who in Paris in 1815 displayed to all comers her buttocks, that "enormous and fleshy mass which at each movement of her body undergoes a singular oscillation," and to the favored few her labia, which apparently hung halfway down to her knees. Once more, Drs. Gould and Pyle supply background information, informing us that "the more coquettish among the Hottentot girls are excited by extreme vanity to practise artificial elongation of the nympha and labia. They are said to pull and rub these parts, and even to stretch them by hanging weights to them . . . this malformation being an attraction for the male members of the race."

Perhaps it is not the law and community standards of decency which prevent the showing of such Freaks, since Hermaphrodites have always been standard attractions at circuses and fairs, but rather the fact that they lack mythological prototypes and, therefore, cannot evoke the *frisson* felt in the presence of truly archetypal monstrosities. They are common enough in folklore and popular culture, in which they are customarily presented, however, as comic rather than awesome figures. The one sex Freak referred to in Jewish tradition, for instance, is a pharaoh once encountered by King Solomon, whom the biblical text describes as "crippled" or "limping": a defect which, the jocular exegetes explain, arose from the fact that his upper body was one yard long, his legs one yard long, and his penis exactly the same length. And in popular songs, like the one about the unfortunate bride who married the man who had no balls at all, or the famous parody of the "Colonel Bogie March" ("Oh, Hitler he only had one ball/ Goering had two but they were small/ Himmler was somewhat similar/ But Goebbels had no balls at all"), the same tone is maintained.

It is a different matter with Freaks deviant in secondary sexual attributes, who are often publicly exhibited, particularly when the parts of the body involved are not barred from exposure by custom and use. Yet though polymastia is fairly common in life and myth (the famous Black Diana of Ephesus, for instance, had seven breasts), women with more than two are not frequently featured on the midway, though they are often pictured in paramedical texts like Gould and Pyle's. But asses are quite another matter, as the case of the Hottentot Venus attests.

Woman with three teats.
From *Anomalies and Curiosities of Medicine,* by George M. Gould and Walter L. Pyle (1896).

It was a kind of sniggering racial condescension which made possible her exhibition, and the very name under which she was displayed betrays a sad sort of irony, which turns to downright burlesque in a nineteenth-century ballad celebrating her charms:

> Oh have you been in London towne,
>   Its rarities to see:
> There is, 'mongst ladies of renowne,
>   A most renowned she.
> In Piccadilly Street so faire,
>   A mansion she has got,
> In golden letters written there,
>   "The Venus Hottentot."
>
> But you may ask, and well, I ween,
>   For why she tarries there;
> And what, in her is to be seen,
>   Than other folks more rare,
> A rump she has (though strange it be),
>   Large as a cauldron pot,
> And this is why men go to see
>   This lovely Hottentot.

But the furor she caused, the shock wave which seems to have run through Europe after her appearance, suggests that the audience which came to mock experienced in her presence a sense of awe not inappropriate to one advertised as embodying, however grotesquely, the Goddess of Love and Beauty.

A similar reaction is occasioned by women stigmatized by excess or lack of what seems only peripherally sexual, namely, hair. To be sure, since sexual maturity means the growth of hair on the faces of males and around the genitals of both sexes, it seems natural enough that women with exceedingly long pubic hair or none at all would be recorded as "medical curiosities." But those with too little hair on their heads or too much on their chins have also been found titillating. Indeed, among the oldest Freak forms of the goddess of love (antedated only by the Fat Aphrodite) are the Bald Venus and the Bearded Venus, who in Cyprus were combined into a single deity believed to preside over childbirth.

Even now, when confronted by a full-breasted, round-flanked human with a luxurious growth on her chin or none at all on her head, we feel called into question—in a troubling but by no means anaphrodisiac way—our belief in the bipolarity of the sexes. Such anomalous women usually mingle unnoticed with the rest of us, disguising their deviance with wigs or depilatories; and I have, in fact, known in my own life two or three heavily bearded females who, by shaving often and close, have managed to function successfully in the traditional roles of wife and mother. Moreover, certain neofeminists are trying to "normalize" such members of their sex—or at least to make us perceive them even with whiskers full grown not as monstrosities but as leaders in the fight to liberate all women from traditional, and presumably debasing, sex roles. Nonetheless, I would guess that even now more Bearded Ladies choose careers as Freaks than as revolutionaries.

Women with uncut hair reaching to their ankles have been shown as Freaks, too, though this occurs less and less frequently. And in any case, looking at them we do not experience, as we do before Bearded Ladies, the sense of a border crossed, or a distinction essential to our customary behavior challenged. Nor do we feel it before the kind of boys often born to bearded mothers, who begin to sprout facial hair in infancy and may be fully whiskered by early childhood. Even the Prodigy of Willingham is remembered less for his precocious beard than his prematurely large penis, which undercut not the distinction of the sexes but that of asexual childhood and genital adulthood.

In this sense, he belongs not with the Bearded Ladies but with figures like Old Parr, preserved in legend and literature ("The fall . . . of a once wallstrait oldparr," Joyce puns on the first page of *Finnegans Wake*, "is retaled early in bed and later on life down through all christian minstrelsy"), who challenged at the other end of life notions about the limits of human sexuality. When he died on November 16, 1635, that "poor countryman of Shropshire" was not merely 153 years and nine months old; but (according to reports), the examining physicians found "his Genitals unimpared, serving not a little to confirm the report of his having undergone publick Censures for incontinency; especially seeing that after that time, *viz*, at the age of 120 years, he married a Widow, who owned, *Eum cum ipsa rem habuisse, ut alii mariti solent . . .*", that he had relations with her, quite like other husbands.

In any event, few super-longhaired women have rivaled in popularity the many Bearded Ladies, though the Seven Sutherland Sisters, the combined length of whose hair was 36 feet 10 inches, were renowned enough to give their name to a best-selling shampoo. Nor have bewhiskered pre-pubescent boys achieved top billing in the side show; while the predecessors of both in the no-man's land between myth and history have gone quite unrecorded. The situation of Bearded Ladies, however, is quite different in this respect, too. It is reported, for instance, that Charles XII of Sweden had a bearded female grenadier among his troops, who was captured at the Battle of Poltava in 1709 and taken as a curiosity to the Czar's court in St. Petersburg. Moreover, at least one such Freak of royal rank is recorded, Margaret of Parma, who was Regent of the Netherlands between 1599 and 1667.

The seventeenth century seems to have been a particularly favorable time for bearded females. John Evelyn writes in his *Diary* for September 15, 1651, "I saw hairy woman, twenty years old . . . A very long lock of hair out of each eare. She also had a most prolix beard and mustacheos, with long locks growing on ye middle of the nose, like an Iceland dog exactly . . ." And on December 21, 1668, Pepys tells us with his customary naïve delight, "I went into Hol-

borne and there saw . . . a plain little woman . . . her voice like
a little girl's, with a beard as much as I ever saw a man with, almost
black and grizly . . . I say bushy and thick. It was a mighty strange
sight to me, I confess, and what pleased me mightily." Indeed, at the
beginning of that same century, Shakespeare had already introduced
on the stage three bearded women as witches. Witches had, in fact,
been portrayed as bearded for centuries, a hairy female chin being
considered at some periods *prima facie* evidence of witchcraft. But
bearded women also include saints in their number, like St. Galla, St.
Paula, and St. Wilgeforte or Vigiforte, the latter also known as St.
Liberata or St. Uncumber, under which names she was prayed to by
women eager to get rid of their husbands. It is told that she was not
born with a beard, but having been affianced, despite her conver-
sion to Christianity, to a pagan, beseeched her Christian God to
afflict her in some way that would make her sexually undesirable.
Her God complied, and her revolted lover rejected her; at which
point her irate father crucified her—thus granting her a consumma-
tion infinitely preferable by her lights to unhallowed copulation.

It is an odd legend—invented backward in the late Middle
Ages, modern iconographers tell us, to explain certain archaic paintings of a draped and hermaphroditic Christ. But it also signals the
resurgence in the mind of Europe of the myth of the Bearded Aphrodite—upon which the Christian Happy Ending of blessed virginity
seems inappositely imposed. It is an ending which, in any case,
strikes us as improbable, since in actual history women with beards
have attracted rather than repelled husbands and lovers. Julia Pastrana, for instance, who was not merely bewhiskered but covered all
over with hair and so ill-favored that she was billed as the "Ugliest
Woman in the World," was married to her manager, a man called
Lent.

Their union was blessed with a daughter no more comely than
Julia, at the first sight of whom she began to languish, dying shortly
thereafter—the sob-sisterly would have us believe—of a broken heart.
But Lent proved unable to let her go, not only preserving her body
in mummified form and displaying it—along with, some witnesses
report, the mummy of her baby girl—but searching the world over
until he had found another young woman as hairy and hideous as
she. Rechristening that reborn Julia, whose name was actually Marie
Bartels, Lenora Pastrana, he presented her at fairs and circuses as

ABOVE LEFT: Julia Pastrana, the Ugliest Woman in the World. From *Anomalies and Curiosities of Medicine,* by George M. Gould and Walter L. Pyle (1896).
ABOVE: Grace Gilbert, a Bearded Lady. Contemporary publicity photograph.
Circus World Museum, Baraboo, Wisconsin
LEFT: Madame Clofullia, the Swiss Bearded Lady, with her bearded son, the Infant Esau. Lithograph by Currier & Ives. Mid-nineteenth century.
Theatre and Music Collection, Museum of the City of New York

Julia's sister. Moreover, he married her, too, thus establishing a record of his own as the sole man in history to have had two bearded brides. His only rival in this regard is a nineteenth-century Italian showman who married successively a Strong Woman, a Fat Lady, and a Bearded Lady, and apparently lived happily with them all. Lent, however, did not end as well, dying—as one might have foreseen—quite mad, though successful enough to leave "Lenora" sufficiently well heeled to retire from show business and acquire another husband some twenty years her junior.

Certainly, other renowned Bearded Ladies, more attractive though equally hirsute, have had little trouble in finding husbands. Rosine Marguerite Müller, for instance, along with Clementine Delait, Annie Jones, Grace Gilbert, Joséphine Boisdechêne, and Lady Olga were all married at least once. True, Frances Murphy, who was featured as the Gorilla Lady in the Strange as It Seems side show of the New York World's Fair in 1940, never managed to acquire a husband; but this seems understandable enough in light of the fact that she turned out to be a man. And to even things up, Lady Olga, who was superabundantly female, had four. "Most bearded ladies are men," her manager is quoted as having told an inquiring reporter. "Even when they're women, they look like men. Lady Olga is a woman."

Moreover, she claimed to have had the longest beard of any woman ever publicly exhibited. Annie Jones, who appeared with the Barnum and Bailey Circus from childhood on, billed successively as the Infant Esau, the Child Esau, and the Esau Lady, had whiskers only two inches long. Grace Gilbert's measured six, though she showed them off to full advantage by peroxiding them bright gold, while Joséphine Boisdechêne's reached eight inches, without, however, any trace of a mustache. Olga, née Jane Barnell, was fully mustached and had a beard of thirteen and a half inches. Even that seems insignificant beside the prize male beard of all time, which measured seventeen and a half *feet* and is preserved in the Smithsonian Institution. But it is the best any woman has ever done, with the possible exception of Jane Deveree, to whom the *Guinness Book of World Records* attributes one of fourteen inches.

Jane Deveree seems, in any case, to have lacked the appeal of Lady Olga, who had a longer career as a side show performer than any other American woman, and in 1943 was featured in Joseph

Mitchell's *McSorley's Wonderful Saloon.* Some ten years earlier
Todd Browning had cast her in *Freaks* as the mother of a baby
whose father is the Living Skeleton. The birth scene is one of the
most moving and humane of that extraordinary film, but Olga apparently hated the whole experience. "Miss Barnell," her manager
reported afterward, "thinks this picture was an insult to all freaks
everywhere and is sorry she acted in it."

Bearded Ladies are reputed to be next to Fat Ladies as the most
benign of all Freaks. But Lady Olga seems to have alternated between drunken rage and what Mitchell calls "apathy . . . the occu-
pational disease of freaks." I find it credible enough that boredom
afflicts all performers doomed to play over and over the role to which
their bodies have destined them, and that it debouches in hatred for
those who pay to see them in that role. But Joséphine Boisdechêne,
or Madame Fortune Clofullia, as she was professionally known after
her marriage, who was at least as famous as Lady Olga (3.5 million
people are reported to have seen her during her brief nine months
with Barnum), was as placid and pleasant as we would prefer to believe such Freaks always are.

Perhaps her good humor is explained by the fact that she married only once, which is to say successfully, and withdrew from show
life relatively early. True, at one point, Napoleon III had sent her
diamonds, flattered because she had styled her beard to resemble
his. But though this allegedly occasioned jealousy on the part of his
Empress Eugénie, it apparently caused no concern to M. Clofullia,
who knew how respectable and discreet his wife really was. Born to
a prosperous Swiss family, she had been sent to a proper boarding
school, where, according to Barnum's publicity, "she excelled particularly in those works adapted to her sex such as embroideries,
lace, network, and all kinds of needle work." Later she turned to
painting, an interest which led to her first meeting with her artist
husband, a young man "of pleasing countenance and," appropriately,
"little beard." With him she had first a girl, then a boy who promised
to become even more hairy than herself.

She brought the boy with her to America, where he was also exhibited by Barnum, partly to verify his mother's gender beyond any
doubt (a skeptic had—perhaps at the instigation of the publicity-
hungry old humbug himself—sued for the return of his price of admission on the grounds of fraud), and partly because he was himself

a genuine Freak. "His body is thoroughly covered with hair," Barnum's flyer reads, "more particularly over the shoulders and on the back; his face is fully surrounded with whiskers, fully marked, and of about half an inch in length, but of light color. The child is strong and healthy, and promises fair to astonish the reader."

Called, like Annie Jones, the "Infant Esau," he was exhibited in dresses until the age of fourteen, causing some beholders to assume that he was a bearded girl. But he disappears from sight late in the nineteenth century without ever having achieved either the fame of Mme. Clofullia or the legendary appeal of figures like Jo-Jo the Dog-faced Boy or Lionel the Lion-faced Man—whose names still produce in many the shock of recognition provided only by the most famous human oddities, Tom Thumb, for instance, or Zip, or Chang and Eng, the first Siamese Twins.

Actually baptized Feodor Jeftichew and Stephen Bibrowsky, Jo-Jo and Lionel were rebaptized to indicate that, like other extreme hairies and furries, they had been assimilated to a category of Freaks so deeply rooted in mythology that, in the teeth of all evidence, we have tried to believe it exists in history as well. These are the animal Freaks or beast-men, ambiguous hybrids who have haunted our dreams ever since *Homo sapiens* first began to think of himself as separate from the other beasts of the field.

As late as the early twentieth century, distinguished scholars like Freud, Frazier, and Robertson Smith were convinced that *all* religions began with the belief that mankind had descended from various animal species and that the existence of separate clans and tribes was explained by the fact that some men considered themselves the offspring of wolves, some of serpents, some of tortoises, etc. Such creatures were, therefore, venerated rather than despised, not just as ancestors but as divine creators of their respective lines. But quite early a counter-mythology began to assert itself, teaching a separate creation for man and a separate destiny outside the chain of metamorphoses in which divine, animal, and human constantly merged and blended. Only in the Judaeo-Christian-Islamic tradition, however, with its myth of a humanity created in God's image, have the boundaries been defined absolutely and man's superiority to his inarticulate brothers and sisters made an article of faith.

Similarly, only in that tradition has the conclusion been drawn that since man alone was made in the image of his Creator, his Crea-

ABOVE: Half Man/Half Pony.
From *Monstres et prodiges*,
by Ambroise Paré (1573).
LEFT: Koo Koo the Bird Girl
with Dwarf jester. Contemporary publicity photograph.
*Circus World Museum, Baraboo,
Wisconsin*
BELOW LEFT: The Frog-
headed Boy. From *Monstres
et prodiges*, by Ambroise Paré
(1573).
BELOW RIGHT: The Minotaur.
Illustration by Doré for
Dante's *Divine Comedy*.
Nineteenth century.

tor could only be portrayed in his. It was, therefore, forbidden to Jews to represent the divine in animal form, much less in any shape which combined the human with the animal: whether in the Egyptian fashion, which customarily placed an animal's head upon a human body, or in the Greek, which more typically attached a human head and torso to animal haunches, genitals, and legs. That way heathenish idolatry lay—as Roman Catholicism proved in its backsliding accommodation to pagan taste by symbolizing Christ as a lamb, a peacock, a fish, and a phoenix. But the Jews stood firm; the Protestants returned to the true way again; and the Moslems leaned over backward, forbidding *all* iconic representation of holy things.

Moreover, the priests of Israel and their descendants, Jewish, Christian, and Mohammedan, have always been forbidden, in the fashion of shamans and medicine men and the servitors of idols, to assume the masks of animals or to mime them ritually, thus becoming creatures lower than themselves. And they have enjoined their congregations to avoid totemism, teaching that no man is descended from a beast but that all have issued directly from the hand of an anthropomorphic God. The theriomorphic *daimones* of Egypt and Greece have, therefore, been remanded in Western cultures to the nursery, where children are permitted in the name of "make-believe" to thrill for a little while at transformations of beasts to men and men to beasts, or even to imagine creatures who share the characteristics of both. Indeed, in the Anglo-Saxon world of the nineteenth century, ancient tales of satyrs and centaurs were themselves turned into nursery stories by writers as eminent as Nathaniel Hawthorne. And in the twentieth, a Christian apologist like C. S. Lewis could smuggle such mythological hybrids into his Narnia books, with the implicit understanding that his child-audience would know they were "just pretend," and the adults, reading aloud to them, would recognize them as "allegorical."

Meanwhile, in the official literature of the Church, they were allowed to live on in Hell, where Freaks once worshipped as gods reappeared as the guardians of the damned. Or more jocularly, they were given a place in the cathedrals, on the walls of which they became ornamental gargoyles and grotesques. Satan himself, the Prince of the realm of darkness, was figured forth as a similar grotesque: a monstrous satyr, half goat and half man, a travesty of the once potent lord of the wilderness, the Great God Pan. Indeed, to Christians,

Greek iconography seemed already to have figured forth, though only half-consciously, an easily assimilable meaning, since its hybrid deities, the lubricious fauns and centaurs, were beastlike not in the head, the seat of reason, but only from the waist down. Nonetheless, the official guardians of morality seemed worried lest the animal/ human Freaks excluded from the Judaeo-Christian pantheon be born again in human society, and they established laws forbidding "unnatural" cohabitation. "Whosoever lieth with a beast shall surely be put to death . . . Neither shalt thou lie with any beast to defile thyself therewith; neither shall any woman stand before a beast to lie down thereto; it is confusion."

One Jewish scholar has argued that "just as the Jewish tradition is the only one to posit an unbridgeable abyss between the Creator and the creature, so it is the only one to be oblivious of these unions (contrary to nature) that result in the births of divine or monstrous beings, which in other traditions, blur the dividing line between man and the animals . . ." But if this is really so, it is hard to understand the tone and tenor of such Mosaic taboos. And in any case, once the Hebraic tradition had been blended with the Hellenic, its inheritors, Jewish, Christian, and Moslem, came to believe in the possibility of a fertile mating of animals and humans, resulting in monstrous off-spring—like the Cretan minotaur. True, Greek scientists and philosophers had denied the possibility of inter-specific breeding. But travelers from the time of Alexander the Great had reported seeing such Freaks in India and Africa, and the first monster spotted by Columbus in the New World was a *Cynecephalus*, a dog-headed boy.

Moreover, the curious could find drawings of such creatures in encyclopedias, geographies, and books of medical lore. The first two illustrations to Paré's *Monstres et prodiges*, for example, show under the heading "Examples of the Wrath of God" a horse with the head of a man and the horned, bird-legged Monster of Ravenna. And the chapter entitled "Examples of the Blending and Mixture of Seed" includes pictures of a boy who was half dog, a half pig/half man, and a hog with human hands and feet. No wonder, then, that later thinkers, as different from each other as Linnaeus, the pious father of modern biology, and Voltaire, the skeptical challenger of most received ideas, shared the belief in miscegenation, and that it persisted well into the nineteenth century.

Moreover, it was suspected that not even the avoidance of inter-specific cohabitation would prevent the appearance of such hybrids, since they could also be produced by witchcraft, by the eating of certain plants, and especially by "impression," i.e., being frightened by animals during pregnancy or gazing at them at the moment of conception. Once more Paré provides ocular proof, in the form of a picture of a frog-faced boy born in 1517, whose father reported that "his wife having a fever, one of his neighbors counseled him, in order to cure her fever, that she take a live frog in her hand and hold on to it until it was dead; that night she went to bed with her husband, still holding the frog in her hand; her husband and she made love, and conceived and by the power of imagination the monster was produced, as you see by this picture."

There were, moreover, Vampires and Werewolves, men who became bats or wolves, like the national liberator of Rumania, the Voivode Vlad Teppish, better known as Count Dracula. Or at least some had believed in their reality for almost as long as they had in the existence of satyrs, half men and half goats, famous in Greek legend as the rapists of nymphs and maidens. Embodiments in hybrid form of what remains bestial in human desire, they reappear as allegorical figures in Spenser's sixteenth-century epic *The Faerie Queene:*

> At night, when all they went to sleepe, he vewed,
>> Whereas his louely wife emongst them lay,
>> Embraced of a Satyre rough and rude,   .
>> Who all the night did minde his ioyous play:
>> Nine times he heard him come aloft ere day,
>> That all his hart with gealosie did swell;
>> But yet that nights ensamle did bewray,
>> That not for nought his wife them loved so well,
> When one so oft a night did ring his matins bell.

At this point, however, they were beginning to be demythologized elsewhere by Renaissance science, which renamed them *Homo ferus* or *Homo selvaticus,* the Wild or Savage Man. And though they were still sometimes endowed with mythological tails, hooves, and horns, they were more likely to be portrayed as naked and shaggy and carrying in their hands some sort of club, often an uprooted small tree.

6

Wild Men and Feral Children

All accounts of the "savage man," whether in poetry or prose, shamelessly mingle legend and fact up to the time of Linnaeus, who first attempted to define *Homo ferus* "scientifically" as a human subspecies, hairy, dumb, and able to walk only on all fours. Even his "scientific" definition seems, however, entangled with myths based on vestigial memories of the hominid creatures against whom *Homo sapiens* struggled for so long to inherit the earth. Moreover, it implies a new mythology of "race," appropriate to an age of expanding imperialism. For Linnaeus, *Homo ferus* was a category parallel not just with *Homo monstrosus* or "monsters," but with Americans, Europeans, Asiatics, and Africans, which is to say red men, white men, yellow men, and black men. No wonder, then, that his followers taught that breeding between, say, Europeans and Africans was quite literally "miscegenation," and that formerly some respectable anthropologists argued that the blacks were themselves products of forbidden sexual connections between Europeans and monkeys.

Nor did the myth of feral men die when it turned out that such a species simply did not exist. It was merely translated into temporal rather than spatial terms, as *Homo selvaticus* was renamed the "Missing Link." That term, invented long before the publication of *The Origin of Species*, was already being exploited as early as 1846 by P. T. Barnum, who advertised a female orangutan as "The Grand Connecting Link between two great families, The Human and Brute Creation." Modern evolutionary theory, or rather popular Darwinism, spurred the quest for such "links" in the form of fossil remains, whose discovery has been periodically announced ever since in the sort of journals which originally persuaded the common reader that he was "descended from monkeys." Not that such publications have entirely lost faith in the existence of living specimens either. Indeed, there lies on my desk at this moment a news item dated February 28, 1976, describing Oliver, the latest " 'missing link' between ape and man," who, his discoverers report, "has 47 chromosomes, while humans have 46 and apes 48."

Nothing is ever given up in the realm of popular fiction, where the "Wild Man" continues to live on side by side with the "Missing Link." We prefer these days, however, to speak of wild or feral children rather than adults, meaning unfortunate boys and girls who return to "civilization" after abandonment and long isolation or, more fancifully, adoption by animals. Labeled according to where they were found and what beasts presumably fostered them, for example, the Hesse Wolf-child, the Lithuanian Bear-child, the Salzburg Sow-girl, the Syrian Gorilla-child, and the Teheran Ape-child, such unfortunates have been recorded for centuries under names more appropriate for hybrids than abandoned children. In *Les Enfants sauvages* (a study published in 1964 and translated into English as *Wolf Children and the Problem of Human Nature*), Lucien Malson lists fifty-three "attested cases" between the Hesse Wolf-child, who reentered human society in 1344, and the Teheran Ape-child, who returned in 1961. And others have allegedly appeared since—particularly in India, where poverty and the pressure of population, as well as the relative abundance of wildlife, provide an ideal setting, or where, at least, the legend is strongest and verification most difficult.

But, of course, the mythological ancestry of such children goes back to antiquity. Greco-Roman legend tells of Thyro raised among

ABOVE: *Homo troglodytus, Homo luciferus, Homo satyrus,* and *Homo pygmaeus.* From "Anthropomorpha," by C. E. Hoppius (1760).

LEFT: Hirsute aborigine. Woodcut from *Anthropometamorphosis: Man Transformed: or The Artificial Changeling,* by John Buliver (1653).

BOTTOM LEFT: Satyr, or goat-limbed boy.

BELOW: Cat-headed child.

the cows, Zeus suckled by the she-goat Amalthea, Iamos fed honey by serpents, Hippothoos nursed by a mare, and Telephus, son of Hercules, by a deer; and most famous of all, Romulus and Remus nurtured by a she-wolf and a woodpecker. Nor have writers of fiction in later times entirely abandoned the theme. In 1966 the eminent American novelist John Barth published *Giles Goat-Boy*, which deals, as its title indicates, with a tragic hero raised by goats. And those who read Barth as adults doubtlessly thrilled as children to the adventures of Rudyard Kipling's Mowgli the Jungle Boy, suckled by a wolf, and Edgar Rice Burroughs' Tarzan, that son of English aristocrats, brought up by the great apes in such total ignorance of his true parentage that he declares at one point, "My mother was an Ape . . . I never knew who my father was."

Not only do those words stir Oedipal resonances in us all, but reading them we become aware of another psychic source for such fantasies: the dream, especially appealing to imaginations kindled by Darwin and to sensibilities offended by the indignities of urban life, that a single human being, cast away in the jungle, might recapitulate the evolutionary experience of the race. We are, therefore, not surprised to discover that the Tarzan archetype has continued to flourish in popular fiction of the kind published by Philip José Farmer in 1974 as "A Feral Man Anthology" called *Mother Was a Lovely Beast*.

But the "wolf children" discussed by Malson refuse to fit the classic myth in one important respect. They do *not* become kings and conquerors, much less supermen and gods, like Mowgli or Tarzan, Romulus or Zeus. When casting-away occurs, its victims tend thereafter to live very unheroic lives. Indeed, they have trouble learning to imitate even the most ordinary human behavior. Speech especially baffles them; but it is also hard to teach them to wear clothes or walk upright or even to smile, laugh, or recognize their own images in a mirror. They are, in short, much more like Linnaeus' *Homo ferus; tetrapus, mutus* and *hirsutus*, which is to say, inclined to walk on all fours, inarticulate, and hairy.

But as Malson remarks of their "hairiness," "The inclusion of the characteristic is probably a literary survival . . . It may also have been because hairy people were presented in traveling circuses as animal men." We are caught here in a circular argument, however, since circuses presented Wild Men in this guise because they were believed to be so in fact. Certainly the Chinese merchants who formerly faked such creatures operated on this assumption, not only (according to Gould and Pyle) rendering them "mute by the destruction of the vocal cords" and forcing them "to use all fours in walking," but also by skinning them alive "bit by bit, transplanting on the denuded surfaces the hide of a bear or a dog"—as if they were using Linnaeus' *Systema naturae* as a recipe book.

There is, moreover, little hard evidence indicating that *any* such children were actually brought up by wolves or tigers or pigs or monkeys or gazelles. Even the most famous modern case—Amala and Kamala, the "Wolf Girls of Midnapore" found in 1920—is based on inference and the word of one witness, the Reverend J. A. L. Singh, whom later investigators have found was regarded by his fellow villagers as a spinner of implausible yarns. Yet as Malson, who retells and believes the story, insists, he was a priest, and thus truthful by definition; besides which, it would appear that according to other observers Amala and Kamala did in fact *behave* like wolves: lapping up liquids with their tongues, eating only in the crouching position, and when hungry, digging up carrion or pursuing chickens. Malson similarly argues of certain other classic cases, "Clemens, the pigboy, befriended thick-skinned animals, Kaspar Hauser became completely absorbed only when alone with horses and some of the Sleeman children were happy only in the company of dogs."

However, the double improbability of a human child surviving at all in the wilderness and of cohabiting peacefully with wild animals inclines me to believe that the legend of Wolf Children has been a fabrication from the start. So skeptical observers have always thought, beginning with Daniel Defoe, who ridiculed stories about Peter the Wild Boy in the late seventeenth century, and ranging in our own time from sober anthropologists like A. J. P. Taylor and Claude Lévi-Strauss to popularizing debunkers like Bergen Evans in *The Natural History of Nonsense*. But legend dies hard for commentators like Malson, motivated by what Bruno Bettelheim identifies in a 1959 article in the *American Journal of Sociology* as "first, our unwillingness to admit that these animal-like creatures could have had pasts at all similar to ours . . . and second, our need to understand and explain" too quickly and easily what at first glance appears to baffle normal understanding. After pointing out how each aspect of the presumed animal behavior of Amala and Kamala (their heightened sense of smell and hearing, their inability to laugh, dumbness, preference for raw food, etc.) has been paralleled in autistic children, never suckled by wolves, he concludes:

> It seems to be the result of some persons'—usually their parents'— inhumanity and not the result, as it was assumed, of animals'— particularly, wolves'—humanity. To put it differently, feral children seem to be produced not when wolves behave like mothers but when mothers behave like non-humans. The conclusion tentatively forced on us is that, while there are no feral children, there are some very rare examples of feral mothers, of human beings who become feral to one of their [autistic to begin with] children.

Nonetheless, Arnold Gesell, widely respected for his studies of learning in children, leaned heavily in his *Wolf Child and Human Child* not only on Singh's reports about Amala's and Kamala's behavior but on his dubious inferences about their having spent considerable time in the care of wolves. Poets and writers cling to such instances for reasons of their own, though, unlike social scientists, they are more interested in Kaspar Hauser and the Wild Boy of Aveyron, who seem scarcely Freaks at all, than in Amala and Kamala. Hauser was never left alone in the wilderness, much less nurtured by beasts, but merely confined to close quarters and deprived of all but minimal sustenance, while the Wild Boy, though abandoned, was befriended by no one, human or animal.

Yet Hauser's romantic figure has haunted the imagination of writers like Verlaine, Melville, and Jakob Wassermann, who have seen in him a symbol of their own alienation, or simply of the impossibility of distinguishing reality from illusion, of knowing the true identity of anyone. The most recent novel devoted to him, Marianne Hauser's *Prince Ishmael* (1963), uses as an epigraph a quotation from Melville's *The Confidence Man:*

> "Odd fish"
> "Poor Fellow"
> "Who can he be?"
> "Caspar Hauser."

"Bless my soul!"
"Uncommon countenance."
"Green prophet from Utah."
"Humbug!"
"Singular Innocence."

And she concludes with what is really a gloss on that quotation: "Peasant or Prince. Angel or confidence man. The mystery remains unsolved, and so the dark continues to be lighted by multiple identities, multiple truths . . ."

Ever since the Cultural Revolution of 1968, however, Hauser has been made into a patron saint by those less interested in "multiple truths" than in finding models for their own role as self-willed "mutants," enemies of the "system," which after Hauser escaped from captivity tortured him further by trying to "normalize" him. Peter Handke, an avant-garde Austrian playwright, has presented that point of view in a play called *Kaspar*, first produced in 1968 and hailed by German critics as "the play of the decade." Typically for its time, it treats language-learning, along with scholarship in general, as the ultimate form of oppression, the tamed "Wild Boy" saying finally, "I am usable . . . I have been made to speak. I have been sentenced to reality." And quite as typically, his figure has been blended by Handke with the favorite movie monsters: "Kaspar [Kasper means clown in German]," an early stage direction reads, "does not resemble any other comedian; rather, when he comes on the stage he resembles Frankenstein's monster (or King Kong)."

The Germans seem incapable at this moment of leaving the old legend alone—as if it figured forth the plight of a whole people, resisting reeducation into bourgeois values after a regression to savagery under Nazism. At the Cannes Film Festival of 1975 Werner Herzog entered a film on the subject called *Every Man for Himself and God Against All*, in which he accuses Kaspar's "benefactors" of "deadening what was spontaneously human in him" by preparing him for reentry "into the life of the philistine bourgeois." The analogy operating in Herzog's mind is not with King Kong or Frankenstein's monster, but with Tarzan thrust into civilization—or with Freaks forced to exhibit themselves in a side show. There is one scene in the film, in fact, in which Kaspar, after having been half educated, is required to play the "Wild Man" he no longer is, side by side with a Dwarf.

Victor, the Wild Boy of Aveyron, on the other hand, has appealed chiefly to educational psychologists with a behavioral bias, who consider his case proof that becoming "human" depends entirely on conditioning and that, therefore, any child, no matter how "autistic" or "retarded" or wild, can be socialized by proper stimulus-response techniques. The first man to work with Victor was, in fact, just such a liberal-behaviorist pedagogue, Jean Itard. Resented and feared by the conservative theoreticians of his own time, he was one of the major influences on later pioneers of "progressive education" like Maria Montessori. Indeed, it was largely to defend him and his successors that Lucien Malson wrote an essay on "Les Enfants sauvages," whose title reveals the presence of a myth in which the Wild Boy is identified with Helen Keller rather than Tarzan, and pedagogy is presented not as a threat to spontaneity but as salvation for the deprived. The basic appeal of this myth explains the popularity of Malson's thesis, which was not only printed in shortened form in the Paris newspaper *Le Monde* but inspired François Truffaut's much-admired film *The Wild Child*. The script of that movie

"L'Enfant Sauvage." Still
from François Truffaut's film
The Wild Child.
*The Museum of Modern Art/Film
Stills Archive*

was then published with Malson's essay and Itard's two reports (the first written in 1799, the second in 1806) on Victor's reeducation in a volume which has become in English translation a kind of minor underground classic: one of those works with an inadvertent scriptural appeal to young Americans, like Theodora Kroeber's *Ishi* and John Neihardt's *Black Elk Speaks*.

Such books, whether like the latter two, dealing with American Indians who never left the wilderness or, like the former, with European babies forced back into the world, find an audience among those to whom a society without savages would seem hopeless desolation. "You've taken away our Wild Men," such readers cry out first in their secret hearts, then aloud to their teachers and parents, "And you have failed to deliver on your promise to dig up for us the 'Missing Link.' Leave us at least the Wild Children!"

To that plea, the Freak show is also a response, at least when the hairies and the furries, the Bearded Ladies, the Crocodile Woman, and the Seal Boy appear in the Ten-in-One beside the Sword Swallowers, the Tattooed Woman, the Armless Wonder, and the Dwarfs. Sometimes furry Freaks are called by such mythological names as the "Wild Man of Borneo" or the "Missing Link." And sometimes, like the Geeks, they reenact the roles attributed to those mythological beings, biting off the heads of living chickens or rats and bolting them down raw, like Singh's Amala and Kamala. The title "Geek" was originally given to any side show "Wild Man," presented in a cage with snakes; while those who chewed and swallowed down living animals with real relish were known as "glomming Geeks." But "Geek" alone has finally come to describe them all.

In his novel *Nightmare Alley* (1946), Lindsay Gresham reproduces the spiel by which such "monstrosities" were typically introduced: ". . . he was found on an uninhabited island five hundred miles off the coast of Florida. . . . Is he man or is he beast . . . he has two arms, two legs, a head and a body like a man: But under that head of hair there is the brain of a beast. Somehow he feels more at home with the reptiles of the jungle than with human kind." The carnival Geek, however, was (according to Gresham at least) neither an island castaway nor a feral child, but only some hopeless vagrant, a down-and-out black or a luckless white wino in quest of a warm bed or a few bucks. And Eudora Welty concurs, portraying the Geek known as "Keela, the Outcast Indian Maiden," in her story of that name, as neither wild nor Indian nor female, but only a "little club-footed nigger man," who learned to do what he had to do every time the "sireen" was blown outside his booth, though "they had to whip on it some to make it eat all the chickens," the boy who blew that "sireen" later remembers.

But Arthur A. Lewis, in *Carnival* (1970), a nonfictional account of traveling road shows, tells about an actual "glommin geek" named Veronica Shant, who seems more like Redfield, the "zoophagous patient" in *Dracula*, than the victims of Gresham or Welty. "She loved her work and put her heart into it," her former manager reports. "In the course of one evening she'd bite off *and* swallow a half-dozen heads from live chickens and three or four field mice whole and maybe a garter snake or two. Half the marks'd throw up just watchin'." But to this the man she wed in 1958, an old carnie called Darby, adds that she was a good churchgoing Christian and a virgin until marriage, and that "what sent Veronica into bein' a geek was comin' home from school when she was fourteen and catchin' her mother in bed with the delivery boy." Eventually she left him, unable to abide his cussing or hard drinking; but first she put their son into a home, since, as she told Darby, "Neither of us was good enough—we was both sick in the head otherwise we wouldn't be carnies."

Yet even the most genuine Geeks are like fakes, turned by their billing, the banners above their heads, and the announcer's spiel into living metaphors for a nonexistent species that straddles the line between us and our animal brothers. The Wild Men of Borneo, for instance, whose name was used in my own childhood as an epithet for ill-behaved kids, had never seen Borneo, much less torn apart unwary Western sailors who had landed in their territory, as the talkers claimed. But exotically garbed and rebaptized Plutano and Waino (they had actually been born in Connecticut or Long Island and christened Hiram and Barney Davis), this pair of wispily bearded but extraordinarily strong Midgets seemed enough like the Wild Men of everyone's dreams to keep the money rolling in at the box office, though they never did anything more ferocious than lift dumbbells and wrestle each other to the ground.

Similarly, Krao, a native of Indochina who appeared in Europe

LEFT: The Wild Men of Borneo. RIGHT: Krao, the Missing Link. Contemporary publicity photographs.
Both: Circus World Museum, Baraboo, Wisconsin

during the early 1880s, was accepted for generations as "Darwin's missing link." It required a major suspension of disbelief to confuse that gentle misshapen creature with the species intermediate between men and the anthropoids, though she did indeed have a "prognathic" face, a thick covering of hair which formed "a virtual mane on the back of her neck," and "extraordinary prehensile powers of feet and lips." Moreover, "when annoyed," one contemporary observer noted, "she throws herself to the ground, screams, kicks and gives vent to her anger by pulling her hair in a very peculiar way." This may sound like the classic temper tantrum of a child (Krao was, after all, only seven when first exhibited), but it was taken at least by that observer as evidence of her "wild nature."

Zip, the long-lived Freak shown by Barnum from 1859 to 1926, was also assimilated to the image of *Homo ferus*, though, unlike Krao, he was not even shaggy, much less mute or given to going on all fours. But he was kept dressed in a kind of furry jumpsuit and permitted in public only to gabble or grunt, lest he betray (he was, in fact, feeble-minded) that he had been born to a poor American Negro family in Brooklyn (or, according to some accounts, Bridgeport, Connecticut), rather than ". . . captured by a party of adventurers while they were in search of the Gorilla. While exploring the river Gambia . . . they fell in with a race of beings never before discovered . . . in a PERFECTLY NUDE STATE, roving about among the trees . . . in a manner common to the Monkey and the Orang Outang." Billed sometimes as a "nondescript" or the "What Is It?" (a name invented either by Charles Dickens or the then Prince of Wales), Zip was more often identified as the "Man Monkey." Yet he was physically anomalous in only one respect, which Barnum emphasized by keeping his coconut-colored and presumably simian pinhead close-shaven except for a topknot. Zip was, in short, a triumph of packaging and "humbug," in which it would be nice to believe that he participated as a co-conspirator rather than a victim and that, therefore, his much-advertised "last words" ("Well, we fooled 'em a long time") were authentic, and not just one more, posthumous con.

Zip and Isit. Publicity photograph, 1905.
Circus World Museum, Baraboo, Wisconsin

Zip, in any case, satisfied for nearly seven decades a deep need in Barnum's audience, which he attempted to satisfy further by providing other counterfeit feral men, one actually called Zup and purporting to be Zip's brother. But somehow neither Barnum nor his competitors could make another "What Is It?" work. They had better luck with bushy-haired Zulus, "genuine Ubangis" with plates in their lower lips, and even a "wild African bushman" called Clikko: i.e., actual "natives" imported from "darkest Africa" whom popular ethnography classified as the equivalents of "Wild Men."

Jo-Jo the Dog-faced Boy, on the other hand, was assimilated to the legend of Wolf Child rather than that of the Missing Link. He was described as having been captured in the virgin forest of Russia, where he had for a long time managed to feed himself on berries plucked from the bushes and small animals which he had learned to hunt down by imitating his neighbors, the wolves. From them, too, he had presumably learned to snap, growl, and bark (*"Looks like a man, barks like a dog, crawls on his belly like a snake . . ."*), as he continued to do throughout his career. Actually Jo-Jo/Feodor had grown up on the fairgrounds of Europe, where he had been exhibited with his almost equally hairy father, who looked (it is reported) exactly like a poodle, and was billed as *l'homme-chien*, the man-dog.

Feodor seems rather to have resembled a Skye terrier, thanks largely to the silky yellow hair which covered his entire face and grew in two especially thick tufts on either side by his nose. Indeed, if the memory of Edward G. Malone, owner of the world's largest collection of Freak photographs, can be trusted, members of Jo-Jo's audience often complained that a real dog had been substituted for him when at the climax of his act he would wrap himself in a blanket, concealing everything but his head, and yelp frantically until he was unwrapped again. Not every animal Freak, however, has so closely resembled the beast after whom he was called. Almost all commentators, for instance, insist that the only thing specifically leonine about Lionel the Lion-faced Man was his ability to roar convincingly enough to frighten his more tender-minded beholders half out of their wits.

Yet he was sufficiently furry to have been presented as a kind of human/animal hybrid. Even in their wildest flights of fancy, how-

ABOVE LEFT: Hairy Girl. ABOVE RIGHT: Hairy Woman. From a sixteenth century collection at Castle Ambras.

BELOW LEFT: Jo-Jo the Dog-faced Boy. BELOW RIGHT: Lionel the Lion-faced Man. Contemporary publicity photographs.
Both photos: Circus World Museum, Baraboo, Wisconsin

ever, modern fairground talkers do not claim that such anomalies are the products of "unnatural" unions, suggesting rather that they are the results of "impressions" arising from prenatal fright. The pitch with which Lionel introduced himself, for instance, told how his mother while carrying him watched his father being torn to pieces by lions—presumably in the jungles of Russia! And, according to Malone, "The public bought the story, hook, line and liar . . . and for a price he'd tell it word for word in whatever language you liked." Similarly, it was reported of Marie Bartels, billed as Lenora the sister of Julia Pastrana, that her hairiness was the result of her pregnant mother's having been frightened by their own "big, shaggy dog."

The belief in "impressions," in fact, still persists in many parts of the world, particularly among the less educated, but also deep in the undermind of the most sophisticated. And this may in part explain why Freaks of quite varied origins are exhibited under names which call into question our conviction that the line separating us from all other beasts is unpassable. The legless Dwarf Samuel D. Parks, for instance, was known as "Hopp the Frog Boy," perhaps with conscious reference to Edgar Allan Poe's story "Hop-Frog." And Prince Randian, an armless and legless native of New Guinea, who at the climax of Todd Browning's *Freaks* is shown inching his way through the mud with a knife between his teeth (in real life he was a kindly fellow with a wife and five normal children), was known not just as the "Living Torso," but also as the "Snake Man" and the "Caterpillar Man." Phocomelics, too, which is to say, humans whose arms and legs seem to grow directly out of their torsos, are easily assimilated into this category. Usually they are called Seal Boys or Girls (the official medical term for them meaning, in fact, "seal limbs"), though one of the more famous was billed as the "Penguin Girl."

Moreover, many victims of skeletal dysfunctions and skin diseases are listed in the annals of medicine and show business as "Koo Koo the Bird Girl," "Priscilla the Monkey Girl," the "Porcupine Man," the "Biped Armadillo," the "Alligator Boy," the "Snake Boy," the "Leopard Family," etc. And where nature does not provide plausible facsimiles of long-believed-in mythological hybrids, they are counterfeited by exhibitors eager to please. Fake Mermaids, for in-

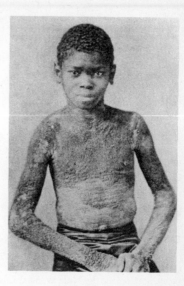

The Alligator Boy. From
*Anomalies and Curiosities of
Medicine*, by George M.
Gould and Walter L. Pyle
(1896).

stance, have been on view since the exhibition of Freaks began, because, though sirenoform fetuses with their legs grown together are
standard items in the "pickled punk" shows, full-grown Sirens do
not exist. The most famous such fake, Barnum's "Feejee Mermaid,"
was portrayed on the banner outside his American Museum as beautiful and larger than life, but inside turned out to be a withered
mummy less than two feet tall, made by grafting a monkey's body
onto a fish's tail. Later exhibitors have preferred to equip normal
young girls with fraudulent fins and green hair, then let them splash
about in tanks to keep the "marks" happy. One of the research assistants, in fact, who helped with this project spent a summer playing
that watery part (advertised these days as an "illusion") at a small-
town carnival.

Even Grace McDaniels, rival to Julia Pastrana for the title of
the Ugliest Woman in the World ("Her flesh was like red, raw meat;
her huge chin was twisted at such a distorted angle, she could hardly
move her jaws. Her teeth were jagged and sharp, her nose was large
and crooked . . . Her eyes stared grotesquely in their deep-set
sockets . . ."), was billed as the "Mule Woman." Grace, as Edward

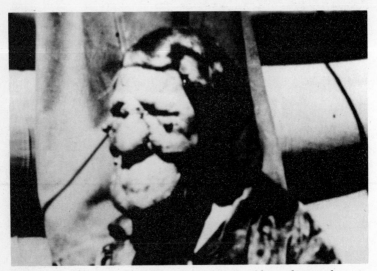

Grace McDaniels, the Mule Woman. Contemporary publicity photograph.
Circus World Museum, Baraboo, Wisconsin

Malone tells us, "didn't actually look like a mule, of course; more
like a hippopotamus—in the face." But she was, he goes on to say,
"attractive to a lot of men, too, believe it or not. I can't tell you how
many proposals of marriage she received before Grace finally accepted a nice looking young fellow who was very much in love with
her . . ."

   John Merrick, the Elephant Man, however, who has no rival for
the title of the Ugliest Male who ever lived, was not so lucky in
love. He is the most discussed of all feral Freaks: an object not just
of wonder and compassion, but of real admiration from Victorian
times to our own. His fame is explained in part, perhaps, by the fact
that his history was first recorded by Dr. Frederick Treves, a gifted
writer as well as a skilled surgeon, and the benefactor who rescued
him from a life of squalor and exploitation. Treves's memoirs in which
the account appears have long been out of print. But the essay has
been recently republished twice: in Ashley Montagu's *The Elephant
Man: A Study in Human Dignity* (1971), and in Frederick Drimmer's *Very Special People: The Struggles, Loves and Triumphs of*

Human Oddities (1973), of which it constitutes the whole final chapter, "a reward for having read this book to the end."

Montagu, a sociologist, though he begins by adducing Merrick's case as testimony to the invincibility of the human spirit, cannot resist using it also to prove a favorite theory of his own about the importance of mothering. He argues, therefore, "that no one could possibly have borne the torment of his later years and emerged from them as Merrick did had he not been fortified by the early experience of adequate love," meaning maternal love, of course. Yet Dr. Treves, who knew the Elephant Man better than anyone, was convinced that his mother had been "worthless and inhuman."

Finally, it seems to me, nobody can write about Freaks without somehow exploiting them for his own ends. Not I, certainly. And not even Dr. Treves, who writing down after many years his memories of the Elephant Man (though he knew Merrick from 1884 to 1890, he did not publish his essay until 1926), seems to have been interested not only in testifying on behalf of the Victorian cult of sentimentality but also in answering certain charges raised again at the time of Merrick's death. It is hard to determine the precise nature of those charges from the circumspect "Report of the Coroner's Inquest" published in the London *Times* of April 16, 1890: "The Coroner said that the man had been sent round the shows as a curiosity, and when death took place it was decided as a matter of prudence to hold this inquest."

It was presumably to protect Merrick against just such exploitation that Treves took him into the London Hospital, and Dr. F. C. Carr Gomm, its chairman, raised by public subscription enough money to keep him there. Yet he was shown thereafter under the supervision of Dr. Treves at various medical conventions, compelled to expose his nakedness for the sake of science, as he had earlier done for his exhibitor's profit. Since the coroner found that he had died in bed of natural causes, however, the only court that could have impugned Treves was his own conscience. And even before so relentless a judge, he could have pleaded as extenuation that the accounts which he prepared for such meetings provide the only reliable evidence we have of what the Elephant Man looked like in his last days.

They are couched in the neutral language of "teratology," so that it is not easy to tell from them alone what made Merrick the wonder of his age: "some congenital exostoses [bony tumors] of the skull; extensive papillomatous growths [small nipple-like growths] and large pendulous masses in connection with the skin; great enlargement of the right upper limb, involving all the bones." At one point, to be sure, Treves pauses to explain the origin of Merrick's mythological name: "From the massive distortion of the head, and the extensive areas covered by papillomatous growth, the patient has been called 'the elephant-man' "; and at another he informs us that Merrick attributed his condition to "a shock experienced by his mother shortly before his birth, when knocked down by an elephant at a circus." It was Merrick's way of dealing with what would otherwise have seemed to him monstrously inexplicable, just as speaking of "congenital exostoses" and "papillomatous growths" was the doctors' way.

But their anti-mythological language gives no sense of the combined repulsion and fascination of his appearance, which made it impossible for him to go into the streets without being mobbed. Nor do later diagnoses of his disease as "generalized hyperstosis [excessive bone development] with pachydermia" or "multiple neurofibromatosis" (tumors of the peripheral nerves, cranial nerves, and skin) help very much in this regard. In his final treatment of the theme, written for the general reader rather than his fellow specialists, Treves does somewhat better, eschewing jargon in favor of literary language:

> The most striking feature about him was his enormous and mis-shapen head. From the brow there projected a huge bony mass like a loaf, while from the back of the head hung a bag of spongy, fungus-looking skin, the surface of which was comparable to a brown cauliflower. . . . The osseous growth on the forehead almost occluded one eye. The circumference of the head was no less than that of the man's waist. From the upper jaw there projected another mass of bone. It protruded from the mouth like a pink stump, turning the upper lip inside out and making of the mouth a mere slobbering aperture. . . . The face was no more capable of expression than a block of gnarled wood.

The Elephant Man, four
views. From the *British Medical
Journal*, 1886.
Reproduced by permission

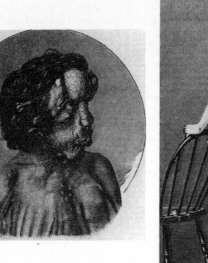

He then goes on to describe Merrick's back, buttocks, legs, and arms in an increasing crescendo of pity and disgust. But even this literary re-creation leaves us feeling baffled in our attempt to re-imagine such a monster, and we turn, in the conviction that only pictures can adequately render what existed in the first instance for the eye, to the photographs of Merrick taken under the direction of Dr. Treves. But he himself had first learned of Merrick's monstrosity from a picture very different from those in the clinical studies he left behind. And forty years later, he still remembered the display banner which hung before the booth where in 1884 all comers willing to pay two pennies could watch the Elephant Man whisk off his dirty blanket to reveal the full horror of his nakedness.

> This very crude production depicted a frightful creature that could only have been possible in a nightmare. It was the figure of a man with characteristics of an elephant. The transfiguration was not far advanced. There was still more of the man than of the beast. This fact—that it was still human—was the most repellent attribute of the creature. There was nothing about it of the pitiableness of the mis-shapened or the deformed, nothing of the grotesqueness of the freak, but merely the loathesome insinuation of a man being changed into an animal . . .

I look up as I write these words at the reproduction just over my desk of a stone carving of the elephant-headed Ganesh from the Great Temple at Karnak, awesome but somehow neither loathsome nor grotesque despite his beast's head and his six arms, and I realize the archetypal continuity which—however Dr. Treves may resist accepting it—joins the sacred Indian icon to a pop-art banner hung out in the streets of late Victorian England. Ganesh's deformity is also traditionally explained in terms of "impression"—his divine father and mother presumably having watched two elephants mating at the moment of his conception. But Treves's account is directed precisely at demythologizing the human/animal Freak; or rather re-mythologizing it in terms more acceptable to the secular, bourgeois world. For that world there is no monstrosity or mystery which cannot be explained by science and alleviated by the efforts of the genuinely concerned well-to-do, as even Merrick's atrocious plight was finally alleviated.

His idyllic last three and a half years are best described, perhaps, in a letter written to the *Times* after his death by F. C. Carr
Gomm, which seems somehow all the more moving for its condescension and self-congratulation:

> Here, therefore, poor Merrick was enabled to pass the . . . re-
> maining years of his life in privacy and comfort. The authorities
> of the hospital, the medical staff, the chaplain, the sisters, and
> nurses united to alleviate as far as possible the misery of his ex-
> istence, and he learnt to speak of his room . . . as his home.
> There he received kindly visits from many, among them the high-
> est of the land . . . he was a great reader and was well sup-
> plied with books; through the kindness of a lady, one of the
> brightest ornaments of the theatrical profession, he was taught
> basket making, and on more than one occasion he was taken to
> the play, which he witnessed from the seclusion of a private box.
>   He benefited much from the religious instruction of our
> chaplain . . . and in the last conversation he had with him
> Merrick had expressed his feeling of deep gratitude for . . . the
> mercy of God to him in bringing him to this place. Each year he
> much enjoyed a six weeks' outing in a quiet country cottage,
> but was always glad on his return to find himself once more "at
> home." In spite of all this indulgence he was quiet and unassum-
> ing, very grateful for all that was done for him, and conformed
> himself readily to the restrictions which were necessary.

His actual deathbed scene, however, was better rendered by
Treves, in part because he was more interested in Merrick's humanity than his piety. It was he who had arranged the outings to the
country, and he lingers over the details of the last of them with real
tenderness, observing that: "The Merrick who had once crouched
terrified in the filthy shadows of a Mile End shop was now sitting in
the sun, in a clearing among the trees, arranging a bunch of violets
he had gathered." Then he concludes:

> Some six months after Merrick's return from the country he was
> found dead in bed. This was in April, 1890. He was lying on his
> back as if asleep, and had evidently died suddenly and without a
> struggle, since not even the coverlet of the bed was disturbed.
> The method of his death was peculiar. So large and heavy was

his head that he could not sleep lying down. When he assumed the recumbent position the massive skull was inclined to drop backwards, with the result that he experienced no little distress. The attitude he was compelled to assume when he slept was very strange. He sat up in bed with his back supported by pillows, his knees were drawn up, and his arms clasped around his legs, while his head rested on the points of his bent knees.

He often said to me that he wished he could lie down to sleep "like other people." I think on this last night he must, with some determination, have made the experiment. The pillow was soft, and the head, when placed on it, must have fallen backwards and caused a dislocation of the neck. Thus it came about that his death was due to the desire that had dominated his life—the pathetic but hopeless desire to be "like other people."

It is a touching and true ending, but Treves was not able to let it go at that, compelled somehow, despite his resolve to avoid a conventional Christian close, to raise the mythological ante of his tale with an allusion to *Pilgrim's Progress:*

He had been plunged into the Slough of Despond, but with manly steps he gained the farther shore. He had been made "a spectacle to all men" in the heartless streets of Vanity Fair. He had been ill-treated and reviled and bespattered with the mud of Disdain. He had escaped the clutches of the Giant Despair, and at last had reached the "Place of Deliverance," where "his burden loosed from off his back, so that he saw it no more."

What remains in my own mind, like an unresolved chord, however, is neither the pathetic nor the pious note, but the erotic: Merrick's imperious need for a woman, exacerbated by the grand ladies who (at Treves's behest) visited him, talked to him, took him by the hand, and even sent him their signed photographs. "His bodily deformity had left unmarred the instincts and feelings of his years," Treves tells us of the young man, who was only twenty-six when he died. "He was amorous." And in his less guarded communication published in *The Transactions of the Pathological Society of London* for 1885, he underlines the irony of Merrick's physical state, writing, "It is remarkable that the skin of the penis and scrotum were perfectly normal in every respect."

Elephant-headed man. Etch-
ing from *De monstrorum*, by
Fortunis Licetus (1616).
British Library Board

The appeal of the Elephant Man was ambiguously sexual from
the start, his early shows a kind of strip-tease, in which his draped
body, after long suspense, was fully revealed. And even Dr. Treves's
later lecture-demonstrations could not quite escape that format, as
the surviving photographs from *The British Medical Journal* illus-
trate. After all, Merrick's total horror could be seen only in total nudity. But he never found—in those early audiences, or in the hospital—anyone willing to play Beauty to his Beast, even that ideally
blind lady he liked to fantasize failing finally to materialize. And so,
unlike his female counterparts Julia Pastrana and Grace McDaniels,
he took to himself no spouse and begot no child; perhaps because in
him, unlike them, the note of erotic titillation was overwhelmed by
"the loathesome insinuation of a man being changed into an animal."

7

Hermaphrodites

In no account of the Elephant Man, or, indeed, of other male animal/
human hybrids, is there the slightest hint of gender confusion; but
female feral Freaks tend to be experienced as androgynous. In a
wall painting from Pompeii, for instance, a bearded woman appears
as an attendant to the god Hermaphroditus, and the ancient Aphrodite of Cyprus was portrayed as, on the one hand, bald and bewhiskered, and on the other, endowed with the genitals of both sexes. Her
sexual doubleness, however, was taken to signify fertility, whereas
those other Bearded Ladies, the witches, have traditionally been
thought of as blighting the child in the womb and crops in the field.

Though we no longer believe that women, however wicked, can
make men sterile, we still fear that some can cause impotence, and a
recent study explains the fear of such "witches" in terms of their
transgression of sexual boundaries. "The incorporation of the male
ego by a female produces a witch . . . The witch turns against her
own body and gloats over its sacrifice . . . The demonic drive of

the witch also aims to destroy the male ego." Moreover, the adoption of the witch as a role model by mysandrist radical feminists serves to reinforce such a view. Yet, as we have already noted, Bearded Ladies have been much desired by certain males—not least, I suspect, by macho types, to whom the masculinity they challenge is especially dear.

But a woman with much hair on her chin or none at all on her head is a euphemized representation of true hermaphroditism, which compels in beholders an ambivalent shudder deeper than that cued by any other Freak. In the past couple of years I have seen Fellini's *Satyricon* twice, and each time the audience has seemed especially moved at the revelation by the author of a world of monsters and *mutilés*—of the desiccated and dying Hermaphrodite, his teeny-tiny penis and pale mini-breasts absurdly juxtaposed. Those breasts were, it turns out, artificial, the actor who played the part being a sexually normal boy. And during the shooting, Fellini had in readiness an artificial penis as well, because he was not sure until the very last moment whether or not to use instead an albino girl. He knew only that his "bisexual" Freak had to be somehow faked, since the Hermaphrodite challenges the boundaries not just between male and female, but illusion and reality. And it worked—stirring a fascinated horror even in the youngest and most hip of those among whom I sat, despite their commitment to the fashionable new cult of androgyny.

A similar cult of androgyny had flourished in the heyday of witch burning in England, without in any way inhibiting the conviction that bearded sorceresses should be destroyed—and, one presumes, actual androgynes allowed to die at birth. No category of Freaks is, in short, regarded with such ferocious ambivalence as the Hermaphrodites, for none creates in us a greater tension between physical repulsion and spiritual attraction, as Marie Delcourt observes in her pioneering study, *Hermaphrodite: Myths and Rites of the Bisexual Figure in Classical Antiquity* (1961):

> Androgyny is at the two poles of sacred things. Pure concept, pure vision of the spirit, it appears adorned with the highest qualities. But once made real in a being of flesh and blood, it is a monstrosity, and no more; it is proof of the wrath of the gods

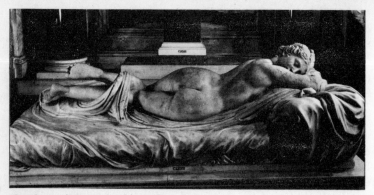

The Sleeping Hermaphrodite. Hellenistic statue.
Galleria Borghese, Rome

falling on the unfortunate group in which it is manifested, and the unhappy individuals who reveal it are got rid of as soon as possible.

But the ancients at least had gods carved from wood or hewn in stone to represent the beautiful dream of androgyny; whereas we must make do with the show Freak, the midway "morphodite," genuine or counterfeit, but in any case human. It is perhaps for this reason that the Half Man/Half Woman of the fairgrounds has, in recent years at least, revealed his/her abnormality not by showing his/her genitals but by playing the role in "drag," assuming a costume as conventional as the masks of different colors which signify male and female in classic Chinese opera.

Typically called by double names like Roberta-Robert, Frieda-Fred, and Joseph-Josephine, such "human enigmas" are rapidly disappearing from the side show. But where still displayed, they are decked out on one side in what fashion formerly decreed as male garb, and on the other, in what was accepted as female. So, too, their hair is trimmed so that one profile is crowned with a manly if archaic crewcut, and the other by long "womanly" tresses, while one side of the face is shaven or depilated and heavily rouged, the other left shadowed with a beard.

Before unisex clothes and hairstyling, even such superficial counterfeits of androgyny seem to have provided audiences with a sufficient thrill, though there were always those who wanted more and were willing to pay to see the "morphodites" strip down and reveal that one breast was full and hairless, the other flat and furry. Their genitals, however, even inside the tent, were usually concealed, though the spieler hinted at their double nature, and sometimes a select few (almost always "gentlemen only") were permitted to gaze at the final mystery. But most performers refused that final revelation, insisting like Mondu, who was billed in the 1920s as "Brother and Sister in One Body—the Ninth Wonder of the World," "Sorry to say, I do not submit to this for I am so sensitive."

Perhaps he spoke the simple truth; though, indeed, he may have had nothing more to show. Some fairground Hermaphrodites must have been true intersexes, freaky enough to satisfy any beholder; but most in all probability were fakes, just trying to make a living— or responding, perhaps, to a psychic dissatisfaction with their physiological gender. In any event, none of them could have been male on one side and female on the other, as their audiences had been led to expect, and as they were made to appear by the use of cosmetics and silicone injections.

Indeed, it is hard to understand how such a mode of presenting Hermaphrodites ever came to prevail. The illustrations in Ambroise Paré, for example, represent them totally nude and with two sets of distinct, if rather small, sexual organs, but otherwise undifferentiated in their bodies; while Montaigne describes a thirty-year-old "monster" he once examined as having "no signe at all of genitorie parts: But where they should be, are three little holes, by which his water doth continually tril from him. This poor man hath a beard, and desireth still to be fumbling of women."

By the seventeenth and eighteenth centuries, however, Hermaphrodites were no longer shown to amateurs in the nude. Yet it was still their genitals the curious came to see—and which they therefore displayed by lifting flaps on their otherwise quite conventional garments, as shown in a drawing made by James du Plessis at the behest of Samuel Pepys. But at some point this peep show technique of presentation was replaced by the Joseph-Josephine strategy, perhaps in the Victorian era in response to pressures

LEFT: Sketch of Hermaphrodite displaying himself. From *A Short History of Human Prodigies and Monstrous Births* . . . , by James Paris du Plessis. Unpublished manuscript, seventeenth century.
British Library Board

BELOW LEFT TO RIGHT: Hermaphroditic joined twins; two-headed Hermaphrodite; Hermaphrodite. From *Monstres et prodiges,* by Ambroise Paré (1573).

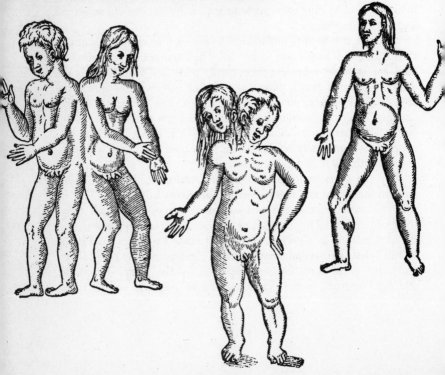

Josephine-Joseph, Half Man/
Half Woman. Contemporary
publicity photograph.
*Circus World Museum, Baraboo,
Wisconsin*

against the Freak show in general and its erotic aspects in particular.
In any case, by the end of the nineteenth century the display of
genitals had moved from the center to the periphery in the showing
of androgynes, except for "pickled punks": those malformed fetuses
in jars, who being not merely dead but never properly born, were
considered immune to the taboos against "indecent exposure."

As difficult as it is to establish the historical origins of the Joseph-Josephine strategy, it is even harder to discover its mythological sources, since the androgyne is never portrayed either in the art
or legend of the West as bilaterally differentiated. To be sure, Pliny
writing about "the race of the Androgynae, who combine the two
sexes, of which they make use turn and turn about" cites Aristotle
to the effect that "in all of them the right breast is that of a man, the
left breast that of a woman." Pliny's comment, however, seems to reflect a misunderstanding of ceremonial sex-shifting among the
Scythian Shamans, who after initiation "put on feminine clothes and
keep them all their life."

It was a custom which the Greeks attributed to impotence caused by being constantly on horseback. "When they go to a woman and cannot have intercourse with her," Hippocrates explains, "they . . . imagine they have committed some sin against the god and put on women's clothing. They declare their impotence, live like women and devote themselves to feminine occupations." But in Greek mythology there are traces of similar rituals, particularly in the legend of Tiresias, the blind prophet whose sex was changed as a result of having disturbed a pair of copulating snakes, or because, taking Zeus's side in an argument on Olympus, he claimed that females find more pleasure in sex than males.

Moreover, ritual sex-shifting was preserved in the Dionysian theater, in which boys played women, even as mortals played gods. It was a practice revived with the revival of drama in Renaissance Europe, incurring the hostility of the Church on the grounds that it led to pederasty and that, in any event, the law of God condemned to death any man "who put on the garments of a woman." Nonetheless, in Christendom as in the ancient world, some women did seem to turn into men at puberty and the menopause, as Pliny had already attested, insisting that "transformation of females into males is not an idle story." And such "metamorphoses," which we now know result from shifts in hormonal balance or the appearance of masculine genitals masked temporarily by feminine pseudo-pudenda, have brought to life half-dead ancient myths.

Aristotle's comment, however, seems to represent a garbled account of the legend of the Amazons, who presumably amputated their right breasts in order to free their spear-throwing arms. Or it may reflect some Anatolian myth of androgyny, which survives still in India, where Shiva is sometimes portrayed with one female breast and one male. Certainly we do not find the Hermaphrodite thus represented in ancient Greek sculpture, which preferred to figure forth the mystery of bisexuality in the human form divided *horizontally*. Since such cult images originated in the draping of a phallic pillar, or herm, with women's garments, they remained throughout the history of Hellas female above and male below. Sometimes they assume the form of Hera or Aphrodite or Demeter, with maternal bosoms swelling under gowns lifted to reveal a quiescent phallus or a shocking erection. But sometimes they appear as a naked Hermes, Priapus, Dionysus, Apollo, or Zeus with female breasts.

There is always a hint in their posture of erotic allure, though in the earliest versions they stand upright, distancing the beholder with their dignity. But as they metamorphose into the true Hermaphroditus, assimilating the softer appeal of the child gods Eros and Ganymede, they lie down invitingly, their heads cradled in their arms. It is in this guise that the new god was venerated when his cult finally triumphed over its mockers, and his worshippers brought to his image on the fourth day of every month offerings of flowers and food. And it is thus that we are likely to encounter him still in the museums of the Western world.

We see such images of Hermaphroditus first from the rear, for it

Pompeiian Hermaphrodite and Bearded Woman. From mural at Pompeii.
From Hermaphroditism, Genital Anomalies and Related Endocrine Disorders, *by Howard W. Jones, Jr., M.D., and William Wallace Scott, M.D., Ph.D., copyright 1937 The Williams and Wilkins Co., Baltimore, Maryland*

is so that their sculptors oriented them. And noting the lovely sweep of flank and back, we may take them for representations of women, a mistake apparently confirmed when we peer round their hyacinthine heads into their beautiful faces. But looking lower, we discover that their bodies are "pricked . . . out for women's pleasure." It was this image, at any rate, which possessed the imagination of writers and artists of the Renaissance, not least of all Shakespeare, as the punning quotation suggests. But Marie Delcourt finds it eminently unsatisfactory. "A homosexual dream," she writes, "expresses itself without doubt in these ambiguous forms. In the past which men were forgetting, the image of the double being had been a symbol of abundance, richness, a promise of eternity. At the very moment when Greek thought was finding its way back to these meanings, the artists, it would seem . . . were concerned only with gratifying a kind of sensuality that was universal and unquestioned in their age."

It seems to me, however, that the image of the androgyne could never have been totally dissociated from the dream of polymorphous-perverse satisfaction. And certainly no one in our time can ever disentangle his reaction to Hermaphroditus from his responses to homosexuals, transvestites, and especially transsexuals: humans of one sex driven, for reasons no one quite understands, to assume the roles attributed by their culture to the other. More "primitive" cultures have permitted male deviants of this kind, whom they tend to lump with actual intersexes, to assume female garb and perform traditional female tasks. But in our own, their situation has remained difficult, since much of the horror felt in the presence of physiological intersexes has been transferred to them.

The word "morphodite," used originally for actual sex Freaks, has been applied, with even greater scorn, to those otherwise labeled "faggots," "queers," or "drag queens." And the side show Half-and-Half, who purports to be the former and is often suspected of being the latter, is doubly despised. Bobby Kork, for instance, also known as Robert-Roberta, was driven on occasion to take a punch at members of his audience who in mockery or freaky desire propositioned his "female side." And once at least, he knocked his tormentor cold, since on his "male side" he was as "hard as nails."

Most transsexuals, however, when they appear in fairs, perform not in the Ten-in-One but in the "Kootch Show," where they assume female garb and disguise their sex organs. Bruce Jackson reprints in *In the Life* (1972) an interview with a transsexual carnie, who begins by saying, "I've travelled with a carnival . . . I was stripping then. At that time I was billed as a woman. Paraffin injections for breasts and an elastic band for a gaff," then continues:

> You put a piece of Kleenex around the penis, just back of the head, and cinchknot with three-quarter-inch elastic . . . And bring all of your equipment . . . down between your legs and then push the testicles up into the stomach . . . and bring everything else as tight as you possibly can up between the crack of your ass. Then you tie the elastic again so that there's another knot right at the base of your spine and the remaining elastic goes around your waist . . . You can show absolute nakedness except you have to wear a back panel . . . The gaff with the elastic band makes the appearance of a vagina . . . the bag which is now empty, brought forward, produced the lips of the vagina . . . I've had men kiss it and never know the difference.

Such a device could, however, be endured for no more than twenty minutes, unlike recent surgical techniques which can turn penises into vulvas permanently, painlessly, and without loss of the capacity for orgasm. Moreover, though hostility to such sex changes has not disappeared, "consciousness-raising" sessions organized by gay males for the benefit of their "straight" brothers have made their lot, as well as that of homosexuals in general, somewhat easier.

Nonetheless, the fear and suspicion of actual intersexes remain strong among those who still naïvely believe that everyone is born unequivocally male or female, and must therefore always behave like one or the other. Granted the organs of both sexes, what is to prevent anybody from exercising the privileges of both? Pliny in the first century after Christ already associated hermaphroditism and bisexual satisfaction. And Plato five centuries earlier puts into the mouth of Aristophanes a myth of androgyny justifying homosexual love.

The primal androgyne, according to that myth, was created double—male and male, female and female, or male and female. Split down the center by the envious gods, however, they became single sexes seeking forever to recover their lost unity. "Each of us when separated . . . is always looking for his other half. Men who are a section of that double nature which was once called Androgynous are lovers of women . . . the women who are a section of a woman do not care for men but have female attachments . . . But they who are a section of the male follow the male . . . they do not act thus from any want of shame, but because they are valiant and manly . . . When they reach manhood they are lovers of youth . . ."

It is an odd conceit; and it becomes even odder when adapted by medieval rabbis—hostile to homosexuality but hard pressed to explain the discrepancy in Genesis, which suggests in one place that mankind was created androgynous ("male and female created he them"), and in another that woman was made after man. According to such Talmudic exegetes, the first bisexual human was dorsally joined so that the two parts could not come together in love. But realizing that "it was not good" for Adam to be thus "alone," and therefore subject to the temptation of incubi, God separated the male from his female other half, thus making heterosexual cohabitation possible.

In both instances, at any rate, it is primal man who is portrayed as androgynous rather than his God or gods. Bisexuality as a divine power, on the other hand, that is, as Hermaphroditus, has attracted to itself few myths. "The poets," Marie Delcourt remarks, "do not ascribe a single adventure to the Hermaphrodite, contenting themselves with embroidering a little on the story of his birth. And late cosmogonies, which were haunted by the dream of bisexuality, did not make it the characteristic of the god best fitted to be its symbol, but attributed it to a number of divine beings, as one of their several perfections." Yet Ovid's *Metamorphoses* makes of that "story of his birth" deeply moving poetry which has possessed the imagination of many later writers, including Shakespeare, who reinterpreted it to signify the unmanning of a youth by a sexually aggressive female. From the first there was implicit in the myth a suggestion that bisexuality, though dreamed as fulfillment, might mean in fact sterility and impotence.

As Ovid tells the tale, the water nymph Salmacis, rejected by

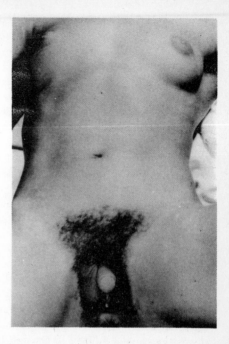

Hermaphroditus Verus with
one testis, one ovary. From
Sex Errors of the Body, by
John Money (1968).
Reproduced by permission of the
Johns Hopkins Press

her beloved Hermaphroditus, prays to the gods to make them forever inseparable and is answered by a miracle:

> And the two bodies seemed to merge together,
> One face, one form . . .
> So these two joined in close embrace, no longer
> Two beings, and no longer man and woman,
> But neither, and yet both . . .

But Hermaphroditus, though he cannot reverse the transformation, is granted his final wish as well: that the dream of androgyny may destroy all who come after him, even as he has been destroyed. He is already a eunuch when he makes it, crying out in "a voice whose tone was almost treble":

> . . . O father and mother, grant me this!
> May every one hereafter, who comes diving
> Into this pool, emerge half man, made weaker
> By the touch of this evil water!

That voice, however attenuated, has continued to ring in our ears ever since—not only when we pursue a love that transcends sexual difference, but when we contemplate creatures born with "abnormal genitals," though conceived by the "normal" love of men and women. And we can escape it only if we are at last persuaded that there are not two physiological sexes but many, a continuum rather than a bipolarity.

Though the myths of bisexuality do not adequately prepare us to deal with this fact, they remind us that behind the question, asked whenever a baby is born, "Is it a boy or a girl?" lurk deeper questions, usually unspoken: "Is it alive or dead?" "Is it a human or a monster?" Both represent pleas to be reassured that life will not cease from the earth, nor so profoundly alter that we would have preferred it had. But just as some children are in fact born dead or two-headed or one-eyed, so some are born so ambiguous phenotypically that wise women or shamans cannot determine their sex. "Monsters!" the naïve are likely to cry out, turning away in horror. And names invented by the more learned, like "androgynes," "Hermaphrodites," or "intersexes," do little to allay that primal fear—suggesting still that they are "unnatural" hybrids of the two "normal" sexes, male and female.

No wonder that some parents even now conceal the genitals of such children and dress them like unequivocal boys or girls. And even less wonder that they themselves continue the masquerade, lying, equivocating, evading until the day of revelation, when, say, in some athletic competition their sexual credentials are challenged. Customarily, it is the ambiguously sexed passing as girls who are thus exposed, or who flee before they can be examined. But in our sexually segregated sports, with whom were they supposed to have competed anyhow? Where are Olympic Games held for those intermediate sexes who, whatever the rulebook says, do exist? Anatomists and geneticists have been telling us so ever since the mid-eighteenth century, when Albrecht Van Haller published the first scientific treatise on hermaphroditism. There is "a relatively wide range of abnormalities in sexual development," one recent medical text puts it, "also a relatively high frequency," perhaps 3 or 4 percent of all births.

But even to recognize many such births we would have to cease making gross ocular sex identifications like medieval midwives and learn to identify a child's sex by seven separate criteria, which do not always coincide: external genitalia, internal genitalia, plus gonadal, chromosomal, and hormonal sex, and finally sex of assignment and gender identity. The latter two are psycho-social rather than physiological in origin—the first depending on how the child is named and dressed, how its hair is cut, how it is trained to pee; the second on how it comes to think of its own body, and especially to which sex it learns to direct its libido. Since both are initially determined by what the external genitalia look like at birth, there is always the possibility that they may contradict chromosomal, gonadal, even internal genital sex, all of which are present before birth.

The first, indeed, exists from the moment of conception, when the sperm brings to the X chromosome in the ovum either a second X, in which case the child is genetically a female, or a Y, in which case it is a male. In both, however, there develops a primal undifferentiated gonad, which becomes (or at least should become) in XX's the ovaries, in XY's the testes, and at the next stage, ducts which are normally suppressed in the male, but develop into the uterus and the fallopian tubes in the female. Then only do the external genitalia, still superficially indistinguishable, differentiate themselves into a scrotum or labia, a penis or clitoris. Meanwhile, different hormonal balances are being established in each of the sexes, which can, however, be upset again at puberty and after, producing those apparent sex changes noticed as early as the time of Pliny.

Children are generally classified as intersexes when there are contradictions between two or more of these factors or anomalies in one, as in those with the chromosomal structure XXX or XYY, or with one testis and one ovary. But about the causes of such abnormalities and their interrelationship there is still much disagreement. The first attempt at systematic explanation was made in 1876 by Klebs, who first distinguished pseudo-Hermaphrodites from "true Hermaphrodites," in whose gonads both male and female elements can be found, and further separated the latter into sixteen subcategories depending on whether the gonadal ambiguity is "bilateral," "unilateral," or "lateral," i.e., found on one side, both sides, or alternating.

Like other biologists of his time, who made taxonomy their be-all and end-all, he seems to have believed that merely renaming the world (preferably in Latin) was enough to demythologize it, i.e., redeem it from wonder to understanding. I suppose that just as it makes a difference in our attitude toward wild animals to think of a lion as *Felis leo* rather than the King of Beasts, so it makes a difference in our view of the sexually anomalous child if we refer to him as *hermaphroditus verus completus masculinus dexter* rather than as a "monster." Yet remnants of an older mythology remain implicit in the word "hermaphroditus" itself, and from such anachronistic resonances no inheritor of the Linnean system of classification has been quite able to escape.

Not that they have not tried. In the area of intersexuality, for instance, later scholars have attempted to replace Klebs's language with the more neutral etiological terms "gonadal aplasia" and "dysplasia," "testicular hypoplasia," "gonadal dysgenesis" and "complete primary agonadism"—all of them Greek in origin. Yet they have never quite managed to get rid of the key term "hermaphroditism" with its inescapable mythic aura. Moreover, the words "male" and "female" are themselves mythological, implying not just a certain morphology but a set of assumptions about behavior and roles. Even the conventional symbols by which the sexes are indicated (♀ and ♂) are hopelessly entangled with astrological and mystic associations: the former, for instance, symbolizing not just the human female but the planet Venus and the ankh, or Cross of Life. Any attempt, therefore, to demythify what is in fact our primary archetype, the myth on which all story and song depends, seems misguided and foredoomed.

But the effort has never ceased, as researchers have sought to substitute letter symbols for words of any kind: signifying the "normal" female by the noncommittal XX, the "normal" male by XY, and indicating "deviants" from these types as XXY, XXXY, XXX, XXXX, XXYY and XO/XY, XO/XX, XXO, XX/XXX, etc. Yet they also call the primary sexes "chromatin positive" and "chromatin negative," on the basis of the simplest test for determining the presence or absence of the Y chromosome. Moreover, it has turned out to be impossible even for doctors writing to each other *always* to designate sexually anomalous human beings so neutrally, and they have, consequently, remythologized their patients by referring, for instance, to the XXX's as "super-females," a term which stirs memories of Wonder Woman and the comics. But the most common practice is to designate certain classes of intersexes by the names of their "discoverers," so that XXY's, XXXY's, and XXYY's, for instance, are ordinarily referred to as "Klinefelter's Syndrome," or more familiarly, "Klinefelters." Similarly, XO's with gonadal agenesis (complete absence of one of the X chromosomes in the female) or dysgenesis are called "Turner's Syndrome," or "Turners." And it is, I must confess (revealing my own inability to conceptualize what has not first been mythologized), only those two classes of intersexuals who remain as vivid in my mind as Joseph-Josephine: the "Turners," web-necked, dwarfed females with underdeveloped breasts; and the

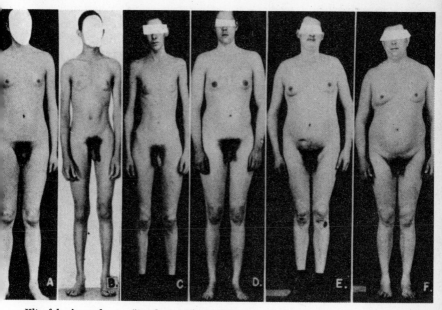

Klinefelter's syndrome. "Syndrome Characterized by Gynecomastia . . . ," by Klinefelter, Reifenstein, and Albright, in *The Journal of Clinical Endocrinology*, November 1942.

"Klinefelters," males with small testicles and bilateral gynecomastia, which is to say, two womanly tits.

The latter especially haunt me, perhaps because they so disconcertingly resemble and differ from classic representations of the god Hermaphroditus. Like him, they challenge our notions of what is fitting by displaying in a single body female breasts and a penis. To be sure, such latter-day avatars of the god—at least in the laboratory photographs illustrating Klinefelter's study of 1942—have a decidedly male habitus and lack completely the ambiguous erotic allure of the statues so dear to Hellenistic pederasts. Nor can we (and it is *not* just the white oblongs that blot out their faces, nor the antiseptic lighting that erases all nuance from their bodies) identify them with the ill-fated youth of Ovid's *Metamorphoses.* Yet we are told in the text that occasionally, like him, they are unmanned, showing "evidence of eunuchoidism, with absence of beard, highpitched voice, small phallus and small prostate." They have been demythified, in short, for their own sake and that of their families, who thus learn to regard them as medical cases rather than legendary horrors.

Most families, however, into which Klinefelters are born have never seen such clinical pictures, much less read the monographs, written by specialists for specialists, in which they typically appear. There exist more popular texts like John Money's *Sex Errors of the Body* (1968), but it seems doubtful that such books reach the lay audience. A distinguished medical psychologist, Money is committed, on the one hand, to enlightened "sex education," and on the other, to propagandizing on behalf of what he calls "a sexual revolution in reaction to the taboos and prudery of Victorianism"—or, as he puts it somewhat less banally, to extending the "sexual freedom" once considered an exclusive "aristocratic privilege" to the "common man."

He addresses himself primarily to the "school-teacher, doctor, pastor, social worker, psychologist, marriage counselor," which is to say, professionals concerned with alleviating sexual anxieties. But, in a kind of peroration, he expresses the hope that certain nonprofessional readers may "by learning the extremes of what can happen in the morphology and function of sex . . . enhance their appreciation of their own normalcy." It is an odd note on which to end, since to some among us, perhaps chiefly feminists, the concept of sexual "normalcy" itself seems a vestige of "the taboos and prudery of

Victorianism." For them the study of intersexuality reinforces a prior conviction that none of us is (or that at least it would be useful to act as if none of us were) exclusively male or female, but rather, to one degree or another, bisexual. Certainly there is a *prima facie* case for this point of view, in the area of "gender" at least, since gender identity and role are clearly matters of convention, socially determined and reinforced.

But they would insist further that morphology and embryology demonstrate that we begin as unisexes, or more precisely, that we are all "female" in the earliest stages of fetal development, so that masculinity represents in some sense a deviance; and, mythically speaking, therefore, it is man who is created "out of woman," rather than vice versa, as the scripture of the patriarchal Hebrews teaches. Such arguments may be specious, insofar as they confuse what is merely homologous with what is identical, and especially because they ignore the chromosomal base of all sex, which makes us male or female in every cell of our bodies from the moment of conception to the moment of death. But they possess genuine mythological and political appeal, which is to say, they can become social fact. And a small group of men and women who advocate them are now rearing their children as if the traditional male-female distinction were *nothing but convention*. Such children are dressed alike, have their hair cut in the same style, are given the same toys, trained for the same vocational roles, the same household functions, etc.

It is still too early to tell what will happen to such children, as the tension grows, on the one hand, between what the larger society expects of them and the behavior to which they have been trained, and on the other, between the differentiation of physical habitus, characteristic of puberty, and the unisex appearance they have learned to cherish. We know that children inadvertently assigned genders which contradict their gonadal and chromosomal sex live lives no more haunted or insecure than other humans, so long as their external genitals do not flagrantly belie those roles. But genital boys or girls deliberately brought up as the opposite sex by neurotic parents, incapable of accepting what fate has bestowed on them, have conspicuously come to grief. But whether children trained in unconventional sex roles for political rather than pathological reasons will fare well or ill is hard to say.

Only one thing is sure. If and when they fall, or, having escaped their doctrinal parents, put themselves into the hands of doctors and psychologists, those tensions are likely to be aggravated, since such professionals, however they stand politically, tend to act in a vocationally conservative way when confronted by an anomalously sexed child in a clinical situation. Almost without thought, they will employ their skills to remake that child into a viable "male" or "female" —capable of pleasurable and, in some instances, fertile intercourse with one of the "opposite sex." Intersexes are, that is to say, typically "repaired" or adjusted to fit current criteria of "normalcy," whether in accordance with their "real" (chromosomal or gonadal) or apparent (external genital) sex.

It is relatively easy, one gathers from the diagrams and descriptions in medical textbooks, to create with the knife or metal probe vaginas and vulvas for "females" lacking them; and possible, though considerably more difficult, to construct adequate penises for "males" only vestigially equipped. Moreover, if the initial operation is properly performed and hormone- or chemotherapy begun early and continued regularly, such "males" or "females" can have satisfactory orgasms; and the "female" can menstruate, too, like her "normal" sisters. Her problem is solved, in other words, not by teaching her to challenge what is called "normal" (as the more revolutionary would urge), much less transcend it, but to accommodate by accepting it—like her doctor before her.

In no standard "treatment" of sexual dilemmas or dysfunctions is this principle ever called into question, not even in the case of male "transsexuals," whose situation seems at first glance so radically different. It is true that they are not in any sense made more like what they were "intended" to be, since surgery and androgen/estrogen therapy for them establishes "contra natura," as it were, the sex they desperately desire but which all seven of their normal criteria seem to preclude. But even though the "sex change" they undergo may shock the conventional, they, too, end up being "normalized." They are, in fact, so totally transformed that even their eventual mates need never know that their sex is the creation of science. Once again, in any case, the "bourgeois" institution, if not of marriage, at least of heterosexuality and "normalcy" has been upheld. But by the same token a whole category of show Freaks has been removed from the "Ten-in-One" and remanded to the medical journals.

8

Siamese Twins

Because they, too, can be surgically "repaired," Siamese Twins are well on the way to obsolescence. In 1964 Nate Eagle, a manager of Freaks, was quoted as doubting that "any true Siamese Twins (the act can be faked easily) are on exhibition in this country today." Yet only a couple of decades ago they were, according to one of his predecessors, "a dime a dozen." Allowing for exaggeration on the part of a couple of men who earned their living by hyperbole, this represents an astonishing change due almost entirely to advances in surgical techniques. It is not likely that fewer joined twins are being born now, since we read accounts of such births two or three times a year in our daily papers, followed sometimes immediately, sometimes a year or two later, by announcements of their separation. They have become events, in short, not in the history of show biz but in that of medicine, like the beneficiaries of open heart surgery or the latest organ transplant.

We know of an attempted separation of living Siamese Twins as

early as 1690, and of an unsuccessful effort at cutting a survivor free
from his predeceased brother in the fifth century A.D. But it was not
until December 12, 1953, that the *Journal of the American Medical
Association* reported "the first case, so far as it is known, of both
members of a pair of Siamese Twins surviving this long [one year]
after a separation operation." There had been, according to an article which appeared a couple of weeks later in *Science News*, only
four similar operations before 1953, in three of which one twin survived, and in the fourth both, though only for six months. Best
known of these earlier cases was that of Radica and Doddica, the
"Orissa Sisters," first shown in Europe in 1893 at age four, and surgically divided at age twelve. But the operation, performed as Doddica lay dying of tuberculosis, amounted to little more than a desperate effort to save her sister by sacrificing her. She died, in fact,
under the knife and in vain, since Radica survived her by only two
years.

Radica-Doddica. From
*Anomalies and Curiosities of
Medicine,* by George M.
Gould and Walter L. Pyle
(1896).

One would have supposed that the names of the first twins to have made it successfully through such an operation would have become as famous as those of the Orissa Sisters. But though the medical techniques involved (the use of vitamin K, streptomycin, and penicillin, as well as an incubator and respirator) were specified in the report, the principals were identified only as "twin A" and "twin B." The names of the physicians in attendance, however, were recorded for posterity: "Drs. Hyatt Keitman, Earl E. Smith and Jac S. Geller, obstetrician, pediatrician and surgeon of Mount Sinai Hospital in Cleveland." Nor do the names of such later successfully separated twins as Santina and Giuseppina Foglia or Clara and Alta Rodriguez or Masha and Dacha, Russian girls brought up in a laboratory, though they appeared in the press, resonate mythically in our memories, since Siamese Twins have become supernumeraries in a psychodrama starring the doctors who make normal humans out of monsters.

To be sure, they can still attain a kind of fame by *refusing* to be separated, like Mary and Margaret Gibb, who died at age fifty-four in 1967 of cancer rather than undergo an operation they had grown up thinking impossible. Or if separated, they can become the occasion for the sort of headline I read in today's newspaper—as I take a break from writing this chronicle. "Father Flees Hospital, Abducts Siamese Twin," the story, datelined Wichita, Kansas, February 13, 1976, is captioned; and it goes on to tell how W. L. Cates, visiting his recently divided daughters in the hospital, suddenly tossed one onto a bed, grabbed the other, and ran—presumably because they were about to be placed in a foster home. "They are taking the twins because of race," Cates, a black married to a Mexican-American, is quoted as saying before disappearing. But the story ends, apparently without irony, "It was the 20th successful separation of Siamese Twins in medical history."

Yet before such "happy endings" were possible, the names of many joined twins became bywords throughout the whole Western world as those of Hermaphrodites had not—perhaps because the former embody the mystery of doubleness without any suggestion of the obscene. Beholders must always have felt a quiver of revulsion in their presence, but it was neutralized by a curious kind of affection, so that accounts, particularly of conjoined females, tend to be

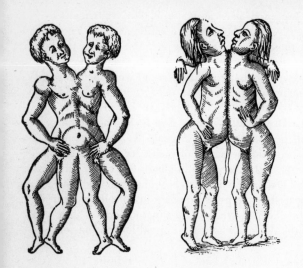

Five pictures of Siamese
Twins. From *Monstres et
prodiges*, by Ambroise Paré
(1573).

laden with terms of endearment. Such "monsters" have been, in any
case, identified by name from the early sixteenth century on. Born
in Glasgow in 1490, just before the discovery of America, the "Scottish Brothers" arrived at the court of James IV of Scotland when
they were eighteen. Some accounts suggest that they had a single
pair of legs and were only divided above the thigh; others insist
that they had four legs, as well as four arms and two heads. In any
case, they won the hearts of the court by playing musical instruments, singing in "two parts, treble and tenor," and making witty
conversation in Latin, French, Italian, Spanish, Dutch, Danish, and
Irish.

And we learn from a sixteenth-century broadside, quoted in the
preface to a nineteenth-century play dealing with a lover's attempt
to win his beloved by disguising himself as a Siamese Twin, of John
and Joan, allegedly "begotten between George Stevens and Margaret his wyfe, and borne in the parish of Swanburne in Bucking-
hamshyre, the 4th of Aprill, Anno Domini 1566 . . . having both
their belies fast joyned together, and embracing one another with
their arms . . ." It would be nice to believe that bisexual pair to be
as real as the "two monstrous girls," referred to in the same preface,
"with their backs fastened to one another . . . born in the kingdom
of Hungary. The one's name is Hellen, and the other Judita . . ."

The latter are the famous "Hungarian Sisters," alluded to by
Alexander Pope and in Buffon's *Natural History*. They lie beneath
an epitaph which reads: *One urine passage serves for both; one
anus, so they tell; / The other parts their numbers keep, and serve
their owners well. . . . Their inner parts concealed do lie, hid from
our eyes, alas! / But all the body here you view erect in solid brass.*
Moreover, at least one theologian gravely debated *post mortem* not
only whether they should have married, but whether on the Day of
Resurrection they would rise in one body or two. John and Joan,
however, are merely legendary, since identical twins, joined or unjoined, cannot be of different sexes. Yet men have long believed in
that possibility.

Even Siamese Twins of the same sex, though they occur with
some frequency, have always been surrounded by fantasy; and before the sixteenth century fantasy prevails over fact. The Biddenden
Maidens, for instance, presumably born in 1100, are often referred to

The Biddenden Maidens,
From *Anomalies and Curiosities of Medicine,* by George
M. Gould and Walter L. Pyle
(1896).

as the earliest such Freaks, though they seem as palpable a fraud as
John and Joan. C. J. S. Thompson tells their story in his *Mystery
and Lore of Monsters* (1930) with every appearance of believing it,
like Drs. Pyle and Gould before him. And though Drimmer qualifies
his account with phrases like "are said to have been" or "according
to tradition," he cannot resist retelling the tale of Eliza and Mary
Chalkhurst, who were joined—improbably enough—at both the hip
and shoulder, though not between.

Dying within six hours of each other at age thirty-four, the
legend runs, they left to their native parish of Biddenden in Kent a
parcel of land yielding an annual income of thirty-five pounds,
which they directed be spent on cheese and bread for the poor. The
practice has continued to the present; and sometime in the years
between, the custom grew up of making the bread into flat cakes impressed with their images "in their habit as they lived." I have seen
pictures of those cakes, and it seems to me that they came first rather
than vice versa, the whole legend having been invented to explain
"effigies" which show, as in a child's drawing, two women with their
arms linked behind each other's shoulders so that it looks as if one
lacks the right arm and the other the left.

Despite the richness of the popular mythology which has grown up around Siamese Twins since the beginnings of the Freak show —unlike Dwarfs and Giants, Fats and Thins, or Hermaphrodites— they seem to have risen out of an archetypal vacuum. There are no recognizable prototypes painted on the walls of caves, nor do they appear in the folk tales of the Mediterranean or the Black Forest. To be sure, images of two-headed men and gods have been left behind by primitive cultures from Anatolia to New South Wales and the Solomon Islands. But these belong to an iconic tradition which signifies divine or demonic super-strength by multiplying the extremities and appendages of a single body. Legendary creatures otherwise as different as the three-headed Hell hound Cerebus, the two-faced Janus, and the many-armed Shiva belong to this archetypal family, memories of which stir in us when we confront Freaks ranging from major terata like Frank Lentini, who played soccer with his third leg, to minor ones like Anne Boleyn, mother of Elizabeth I, who had an extra finger on each hand, and our one-time washerwoman on the island of Ischia, known only as the Lady with Twelve Toes.

Even sexual *monstres par excès*, with double penises or clitorises, three balls or several breasts, ordinarily fall into this category, though at their most outlandish and terrifying they call into question not just the integrity of the body but the parameter of symmetry which bounds our notions of the beautiful and the human. It is as *mutants* we perceive and fear them, as threats to what we cannot help feeling is, or ought to be, the end of the evolutionary line: a final adjustment so effective and elegant that any change would be a regression. And in this they resemble the hairies, the uglies, the Half Men/Half Women, even Midgets and Living Skeletons.

Siamese Twins, on the other hand, challenge our individuality, along with the distinction between self and other upon which that individuality depends; in other words, not the uniqueness of our bodies but of our consciousnesses, or what used to be called our souls. Indeed, all identical twins pose for us such a challenge. And for the unjoined there are prototypes of great mythic resonance, including Castor and Pollux, Romulus and Remus, Jacob and Esau, Polyneices and Eteocles. Most of them, as my examples suggest, turn out to be *enemy* twin brothers, one of whom must go down to bloody

death so that the other can become the founder of a city or the
savior of his people. Chroniclers of actual Siamese Twins have
adapted this aspect of the myth, portraying male pairs in particular
as opposed in temperament and taste. It is reported, for instance, of
the Scottish Brothers that one was extraordinarily stupid, the other
remarkably intelligent, and "they would carry on . . . curious debates, on which they sometimes disagreed, and occasionally came to
blows."

Though some biographers speak of the good humor with which
Chang and Eng bore each other's foibles, others dwell on the growing bitterness between them as they approached death and an ailing
Chang took to drinking heavily. Moreover, we are told that Chang
"loved the ladies," as his brother did not; liked highly spiced Oriental
foods, while his brother preferred a bland vegetarian diet; and told

Chang and Eng, the original
Siamese Twins. Nineteenth-
century photograph.
*Circus World Museum, Baraboo,
Wisconsin*

dirty jokes in public, embarrassing the more circumspect and scholarly Eng. In fact, if Malone is to be believed, "they fought both publicly and privately, from the time they learned to walk to the day they died." The last words they ever spoke to each other were in anger, though at that point they customarily avoided talking to prevent quarrels. It was those temperamental differences which Mark Twain exploited in 1868 in a farcical essay portraying one as a drunkard and the other as a teetotaler, who during the Civil War "both fought gallantly, Eng on the Union side and Chang on the Confederate. They took each other prisoners at Seven Oaks . . ." And he ends by describing a combat in which they beat each other mercilessly, until "the bystanders interfered, and tried to separate them, but they could not do it, and so allowed them to fight it out."

It is his way of dealing with the fact that the conflict of enemy twins turns comic when they are joined, the classic solution of fratricide being obviated because the death of one brother entails that of the other. Such a perception of its absurdity, however, does not annul the sense of the uncanny implicit in the notion of two humans so indistinguishable that one can usurp the other's place even in the arms of his beloved. That sense is better captured in Gothic tales of the double, or classic myths of the divine imposter, who by counterfeiting such a resemblance robs his victim of his identity and fate; and it is reinforced when, seeing our reflections in a mirror or a limpid pool, we relive the archetypal terror of Narcissus.

In our ancestors' awareness of Siamese Twins, the myth of the double merged with that of the multiple monster to create a myth of the Monstrous Self and an identically Monstrous Other *joined together till death do them part*. And this myth created a *frisson* no longer available to us, alas, even when confronting those who have chosen not to be separated. Recalling older show Freaks, however, who still felt themselves "chained for life," we can almost, *almost* re-create the original thrill. I myself think first of Daisy and Violet Hilton, who made a film with that grim title, and were perhaps for that reason chosen to represent their kind in Todd Browning's *Freaks*. THE STORY OF THE LOVE LIFE OF THE SIDESHOW, its publicity posters were headed, and the first question which followed, taking precedence over "Can a full grown woman love a midget?" and "What sex is the half man half woman?" was "Do Siamese twins make love?"

Ritta-Christina. From *Anomalies and Curiosities of Medicine,* by George M. Gould
and Walter L. Pyle (1896).

That question reporters never ceased putting to Daisy and Violet, along with the follow-up the posters leave implicit: "And if so,
how?" Violet answered both: "Sometimes I quit paying attention,"
she is reported as saying. "Sometimes I read and sometimes I just
took a nap . . . we had learned not to know what the other was
doing unless it was our business to know it." In all ages, joined twins
have evoked erotic fantasies in their audiences, since they suggest
inevitably the possibility of multiple fornication—or at least the impossibility of sexual privacy. Violet and Daisy apparently proved
more titillating than most, since they were attractive even as little
girls, with bottle curls and bows in their hair, and all the more so
when they continued in that guise of innocence long after puberty
and various failed marriages. They have in fact only one pair of
rivals for the title of the sexiest of all Siamese Twins, Rosa and Josepha Blazek.

For a little while Rosa and Josepha were in competition with
the Hiltons, though, born in 1878, they were somewhat older. But

they continued to dance old-fashioned Bohemian dances and play gypsy violins up to 1922; so that even in 1971, Edward Malone, then eighty-three, still remembered their charms. "These two dames were like two Mae Wests, joined at the tail bone," he told an interviewer. "One would wiggle, while the other would waggle, and brother could they put on a great show." And he went on to recount how, when they had begun "to hit the big time" in 1921, Josepha announced that she was (a) pregnant and (b) still a virgin: a "misconception" which tickled the reporters of the period. At that point, however, a carpenter called Franzel embarrassed them both (Rosa having sworn that her sister was telling the truth) by claiming to be the expectant father and offering to marry Josepha. But when after much shilly-shallying, the twins acknowledged that he might after all have been responsible, no minister or judge would perform the ceremony, lest he compound their previous "moral turpitude." It is a story I would dearly love to believe. But Malone's credibility is damaged when he tells us that they moved to Europe, where all three got married and "settled down for the rest of their unnatural lives," since Rosa and Josepha never left the States, dying in Chicago long before the presumed date of their marriage.

The Bohemian Sisters have, in any case, faded from the memory of all but the most ardent Freak fans, while the Hilton Sisters are still fondly recalled. I sit looking at this moment, for instance, at a recently published postcard reproducing one of their old posters. Headed "San Antonio's Siamese Twins Daisy and Violet Hilton, the Sensation of Vaudeville," it shows them back to back, but swiveled away from each other so that both face outward, a saxophone in the hands of each, and a fixed smile on each cupid's-bow mouth. Clearly, it is our nostalgia for the Jazz Age which has given them a second life. "We are our own Jazz Band," they told a reporter in 1924, when they were only fifteen. "We have been studying music . . . and we have now reached the point where we can make the big horns moan and whine and cry and gurgle." They could also dance the black bottom, having learned that step from Bob Hope, even as they had taught themselves the saxophone by listening to Rudy Vallee. And as, in a final link to the mythological figures of the era, they had been instructed in turning themselves off during each other's moments of sexual pleasure by the great Houdini.

LEFT: Violet and Daisy Hilton, the United Twins.

RIGHT: Millie-Christine, the United African Twins. Contemporary publicity photographs.
Both photos: Circus World Museum, Baraboo, Wisconsin

They did not survive long as performers, though they managed to find work in Hollywood during the thirties, after "talking pictures" had doomed big-time vaudeville, to which they had graduated from the side show. It was not until 1932 that they really came into their own, since up to then they had been victimized by self-appointed "guardians," who even after they reached their majority managed to do them out of their earnings. In that year, however, they won a judgment awarding them $100,000 in damages and making them responsible only to themselves. SIAMESE TWINS UNFOLD TALE OF BONDAGE, the headlines ran as their suit began, but when it was over they could say to the reporters, "It's good to be free!" Unfortunately, they proved incapable of profiting by that freedom, though shortly thereafter they were earning $5,000 a week and for a while owned a hotel in Pittsburgh. When they died of the Hong Kong flu in 1969, they were working in a supermarket near Charlotte, North Carolina, as a double checkout girl—one bagging, no doubt, as the other rang up the bill on the cash register. It is an apt ending, somehow, for Freaks who though declared "free" at the close of a headlined courtroom drama, remained slaves to each other to the end of their lives.

Even more ironic is the case of the "Millie-Christine Sisters," also known as the "United African Twins," who being black and born in the pre–Civil War South, were from birth slaves to others as well as each other. By the time of the Emancipation Proclamation, they had already been exhibited for nine of their ten years by their first "master," a Mr. Jos. P. Smith, who had paid $30,000 for these "two strange lumps of humanity." But they were stolen away by a less scrupulous showman, who moved them, like disposable pieces of property, back and forth across state lines and finally to England, where their legitimate "owner" won them back in a hotly contested court case. Between shows he left them in the care of his wife, their "white ma," who indoctrinated them in "the fundamental principles of the established Church of England." And after his death they continued to support her—in imitation, they tell us, of "that deep devotion which Ruth evinced toward Naomi." Moreover, according to a pamphlet presumably written by them, they stayed good Christians always, singing to their audiences a pious song which concluded:

> None like me, since the days of Eve—
> None such perhaps will ever live;
> A marvel to myself am I,
> As well as to all who passes by.
> I'm happy, quite, because I'm good;
> I love my Saviour and my God;
> I love all things that God has done,
> Whether I'm created *two* or *one*.

According to Malone, however, neither remained an Anglican, Millie becoming a hard-shell Baptist, and Christine preferring to belt out bawdy songs rather than hymns of any kind. Moreover, if they kept on providing, as they claimed in their "plain unvarnished tale," for their "white ma," it was not by sacrificing their own interests. When they retired in the early 1900s, Malone asserts, they had "stashed away" perhaps a quarter of a million dollars, on the income of which—minus some gifts to Baptist African missions—they lived until October 9, 1912, when first Christine, then Millie died. But it is hard to trust Malone, since his views represent the debunking of a carnie insider: the "straight skinny" as opposed to the "bunkum" fed by publicity men to credulous "marks." He was, in any event, a garrulous old man far from the events he describes before Bill Carmichael got around to recording his pitch in *Incredible Collectors* (1971). But Malone was trying at least to recover some sense of Millie-Christine's humanity from the ballyhoo created in utter contempt of it.

Barnum's pamphlet has quite the opposite intent, mythologizing what it claims merely to describe, beginning with the very picture on its cover. Immediately below a caption reading "The Two-headed Girl," we see Millie-Christine endowed with only two arms, and apparently fused all the way from shoulder to kneecap. That they actually had four and were joined only from the sacrum to the coccyx, however, the appended "Medical Descriptions" make clear, informing us, too, that, like the Hungarian Twins, they had "a common anus . . . and actually discharge their faeces and urine at the same time." Perhaps, indeed, two bodies with a single urogenital tract is a monstrosity equivalent to one body with two heads.

But the latter anomaly has seldom survived long enough to be shown in the Ten-in-One, though there have been a number of still-born janiceps babies, whose images can be found to this day in medical textbooks. John Hunter used to display in his private collection, along with the skeleton of the Irish Giant, that of an Indian child with a second skull on top of the first (the famous "Home's Case"), who died in infancy of a cobra bite. And William Durks, the "Man with Three Eyes," was still being exhibited in 1970 as a "Single O," an attraction weird enough to stand by itself, though he had been talking about retirement ever since the death of his wife, the "Crocodile Woman," in 1968. He actually had, I suppose, two heads imperfectly separated—or oddly fused—so that he ended up with a double nose and a split lip, as well as the Cyclopean third eye.

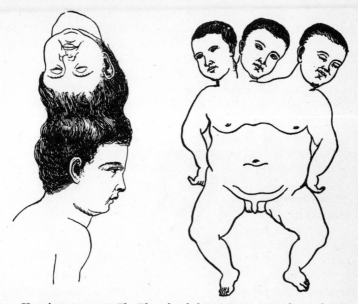

LEFT: Home's case. RIGHT: The Three-headed Boy. From *Anomalies and Curiosities of Medicine*, by George M. Gould and Walter L. Pyle (1896).

The closest thing to what ordinary viewers think of as a two-headed man, however, are the Tocci Brothers. Christened Giovanni Battista and Giacomo, presumably because canon law and common law agree that two heads mean two persons in God's eyes as well as man's, each also possessed a distinct set of lungs, a heart of his own, and a usable pair of arms. From the sixth rib downward, however, they were completely joined, having not merely a single anus and penis, but only two legs. Their perfect amalgamation was marred only by the presence of three buttocks, and their value as show Freaks by the fact that they could never manage to walk. Giovanni Battista was considerably less well developed than his brother, so that "his" foot did not reach the ground when they tried to stand, and both their legs consequently atrophied from disuse. Understandably enough, they found their lot intolerable, and after a brief career in show business withdrew to Italy, where they nursed their melancholy in private until death released them. But they live on in Amer-

ican literature, though as figures of fun rather than of pathos, since Mark Twain was inspired by one of their publicity posters to start a short story called "Those Extraordinary Twins."

As he continued to work on that "extravagantly fantastic" little tale, it grew into a full-scale comic novel, involving a "human philippene" called Luigi and Angelo, the first of whom is eventually hanged for a capital crime, after considerable argument among their would-be lynchers. "No, Count Angelo is innocent," one of them protests; but another answers, "Who said anything about hanging him? We are only going to hang the other one." "And so," Twain concludes coolly, "ends the history of 'Those Extraordinary Twins.'" But a pair of garden-variety identical twins—or rather two babies at first totally indistinguishable, despite the fact that one is white and the other black—began to take over Twain's story, demanding a fate too grim for farce. And Twain sacrificed his Freaks to them, splitting Angelo and Luigi down the middle, long before any surgeon had learned to do so.

Yet for an instant he seems to have sensed the poignant analogy between the biological plight of conjoined twins and the social plight of black slaves and white masters in antebellum America. It would, however, have required a commingling of the tragic and comic he could not handle at that point to make that insight into a convincing fiction, and he lost his nerve. Nonetheless, in the scraps of his original story, which appear as an appendix to some editions of *Pudd'nhead Wilson*, hints remain of his awareness that "monsters" like Giovanni Battista and Giacomo are the more tragic because their indignity stirs us to laughter rather than tears.

Most of us choose to recall Chang and Eng rather than the more tragic Toccis or the Hilton Sisters, because it is possible, despite certain difficulties, to read their story as one with a happy ending. Not only did they die respected by a tough-minded rural community that had begun by resenting and fearing them for both their skin color and their freakishness, but (unlike most joined twins) they died still married after more than thirty years to Sarah Ann and Adelaide Yates, the "normal" and unimpeachably "white" daughters of a local clergyman-farmer. On them they begot twenty-two children: twelve out of Sarah, presumably by Eng, and ten out of Adelaide, presumably by Chang, though they were listed in the family Bible unsorted and unassigned. The families lived, however, in different houses, one presided over by Eng, the other by Chang. It is generally said that their practice of spending three days at one and three at the other began when the sisters proved incapable of getting along with each other. But I suspect that Chang and Eng came to feel that though neither could escape his other self ever, at least they did not have to spend all their waking hours in the presence of two wives and two sets of children.

To whom those children "belonged" I do not think they much cared—regarding themselves as a single person, and signing legal documents and personal correspondence not Chang and Eng, but simply Chang Eng. Moreover, their neighbors, who had threatened to burn the crops of their prospective father-in-law before the wedding took place, accepted the double union after it had been sanctioned by the Baptist Church. If jokes were made about the fact that each bridegroom had two marriage beds and each marriage bed two bridegrooms, they have not come down to us, except as reworked long afterward by Mark Twain:

By and by Eng fell in love with his sister-in-law's sister, and married her, and since that day they have all lived together, night and day, in an exceeding sociability which is touching and beautiful to behold, and is a scathing rebuke to our boasted civilization.

Both brides, if the photographs can be trusted, grew as respectably dowdy and grim as any of their fellow townswomen; and their husbands proved that they could pull their weight and pay their way —chopping down trees or raising a roof beam as quickly as any pair of men. They became, in short, as none of their freakish counterparts had ever quite done before, their own masters, and what is more, the masters of others. Like their neighbors, that is to say, *they owned slaves*, men and women presumably "normal," though undoubtedly black. It is for me the most astonishing fact about their astonishing lives; though the accounts I have read do not pause to reflect how, holding other humans in bondage, they must have felt their own monstrous bondage mitigated or annulled. The Civil War, however, freed those slaves, and, indeed, so disrupted the economy of the region that Chang and Eng were forced to put themselves on public exhibition for one last time.

They had interrupted their farming careers on a couple of earlier occasions, partly to consult European doctors about a surgical separation, though they had promised their wives that they would never sever that bond, stronger than matrimony itself. The closest they had come to doing so was just prior to their wedding, when Adelaide and Sarah had burst in just as a group of Philadelphia doctors was ready to begin cutting. Yet once more they felt driven to try. Only an inch and a half at the thinnest place and no more than three at its thickest, the "ensiform (sword-shaped) appendix," which connected them just below the sternum, was flexible enough so that the "United Twins," though born face to face, had learned to turn away from each other. But this time the doctors assured them that separation would mean death.

Their trip was financially successful at least, though they by no means created such a furor as they had nearly half a century before. No country, to be sure, banned their appearance, as France had once done lest they terrify pregnant women into producing babies as "monstrous" as themselves. On the other hand, the old thrill seemed gone—the great pathologist Rudolf Virchow, who had first examined them, thought it was because they had grown too old to do the handsprings and somersaults which had delighted their first audiences. It was not, however, their declining strength which made the difference, so much as a new sense of themselves. No longer were they young performers eager to please and having nothing to offer except the abnormality which made them two in one. They were sixty-year-old solid citizens, temporarily down on their luck and therefore deigning to perform one more time. Besides, how could they not have been aware that they had become the living prototype of all joined twins, their show name a common noun for all their anomalous brothers and sisters.

It had not always been thus, of course. Just after their birth in 1811 to a poor Chinese family ("Siamese Twins" is in this sense a misnomer) living in Siam, they had been on the verge of extermination twice: once when local superstition demanded their death, and once when local doctors proposed to separate them by primitive techniques whose results could only have been fatal. But they survived, throve, and won the approval of the King, appearing before him in a ceremony which involved much double bowing and banging of their heads on the floor. Later, the Siamese were to complain that their country was known to the outside world as a source of cats, elephants, and joined twins; but at first they seemed proud to have added one more valuable export item to the first two. And valuable indeed Chang and Eng proved to be, bringing in $30,000 as a down payment to be split between their parents and the government officials who expedited their export.

When they had been duly paid for and carried off to America in 1829 by a pair of Yankee merchant skippers called Hunter and Coffin (the former of whom also dealt in opium), it appeared as if they would remain chattels, like Millie and Christine. They even took the name of one of their "owners," as slaves were accustomed to do. But if Coffin believed he was dealing with helpless victims, he was soon disabused of the notion. Even before they became show Freaks, Chang and Eng were already businessmen, dealing in poultry and preserved "hundred year eggs"; so that when their stock in trade became their own freakish selves, they were prepared to show the traditional acumen of their Chinese ancestors. By the time they reached their majority and could act as their own managers, they had proved themselves such stellar box office attractions that even P. T. Barnum had to accept them on their own terms. He seems, in fact, never to have forgiven them for the hard bargain they drove, referring to them years later in his *Autobiography* with a coldness and brevity inappropriate to their fame.

In any case, they thought they were through with show business by 1839, when they took up residence in rural North Carolina, becoming American citizens and, as if to indicate a break with their past, cutting their queues and adopting the name Bunker, under which they lie buried, and which many of their descendants still proudly bear. It seems to me an extraordinary name to have chosen —evoking not just a legendary battle, but also that good old word "bunkum." The biographers tell us, however, that Chang and Eng borrowed it from a "New York friend." Yet whether intended as a charm or a joke, it has worked like a charm; for despite an occasional dark-skinned or slant-eyed descendant, the Bunkers have become completely assimilated to American "normalcy."

Not one of Chang Eng's children turned out to be a Freak, though two were born deaf and dumb; and the same has apparently remained true of the three following generations. "There are probably at least one thousand living grandchildren, great-grandchildren, and great-great-grandchildren scattered around the country," we learn from an article written in 1953, the year after the last of their children had died. "These have included such distinguished citizens as a president of the Union Pacific Railroad and a major general in the U.S. Air Force, as well as a large number of average taxpayers." But even among the latter, those who have remained in the vicinity of Mt. Airy at least are rated by a neighbor as "a little better than average farmers." And he adds, "I don't hardly know any Bunkers that don't own their own land."

It seems, in short, a success story all the way; though when we look closer, we discover that from the beginning Chang had been a little more successful than Eng. Indeed, he seems always to have tried a little harder, and when they fought physically, to have been the bitterer and more vindictive of the two. Perhaps the root of the matter was that, starting smaller, he ended both slighter and an inch shorter, a fact he tried to conceal by wearing special thick soles. To make things worse, he became paralyzed on the side next to Eng during their return trip from England, where they had gone in 1872 to find a doctor who would separate them. It was a condition both brothers believed was aggravated by Chang's heavy drinking (Eng neither drank nor got drunk vicariously), which grew ever heavier, leading to increased bitterness between them.

At one point, a peace bond was imposed on both to keep them from inflicting physical harm on each other. But in their final years nothing could allay Chang's rage, or his tendency in moments of frenzy to toss the household valuables into the fire. All the while, Eng had to bear more and more of his weight, as his disability turned him into a clinging, surly child. Moreover, they were both aware that nothing but death could deliver them from this lifelong bondage. When Eng finally died, sometime during the early morning of January 7, 1874, it was after a horrendous night, which had begun with their customary move from household to household, exactly on schedule despite Chang's growing distress. And it ended with the customary bickering over when to go to bed, Chang holding out— perhaps in the premonition that he would never rise again.

What happened the next morning is related in the phonograph-ically recorded proceedings of the Philadelphia College of Physi-cians for February 8, according to which Eng woke unaware that his brother was dead—or perhaps merely unwilling to acknowledge that fact. Instead, he asked his son, " 'How is your Uncle Chang?' The boy said, 'Uncle Chang is cold—Uncle Chang is dead.' Then great excitement took place. Eng commenced crying out immedi-ately—saying to his wife, whom they called in, 'My last hour is come,' and finally sank away." A few details are added by the state-ment made by Eng's widow:

> When Eng saw his wife after learning that Chang was dead, he said, "I am dying," but did not speak of his brother's death. He soon afterwards expressed a desire to defecate, and this con-tinued for half an hour. He rubbed his upper extremities, raised them restlessly, and complained of a choking sensation. The only notice he took of Chang was to move him nearer. His last words were, "May the Lord have mercy on my soul."

It would seem that Chang's death resulted from a second stroke, though the postmortem was limited by a family stipulation that no incisions be made that would disfigure their heads and faces, and that their bond be entered only from the back. The question of what caused Eng's death remains open. It occurred so quickly that the doctors who attempted at the bedside to separate his still living body from his brother's corpse did not have time to begin. And Drs. Ruschenberger, Pancoast, Allen, Hollingworth, and Abraham Jacobi, who assembled for the postmortem, had other things on their minds, chiefly a desire to determine the nature of the "ensiform appendix" that connected them, and to convince themselves that the twins could not have been safely severed in life. In any case, they began, even as they opened up the bodies to claim them for science, renaming the pair known in show business as "United Brothers" or "Siamese Twins," first a "monster of symmetrical duplex development," and then, "an *Omphalopagus Xiphodydimus*" (twins joined at the umbilical region).

Before they were through, however, the question of Eng's death recurred, and when Dr. Pancoast hedged, Dr. Allen rose to say, "Eng probably died of fright, as the distended bladder seemed to point to a profound emotional disturbance of the nervous system, the mind remaining clear until stupor came on . . ." It is a remark quickly lost, as they returned once more to scrutinizing the cord, and Dr. Jacobi concluded with a history of famous "Xiphophages" of the past, from the Hungarian Sisters to the purely mythological "Biddenden Sisters." After which the transcript adds only, "None of the Fellows desiring to say anything further on the subject, on motion, the College adjourned."

But the phrase "died of fright" resonates in my mind, evoking the terror of lifelong mutual dependency. In their relationship I feel caricatured symbiotic relations more familiar to me—not sealed in the flesh, like theirs, but quite as inescapable: parents and children, unjoined siblings, lovers, husbands and wives. Like Chang and Eng, such pairs, however equal in theory, are never equal in fact, since one of them inevitably leans a little harder, clings a little longer, demands a little more. And both live always with the threat of that ultimate disparity which will occur when one begins to die, and finally—the other still living—is dead. But there is another kind of show Freak in whom the horror of joined inequality is figured forth even more dramatically than in Chang and Eng, or Millie and Christine, the latter of whom used to sometimes bend over until her weaker sister was left flailing helplessly in the air, or the Toccis, whose deformed leg, considered by both as Giacomo's, could never quite touch the ground.

These are the One-and-a-Halfs, full humans with incomplete "parasitic" bodies attached to their own. One of the most famous was Laloo the Hindu, who in 1899 participated in the protest meeting at which Barnum's prize human oddities asked to be called "prodigies" rather than "Freaks." He looks at us in mute protest still, out of the photographs that have survived him (he died in a train wreck in Mexico in 1905), holding his parasite up and away from his body, as if to evoke our wonder or challenge our belief. That not-quite-human extension of himself is dressed as exotically and extravagantly as he, though in the costume of a female. Actually, it had a rudimentary penis, and outside the show Laloo liked to boast that it urinated and had erections—perhaps in response to its own unimaginable dreams. But where such dreams could have occurred is hard to say, since its head, if it had one at all, was buried deep in its brother's epigastrium.

Sex differences between autosite and parasite may be impossible, but exhibitors find that the notion attracts audiences; so that Perumal, another Hindu One-and-a-Half, was advertised as having a female twin buried head-first below his chest. He went so far as to name her Sami, attributing to her a separate consciousness as well as a different gender. As a matter of fact, only Laloo among Freaks with upper-body parasites refused to give his attached companion a name of her/his own. Those with lower-body parasites, on the other hand, almost never do, presumably because what little of an attached "other" they have to show cannot be exhibited without exposure of the genitals. They are, therefore, typically presented as multi-limbed rather than double-bodied.

Frank Lentini, the most celebrated of such Freaks, was billed during the early part of this century as the "Three-legged Wonder," and the publicity about him concentrated on his ability to kick a soccer ball with his "extra" leg, which in fact belonged to a rudimentary twin, who weighed only twenty-five pounds but possessed a pelvis and an imperfect penis. A generation later, Betty Lou Williams, an attractive black woman who used to appear in a two-piece bathing suit, was advertised as the "Girl with Four Legs and Three

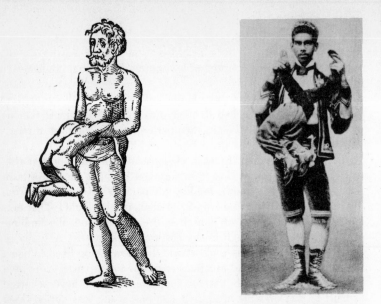

ABOVE LEFT: "A Monster Out of Whose Bellie an Other Man, All Whole, Reserving the Head." From *Monstres et prodiges*, by Ambroise Paré (1573).

ABOVE RIGHT: Laloo and parasite. From *Anomalies and Curiosities of Medicine*, by George M. Gould and Walter L. Pyle (1896).

BELOW LEFT: Perumal and Sami. Contemporary publicity photograph.

BELOW RIGHT: Francisco (Frank) Lentini, the Three-Legged Man. Contemporary publicity photograph.

Both photos: Circus World Museum, Baraboo, Wisconsin

Arms," though her twin had, in fact, not only a whole lower body but a token piece of an upper. And long before her time, Louise L., who delighted French fair-goers in the nineteenth century, was similarly known as "La Dame à quatres jambes." In addition to two complete pelvises and two sets of legs, she had an extra pair of breasts, just below the belly button. But she possessed, it would appear, only one set of sexual organs.

Myrtle Corbin, on the other hand, called the "Four-legged Woman from Texas," had two vaginas, out of one of which she allegedly bore three children, and out of the other, two. Most sub–Siamese Twins with duplicate lower bodies have been perceived, like Myrtle, as sex Freaks rather than identity Freaks or polymelics. Drs. Pyle and Gould, for instance, classify the male counterparts of Myrtle and Louise not as autosite-parasite "monsters" but as *diphallic terata*, observing that "by their intense interest to the natural bent of the curious mind," such Freaks "have always elicited much discussion." Most of their own discussion is devoted to Jean Baptista dos Santos, a Cuban who had, in addition to a pair of fused supernumerary legs, two large, fully operative male organs, and who, they report, "was possessed of extraordinary animal passion, the sight of a female alone being sufficient to excite him. He was said to use both penises, after finishing with one, continuing with the other . . ."

Clearly, Jean Baptista did not consider the pelvically attached vestigial body from which his second phallus hung a second self worthy of a name, as most Freaks with epigastric parasites have done. The early twentieth-century Roman autosite Jean Libbera, for instance, though he was a married man with four children and off the fairgrounds wore a voluminous cloak to conceal his parasite brother, insisted on calling him "Jacques." He was, morever, proud that, unlike most parasites, Jacques had perfect nails on his fingers and toes, as well as a rudimentary hidden head, and therefore really qualified as a person. Perhaps Jean was following the example of his seventeenth-century forerunner Lazarus Colloredo, whose shunken, barely sentient brother Joannes Baptista grew out of his chest. Though the head of Joannes was totally visible and grew whiskers, his eyes never opened, and his mouth, which never closed, could utter no sound. He was nonetheless baptized in the belief that he, too, possessed an eternal soul.

LEFT: Betty Lou Williams and parasite. Contemporary publicity photograph.

BELOW LEFT: Louise L. From *Anomalies and Curiosities of Medicine,* by George M. Gould and Walter L. Pyle (1896).

BELOW RIGHT: Myrtle Corbin. Contemporary publicity photograph.
Both photos: Circus World Museum, Baraboo, Wisconsin

For the audience, however, such autosite-parasites do not evoke the terror associated with the interdependence of the self and the other, tending rather to be assimilated to a category of Freaks which challenges our sense of the integrity of the body: Half Men like Johnny Eck, who lacking buttocks, legs, and feet, moves on his hands through the climactic frames of *Freaks* in pursuit of what is beautiful and whole. But since, unlike Johnny, upper-body parasites are typically headless, they blur into the nightmare of the acephalon: that ultimate monster, lacking not just a skull, but the brain in which we have come to believe resides consciousness, memory, identity itself.

Even more marginal are epignathic parasites, lumps of subhumanity with limbs more suggested than defined, who seem to be emerging from the mouths of their autosites. A form of what were earlier called dermoid cysts but are now known as teratomas, they also resemble fetuses *in fetu:* "strange instances," Drs. Gould and Pyle call them, "in which one might almost say that a man may be pregnant with his brother or sister, or in which an infant may carry its twin without the fact being apparent." And they cite the case of a tumor cut out of the abdomen of a man which turned out to contain teeth and hair; and another, in which there issued from a twenty-seven-year-old male, after great pain, "fetal bones and a mass of macerated embryo."

It was hard for doctors in earlier times to avoid mythologizing such events, associated in the minds of believing Christians with the "miraculous birth" of Eve out of Adam. As late as 1891, such a case occurring in Mexico City was blazoned to the world under the headline A MAN-MOTHER, and was illustrated by a woodcut showing a weeping baby emerging from the tumor on the back of its "father." Formerly, when such cysts were discovered in the urogenital tracts of unmarried women, they were taken as proofs of "unchastity." But in the case of girls safely pre-pubescent, they were more likely to be explained as a "miracle" of parthenogenesis—like the fatherless baby taken from the belly of a girl two years and nine months old, which allegedly throve for more than nine months, displaying from the first "a precocious longing for ardent spirits."

It seems like waking from nightmare to reality to move from such legendary tales to the case histories in modern medical text-

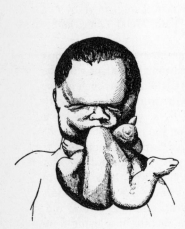

LEFT: Lazarus-Joannes Baptista Colloredo. BELOW LEFT: Epignathic "monster." Both from *Anomalies and Curiosities of Medicine,* by George M. Gould and Walter L. Pyle (1896).

BELOW RIGHT: Giacomo and Matteo, autosite and parasite. From a seventeenth-century print.

books. Diagnosing teratomas as "tumors consisting of tissues derived from ectoderm, mesoderm and entoderm," modern doctors resist dubbing them failed twins or aborted embryos merely because their components include "skin, central nervous tissue, teeth, glands or respiratory and alimentary mucosa." But they are given pause by the fact that though other tumors share the chromosomal sex of their hosts, teratomas can be male, female, or hermaphroditic, as if they had some kind of vestigial identity. Moreover, they occur more frequently in women than in men, and in white men more often than in black, as other cancerous growths do not; so that mystery remains, no matter how thoroughly myth may have been dispelled.

Nor does the distinction between teratomas and fetuses *in fetu*, which the teratology of the past confused with each other, hold up under examination. Modern researchers have contended that the latter are "quite clearly the monozygotic twins of their hosts," as the former are not; and that unlike "pseudo-anthropomorphic terato-mas," they always possess " a vertebral axis, sometimes accompanied by the appropriate arrangement of the organs and limbs with respect to the axis." But in a case reported in 1951, five fetuses *in fetu* were found in "a newborn hydrocephalic infant who was apparently free of congenital malformations with the exception of those of the brain and skull"; and though three of these siblings had "well-defined spinal rudiments," two did not. Those unborn quintuplets, nested in the swollen head of their stillborn brother as in a womb, continue to haunt me as no atrocity in Paré or Gould and Pyle has ever succeeded in doing.

It is not just a matter of the dead yielding up the dead under the surgeon's knife in an ultimate parody of Caesarian birth; nor even the suggestion of a process of parthenogenic reduplication run mad or gone wrong. What troubles me most, I think, is the realization that sometimes the second self so troublingly revealed in the series that runs from unjoined twins to joined ones to autosite-para-site can also be carried in secret, until like an unsuspected preg-nancy or an undiagnosed disease, its presence is betrayed by pain. But where and when, I am left asking—no longer sure that one body equals one self, and one self one body—does my own "I" begin and end? And how will I ever know till the brother I perhaps carry un-seen and unfelt declares himself in malignancy?

PART TWO

PART TWO

9

From Theology to Teratology

Like all men, Christians first encountered Freaks not as creatures from elsewhere but as monstrous children born into their own families. Yet for them such anomalous births could not be considered, as they had been by pagans, avatars of equally freakish gods. They could, therefore, no longer mummify and worship them like the ancient Egyptians, or kill them ritually like the Greeks and Romans, since for them the divine was identified not with the monstrous but with perfection and infanticide was forbidden by God's Law.

What to make, then, of congenital malformations that disconcertingly resembled the daimons of the "Ethnicks": sympodial monsters looking like Sirens, diprosopus or dicephalic ones like Janus, infants with occipital encephalocele like Atlas, and victims of exomphalos like Prometheus? And how to come to terms with the murderous impulse felt by a parent reaching out to embrace his child, and finding a being more like some pagan deity than its own father or mother? To be sure, if the child were spared by God, the troubled parents soon discovered that people would come to gape

229

and wonder—and pay for the privilege. Besides, in time they learned to love the child. Nonetheless, waking at night to its cry, or kneeling before the altar to pray for the salvation of its soul, they could not help asking, "Why?"

And the learned tried to answer, fitting such births into the system of total explanation created by the Fathers of the Church. Some things, that system taught, had to be left to faith; but monsters were, after all, a part of the rational natural order and, therefore, explicable in terms of reason. It was argued that they existed for one of three reasons: as signs of God's wrath, occasioned by sin; as a reminder that each birth was as miraculous as the original Creation; and as omens and portents, intended for our good. Even the ancients had believed the last, and in this they had, the Fathers asserted, anticipated revelation.

All three reasons explain the existence of Freaks not "etiologically," in terms of what has occasioned them, but "teleologically," in terms of what they are intended for. None of them, therefore, suggests anything that can be done about their condition beyond accepting it and learning from it to amend our own ways. Yet some who called themselves Christians murdered such unfortunates at birth, arguing that they were the products of witchcraft. Even learned churchmen seemed unwilling to deny—blinded, perhaps, by the witch hysteria that swept periodically through Europe—that God might on occasion permit the agents of Satan to alter the child in the womb into such horrific forms. And in these cases it was arguably the duty of the pious to destroy his evil work.

In our own country, the view of Freaks as tokens of the Lord's vengeance or as instruments of the Devil was especially strong between the first landings and the Salem witch trials. In 1638, for instance, Governor Bradford wrote to Governor Winthrop about a certain Mrs. Hunkington and her monstrous child:

> I heard since of a monsterous and prodigious birth which she should discover amongst you; and also that she should retracte her confession of acknowledgemente of those errours, before she went away . . . If your leisure would permite, I should be much beholuden unto you, to certifie me in a word or two, of the trueth and forme of that monster . . .

And Winthrop on his part, we are told, "had the bodies of still-born children examined for evidence of witchcraft." Moreover, such attitudes prevailed in New England as late as 1838, when the grandfather of General Tom Thumb said of his birth, "It is evidence of God's wrath against the Strattons."

The mind of Christian Europe was divided from the first, entertaining side by side with such theological explanations others derived from ancient philosophy. The Thomist synthesis had sought to cast out pagan superstition without losing pagan wisdom, especially as formulated by Aristotle; and Aristotle had argued that Freaks were *lusus naturae*, jokes of nature. The tradition which derives from him, therefore, views such creatures as sources of amusement rather than of terror, thus justifying showing them for profit among the lowly, and keeping them for pets in the households of the wealthy.

But Aristotle was also responsible for passing on to the Middle Ages and the Renaissance theories current in his own time about the causes of Freaks, which later scholars embraced whether he himself had accepted or rejected them. Examples of the former include a belief that intrauterine traumas, produced by constriction or sudden blows, can cause malformations, and that the introjection of too much or too little semen at conception is teratogenic; while among the latter is the conviction that "impressions" on pregnant women, resulting from fright or exposure to hideous objects, produce monsters, and that hybrids result from mating with lower animals. Indeed, the only theory Aristotle cited that was universally rejected was Empedocles' hypothesis that all extant species have arisen from the combination of separately created limbs and appendages. But this too patently contradicted the account of Creation in Genesis to be adopted by even the most heterodox Christian.

By the end of the sixteenth century such theories had been amalgamated with the theological ones to create a standard teratology at once teleological and etiological. Sometimes embodied in scholarly Latin works, sometimes in more popular compendia in the vulgar tongues, such monster lore was illustrated with pictures deriving from a tradition older than the printing press or woodblock engraving. They represented side by side palpable hoaxes, allegorical figures, and anomalous humans. The convention was to draw the

Monstrous tribes from India. Woodcuts from *Liber chronicarum*, by Hartmann Schedel (1493).

latter as full adults, whether they had been small children, infants, or even aborted fetuses, thus rendering them as fabulous as any Mermaid or Centaur. Moreover, plates were often reproduced from one work to another, so that their subjects seemed more like immutable images of mythology than real monstrosities.

Among these works, which included Aldrovandi's *Monstrorum historia*, Boiastuau's *Histoires prodigieuses*, Lycosthenes' *Prodigiorum ac ostentorum chronicon*, and Rueff's *De conceptu et generatione homines*, Ambroise Paré's *Monstres et prodiges* (1573) seems to me the most appealing, and it has been the most often reprinted. At first, however, it was attacked on the grounds of plagiarism, inadequate scholarship, and pandering to the lowest levels of taste by certain physicians who resented the pretensions of a mere surgeon, uneducated in the classics and, like all of his profession, little more than an artisan.

Paré did borrow shamelessly, and did mistranslate the few Latin works from which he tried to quote. Nor was he above introducing gratuitous pornographic passages, like one about the over-developed *nymphae* of certain anomalous females "which could stand up stiff like the male member," making it possible for them to give erotic pleasure to members of the same sex. He tried to make amends by recommending that such labia be surgically trimmed. But the offensive paragraph was, like the rest of his book, in French, and available therefore not just to the surgeons for whom he wrote but to a popular audience, including, as one indignant critic put it, "women and girls who speak no other language than this."

No one objected on doctrinal grounds to a work which Paré prefaced with a list of sources (most of them window-dressing), ranging from the Prophet Ezra, St. Paul, and St. Augustine to Empedocles, Hippocrates, Aristotle, and Pliny. He owes less, in fact, to any of them than to his contemporaries, particularly Boiastuau, from whom he derives most of "The Causes of Monsters" which constitute his first chapter.

> The first is the glory of God. The second, his wrath. The third, too great a quantity of semen. The fourth, too small a quantity. The fifth, imagination. The sixth, the narrowness or smallness of the womb. The seventh, the unbecoming sitting position of the mother, who, while pregnant, remains seated too

long with her thighs crossed or pressed against her stomach. The eighth, by a fall or blows struck against the stomach of the mother during pregnancy. The ninth, by hereditary or accidental illnesses. The tenth, by the rotting or corruption of the semen. The eleventh, by the mingling or mixture of seed. The twelfth, by the artifice of wandering beggars. The thirteenth, by demons or devils.

For each of these categories, Paré specifies a particular class of monster, arguing, for example, that a frog-faced child or a girl covered with hair is the result of "imagination," while dog-headed or pig-headed boys are produced by the mixture of human and animal seed. Similarly, he contends that headless creatures and half-men result from too little semen, conjoined twins or autosite-parasites from too much, Hermaphrodites from a mixture of maternal and paternal seed in which neither predominates.

Later writers, denying the existence of maternal seed, speak rather of an inconclusive balance of semen from the left testicle and the right. Neither theory, in any case, fits into any of Paré's thirteen original causes. Nor does his suggestion that the configuration of the planets influences monstrous births; nor, indeed, his attribution of particularly hideous malformations to copulation during menstruation, a practice forbidden by Mosaic law. Finally, it seems to me, Paré's resolve to impose order on a traditionally confused subject is overcome by a stronger impulse to leave nothing out; though, puzzlingly, he does not deal with Giants and Dwarfs. Nor is he alone in this regard. As late as the eighteenth century, size or scale Freaks were treated separately from identity Freaks, sex Freaks, or human/animal Freaks—Gaspar Schott, for instance, calling them "human marvels" as opposed to "monstrous marvels." In short, the words *monstres* and *prodiges* as Paré uses them are not quite synonymous either with what the side show calls "human oddities" or the medical researcher "congenital malformations."

He defines them as all things which go beyond or against nature, which is to say, any phenomenon that stirs fear and amazement: a long-credited legend, an anomalous child, an extraordinary illness or accident, or simply an unfamiliar breed of animal. Such a creature or event does not have to be unique to evoke the appropriate response; the rhinoceros, for instance, does not lose its mon-

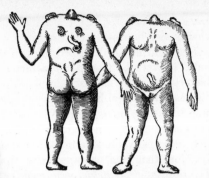

Five monsters. From *Monstres et prodiges*, by Ambroise Paré (1573).
LEFT: "Two-headed Girl, Example of Too Great a Quantity of Seed." ABOVE: "Headless Monster of the Female Sex, Example of Too Little Seed." RIGHT: "One-armed, Two-headed Boy, Example of Too Little Seed." BELOW LEFT: "Goat-Boy, Example of a Monster Created by Mixture and Mingling of Seed." BELOW RIGHT: "A Hairy Girl and Black Child, Example of Monsters Produced by the Power of Imagination."

strous status because it has existed for hundreds of thousands of years. Even what is merely *exotic*, i.e., associated with places still inaccessible to mass tourism but described in popular mythic geographies like André Thevet's *La Cosmographie universelle*, makes it into a work which combines the satisfactions of a trip to the zoo, the circus side show, and the natural history museum, plus a long day's browsing through *Scientific American*, the *National Geographic*, and some piece of pop occultism like the tetralogy of Carlos Castaneda.

Such encyclopedic marvel-mongering never disappeared from popular culture. More than four centuries later, Gould and Pyle's *Anomalies and Curiosities of Medicine* performed the same function for a Victorian audience, and eighty years after publication, it has once more become a best-seller. I suspect, too, that there must still exist the kind of boys' books of marvels through which I used to thumb breathlessly at age nine or ten, and the illustrations in which I can still remember: Chinese women with bound feet and mandarins with long nail-cases, Polynesians tattooed from head to foot, Hindu fakirs on beds of nails, and Ubangi maidens with pendulous lower lips and bare breasts. Moreover, a century or more ago, P. T. Barnum re-created the effect of such books "live" in his American Museum, beginning a tradition which survives, however diminished, in the Ten-in-One and the small-town carnival.

But modern science has split that heterogeneous unity into separate fields, each amenable to analysis by a specialized discipline. Paré's *monstres et prodiges* were first divided into extraordinary species and anomalous individuals, the former consigned to cosmography, the study of the heavens and the earth, the latter made the subject of teratology, the study of the causes of Freaks. Then out of cosmography emerged cartography and modern geography, physiology and zoology, and finally, ethnography and anthropology. Meanwhile, primitive teratology was differentiating itself into embryology, morphology, and genetics, later reunited in modern clinical and experimental teratology.

In the seventh book of his *Natural History*, Pliny had digressed from sweeping generalizations about man to observe that "India and parts of Ethiopia especially teem with marvels," specifying among others Dog-head Men, Giants, Pygmies, and creatures whose feet are turned backward and who have eight toes on each. But centuries earlier, Homer and Herodotus had already mentioned the monstrous races of those lands, which they hopelessly confused with each other, perhaps because, thinking of themselves as inhabiting the cultural and topographical center of a spherical world, they tended to regard all places on the periphery as close to each other. In any event, as late as the time of Alexander, Greek explorers expected to find on the banks of the Ganges fabulous creatures earlier reported living on those of the Nile.

A half-century after Herodotus, Ktesias has reported seeing such creatures; and when Alexander's armies had come and gone, Megasthenes, an ambassador at the court of Chandragupta, verified his observations, creating what remained for two millennia the standard ethnography of that region. In an essay called "Marvels of the East," Rudolf Wittkower has traced its persistence, based on a need to believe that somewhere human monsters exist not as occasional "sports" born into "normal" families, but as anomalous peoples reproducing themselves after their kind. The Doctors of the Church debated whether such beings were descendants of Noah, i.e., humans with souls, or lower animals, even as later they were to debate the status of American Indians. And they decided finally in favor of the humanity of both, explaining their differences from *Homo mediterraneus* as the result of the diffusion of humankind after the fall of Babel.

In any case, they doubted the existence of fabulous monsters no more than that of Indians. And, indeed, why should they? Pliny after observing that some of the monstrous peoples about whom he writes "will appear portentous and incredible to many," adds, "For who ever believed in the Ethiopians before actually seeing them?" He might have argued similarly that a tribe "which live only on the air they breathe and the scent they inhale through their nostrils" is no less believable than one which walks unshod on burning coals, or another which stands "from sunrise to sunset, gazing at the sun with eyes unmoving." Indeed, Shakespeare is implicitly making the same point when fifteen hundred years later he has Othello mention in the same breath "men who do each other eat" and those whose "heads do grow between their shoulders."

Moreover, the list of such miraculous creatures was confirmed and reconfirmed without major variation from the works of Ktesias,

Megasthenes, and Pliny to Solinus, Isidore of Seville, Brunetto La-
tini, Vincent de Beauvais, and André Thevet. For those who could
not read, the unchanging image of the East Indian monsters was
preserved in mosaic murals, manuscript illuminations, sculptures on
the façades of cathedrals, and drawings on the margins of otherwise
reliable maps. But how did it all begin? Why did those first European travelers believe they saw, or lyingly report having seen, what
our own best wisdom tells us never could have existed? And if they
were fantasizing, how did they manage to conjure up the *same* array
of human monstrosities: the Gigantes, Cynocephali, Skiapodes, Cy-
clopes, Pygmies, Androgynes, Troglodytes, Phanesians, Astomi, and
Blemmyae, which is to say, Giants, Dog-heads, Umbrella-foots, One-
eyes, Midgets, Bisexuals, Cave-dwellers, Long-ears, Mouthless Ones,
and creatures with their heads beneath their shoulders?

A traditional answer is that the East Indians lied to gullible
European travelers, but more probably, they had not yet made the
distinction between myth and history which their foreign guests
took for granted. Or such Europeans may have mistaken icons portraying local gods for representations of tribesmen from regions they
had not yet reached. In any case, they found it especially easy to
believe in creatures who had prototypes in pre-Christian European
mythologies, or who resembled terata occasionally born into the
families of their world. It was a way of mitigating, perhaps, the
shock of meeting men who transgressed, racially and culturally,
what they had grown up accepting as the limits of the human.

That shock seems to have destroyed for some the grid of perception which had enabled them to distinguish between dream and
reality, so that they appear to have *seen*—not just heard of or believed in—tribes even more different from themselves than their disturbing "normal" hosts. It is possible, I am suggesting, that the
legend of Ethiopian and Indian monsters arose not from anything
those foreign peoples said, but simply from what they were: alien
races perceived as monstrous turned by the dialectic of nightmare
into monsters perceived as alien races. Certainly, when European exploration of strange lands again began in earnest in the fifteenth
century, the dream of monstrous races recurred—though trans-
planted now to America, Patagonia, Polynesia, and the islands of the
South Pacific.

Pigafetta, for instance, who wrote the account of Magellan's trip around the world after the death of its leader, reports having encountered not only Gigantes in Tierra del Fuego, but at various other points, Amazons, Pygmies, even the fabled people who sleep wrapped in their own long ears. Dog-faces turn out to be the most often spotted of all prodigies. They were reported in the Andaman Islands, the Micobar Islands, Burma, and Russia; while Columbus testifies that they were on American soil, along with tailed men and hairless humans, long before he landed. And in the later Middle Ages a fabulous home was invented for such fabulous creatures: that oddly movable kingdom of Prester John, in which everyone seemed to believe, though they could never agree whether it was located in China, India, or South Africa—or, indeed, in some geographical space discontinuous with our own.

Even in our time, we have not given up trying to persuade ourselves that monstrous races inhabit the remote places of this earth, rather than of our deep psyches. But we are running out of territory remote enough to qualify, except, perhaps, for the Himalayas, where giant hairies, rebaptized yeti or Abominable Snowmen, are still reported from time to time. To be sure, that same monster also reappears in North America, under the name Sasquatch or Big Foot; but he seems in that context more the product of publicity for a new movie than of an old obsession.

In any case, it is these days future shock and the anticipation of space travel which alter consciousness, as the consciousness of pre-industrial Western man was altered by a confrontation with non-European races. We are more likely to hallucinate flying saucers than Blemmyae or Skiapodes. Yet we can reasonably expect that when the first terrestrials set foot on other planets, the old imperialist nightmares will repossess us, and reports come back over TV of Martian Astomi or Venusian Cynocephali. American science fiction has been preparing us for such encounters for a long time; though in the Soviet Union writers of s-f are required to believe that wherever sentient life is found, it will have passed through the same stages of organic evolution and social development as on earth. What science teaches, the Russians would have us believe, is that *there are no monstrous humans anywhere*, whatever decadent, petit-bourgeois fantasy may say.

But the "science of man" postulated in its beginnings the existence of radically deviant human species, which it tried to demythologize by including them in a single system of classification with "normal" men as well as plants and lower animals. In the tenth edition of his *System of Nature* in 1755, Linnaeus introduced the binomial system of nomenclature, according to genus and species, which enabled him to separate *Homo sapiens* from *Homo monstrosus* and *Homo ferus*. Implicit in such a classification is the assumption of a hierarchal order, which beginning with "monstrous man," mounts to "wild man," and climbing upward through black, brown, yellow, and red men, climaxes in the white European. The inclusion of humanity, wild and civilized, monstrous and normal, in the same taxonomic system may have served, then, to demythologize "monsters," but it did so at the price of creating an invidious mythology of "race."

Voltaire, for instance, proclaimed in the late eighteenth century that "the white man is to the Black as the Black is to the monkey, and as the monkey is to the oyster." And Fabricus, a pupil of Linnaeus, tried to explain what he considered the self-evident inferiority of the Negroes as the result of cross-breeding between humans and simians. Though parts of South America and sub-Saharan Africa have the same climate, he argued, there are neither anthropoid monkeys nor blacks in the former, while *both* are found in the latter. Moreover, further mating between black and white, which is to say, miscegenation in the second degree, produced—according to nineteenth-century anthropology—mulattos, sterile offspring like the mating of horses and asses.

Such racist mythology did not play a determining role in the perception of non-Europeans by Europeans until the triumph of the theory of organic evolution in Darwin's *Ascent of the Species* (1859), and its extension by analogy into early developmental anthropology. It was theoretically possible that a new tolerance for mutants might have been created by Darwin's conviction that without deviance, adaptation, and the "survival of the fittest," evolution would never have occurred, but such was not the case. Almost all his early readers took him to be saying that beyond *Homo sapiens* organic evolution is neither possible nor desirable, and the struggle to survive, therefore, though it does not cease at that point, moves from the biological to the social or cultural plane. This second "ascent of man," the new anthropology taught, has raised men from "primitivism" or "savagery" to "civilization," from a culture without the alphabet or the wheel to one with a printing press and an advanced technology, from, in short, the "nasty, brutish and short" life eked out in most of the world to the kind enjoyed in Europe—and after a while, the United States.

Anthropology did not really flourish until Western imperialism had made possible a confrontation between certain restless wanderers, usually white, and those defined as "lesser breeds" in part because they passively awaited such an encounter. After its invention the races of mankind, once experienced as bewilderingly various, are perceived as divided into two groups: one of which can "understand" the culture of the other, collect its artifacts, and write treatises on its myths and customs; and a second which can only go mad or adapt or die.

The earlier European myth of freakish aliens located at the ends of the earth when crossed with the myth of evolution spawns two others that have profoundly influenced our notions of what it means to be human. The first is the myth of the missing link: the belief that since we are "descended from monkeys" (the turning upside down of Darwin's metaphor seems a regression to totemism), there must exist somewhere the remains of a creature intermediate between hominids and anthropoids, perhaps the *Pithecanthropus erectus*, or Java Man. And the second, intimately related to the first, is that of devolution: the nightmare fear that through "miscegenation" our children or our children's children may create in the future the subhuman we cannot find in the past.

Shared by Darwin and Marx and the founding fathers of modern anthropology, that mythic racism is made brutally explicit in Thomas Dixon Jr.'s popular novel *The Leopard's Spots*. Published in 1902, it inspired in 1915 D. W. Griffith's great film *The Birth of a Nation*, which, as its subtitle, *A Romance of the White Man's Burden—1865–1900*, makes clear, sought to justify the Ku Klux Klan. In its climactic scene, a white father says to the Harvard-educated "mulatto" who has asked for his daughter's hand, "I happen to know the important fact that a man or woman of Negro ancestry, though a century removed, will suddenly breed back to a pure Negro child, thick-lipped, kinky-headed, flat-nosed, black-skinned. One drop of your blood in my family could push it backward three thousand years in history."

More recently, however, anthropologists have been trying to deliver their discipline from the ethnocentrism with which it began. Many of them, indeed, have swung to the opposite extreme, celebrating those "societies without writing," considered retrograde by their predecessors, as models of a balanced relationship between man and nature as well as man and man. Certain dissident young, moreover, have sought to emulate in the interstices of industrial civilization what such anthropologists have taught them is "tribal life." But their efforts seem merely to stand the old distinction between "primitivism" and "civilization" on its head. And in any case, the rioters against busing, who, even as I write, are smashing windows and heads in the streets of Chicago and Detroit and Raleigh, are moved by a mythology more like that which possessed the imagination of the West from Voltaire to Dixon than that currently sponsored by Claude Lévi-Strauss when he speaks of "those 'primitives' whose modest tenacity still offers us a means of assigning to human facts their true dimensions."

Meanwhile, elsewhere in the world, particularly in the Soviet Union and the Middle East, analogous notions about monstrous "races" are being applied to Jews, despite the general revulsion from that view after Nazism had been destroyed. It was not only Jews, but Freaks as well, whom Hitler tried to liquidate. And he found support in the work of experimental teratologists, scientific students of the causes of "monsters," like Etienne Wolff of the University of Strasbourg, and Professor Hirt, the holder of the chair of anatomy at that school, to whom in gratitude he shipped a collection of Jewish skeletons. Registering satisfaction with the gift, Hirt observed toward the end of 1942 that "by procuring the skulls of Jewish-Bolshevik Commissars, who personify a repulsive yet characteristic subhumanity, we have the opportunity of obtaining tangible scientific evidence"—presumably of the truth of Nazi theories about "racial purity."

Professors Wolff and Hirt, however, do not belong to the line which descends from Ktesias to Paré, then via Linnaeus and Darwin to early modern anthropology. They are the heirs of an alternative line, which passing from Paré to Etienne and Isidore Geoffroy Saint-Hilaire, the inventors of the term "teratology," was profoundly altered by the rediscovery after 1900 of the laws governing the inheritance of characteristics like dwarfism, and the replacement of taxonomy by experiment as the central concern of the biological sciences.

The term "teratology" is still used by modern researchers, though not without apology. Dr. Josef Warkany, for instance, author of the standard medical textbook *Congenital Malformations* (1971), tells us that "because there was no word available for a science of congenital malformations," his immediate predecessors took over a term formerly used chiefly in reference to major terata like "conjoined twins and severe malformations not compatible with life." In the beginning, studies of such monsters were descriptive and etiological, and though description has grown more precise as it has become less mythological, the system of classification has been little altered since Geoffroy Saint-Hilaire's *Histoire général et particulière des anomalies d'organisation chez l'homme et les animaux* (1826). As Warkany himself admits, "In systematic and taxonomic teratology the masters of the nineteenth century have not been equaled by their successors and much known to these scientists has been forgotten."

Substantial changes have occurred, however, in the realm of causation, as the old division between proximate and final causes has been replaced by a new dichotomy between intrinsic, i.e., hereditary or genetic causes, and extrinsic, i.e., post-conceptual or environmental causes. In the latter category, indeed, some of Paré's thirteen hypotheses have returned in only slightly altered form. Though no more than 2 percent of congenital abnormalities are *known* to be of extrinsic origin, an extraordinary number of theories have been advanced to explain them, including two of that French surgeon's favorites: external physical traumas and position or constraint in the womb. Even the belief that psychological shock or extreme emotional stress can produce malformations has recently begun to make headway with hard-headed scientists.

Similarly, astronomical if not astrological influences begin once more to be acknowledged, perhaps in response to the revival of interest in the "pseudo-science" of astrology. The reports, however, in

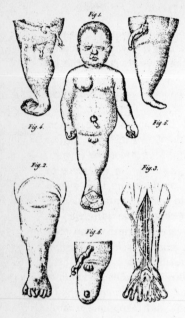

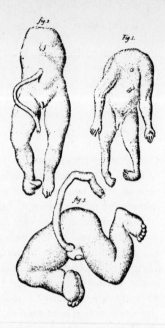

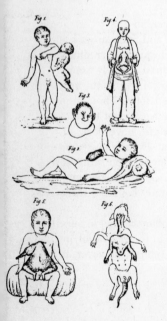

Four plates from Geoffroy Saint-Hilaire's works in teratology. TOP LEFT: Sireno-melics. TOP RIGHT: Ace-phalics. BOTTOM LEFT: Auto-site-parasite. BOTTOM RIGHT: Siamese twins joined at tops of skulls.

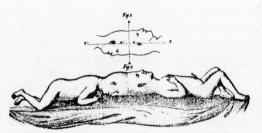

HISTOIRE

GÉNÉRALE ET PARTICULIÈRE

DES ANOMALIES

DE L'ORGANISATION

CHEZ L'HOMME ET LES ANIMAUX,

OUVRAGE COMPRENANT DES RECHERCHES SUR LES CARACTÈRES,
LA CLASSIFICATION, L'INFLUENCE PHYSIOLOGIQUE ET PATHOLOGIQUE ;
LES RAPPORTS GÉNÉRAUX, LES LOIS ET LES CAUSES

DES MONSTRUOSITÉS,

DES VARIÉTÉS ET VICES DE CONFORMATION,

ou

TRAITÉ DE TÉRATOLOGIE,

PAR M. ISIDORE GEOFFROY SAINT-HILAIRE,

Docteur en médecine, professeur de zoologie et d'anatomie générale à
l'Athénée royal de Paris, aide-naturaliste de zoologie au Muséum royal
d'histoire naturelle, membre de la Société d'histoire naturelle de Paris,
des Sociétés royales des sciences de Lille et d'Arras, du Muséum d'histoire
naturelle de Douai, etc.

TOME PREMIER.

AVEC ATLAS.

PARIS,

J.-B. BAILLIÈRE,

LIBRAIRE DE L'ACADÉMIE ROYALE DE MÉDECINE,
RUE DE L'ÉCOLE DE MÉDECINE, No 13 bis,
LONDRES, MÊME MAISON, 219, REGENT-STREET.
BRUXELLES, AU DÉPÔT DE LA LIBRAIRIE MÉDICALE FRANÇAISE.
1832.

RIGHT: Title page from first edition of *Histoire générale et particulière des anomalies* . . . , by Geoffroy Saint-Hilaire (1832).
BELOW: Plate from the same work indicating Saint-Hilaire's classification of Hermaphrodites.

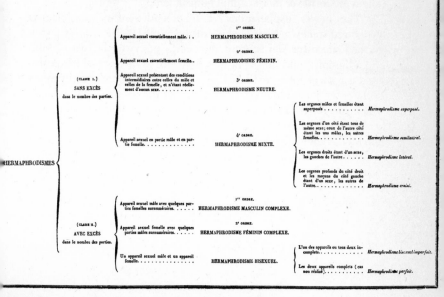

TABLEAU GÉNÉRAL ET MÉTHODIQUE DES HERMAPHRODISMES.

HERMAPHRODISMES	**(CLASSE I.)** SANS EXCÈS dans le nombre des parties.	Appareil sexuel essentiellement mâle. : .	1ᵉʳ ORDRE. HERMAPHRODISME MASCULIN.	
		Appareil sexuel essentiellement femelle.	2ᵉ ORDRE. HERMAPHRODISME FÉMININ.	
		Appareil sexuel présentant des conditions intermédiaires entre celles du mâle et celles de la femelle, et n'étant réellement d'aucun sexe	3ᵉ ORDRE. HERMAPHRODISME NEUTRE.	
		Appareil sexuel en partie mâle et en partie femelle.	4ᵉ ORDRE. HERMAPHRODISME MIXTE.	Les organes mâles et femelles étant superposés . . . . *Hermaphrodisme superposé.*
				Les organes d'un côté étant tous de même sexe ; ceux de l'autre côté étant les uns mâles, les autres femelles. . . . . *Hermaphrodisme semilatéral.*
				Les organes droits étant d'un sexe, les gauches de l'autre . . . . . *Hermaphrodisme latéral.*
				Les organes profonds du côté droit et les moyens du côté gauche étant d'un sexe, les autres de l'autre. . . . . *Hermaphrodisme croisé.*
	(CLASSE II.) AVEC EXCÈS dans le nombre des parties.	Appareil sexuel mâle avec quelques parties femelles surnuméraires.	1ᵉʳ ORDRE. HERMAPHRODISME MASCULIN COMPLEXE.	
		Appareil sexuel femelle avec quelques parties mâles surnuméraires.	2ᵉ ORDRE. HERMAPHRODISME FÉMININ COMPLEXE.	
		Un appareil sexuel mâle et un appareil femelle.	HERMAPHRODISME BISEXUEL.	L'un des appareils ou tous deux incomplets. . . . . *Hermaphrodisme bisexuel imparfait.*
				Les deux appareils complets (cas non réalisé). . . . . *Hermaphrodisme parfait.*

which such a position is reasserted are based on research indicating "a small but statistically significant synodic lunar (or sun-moon) influence on the human birth-rate, and presumably on the conception rate and, perhaps, on the ovulation rate"—and finally, one gathers, on the incidence of monsters as well. Similarly, we have become convinced once again that "corruption," if not of the male seed, at least of the female ovum, which degenerates with age, increases the probability of malformed babies. Of the most dearly held ancient theories, only that of "hybridization" has been entirely rejected, though in our time inter-specific breeding has been successfully accomplished.

Perhaps our resistance is especially strong because that theory was bound up with the most repressive aspects of early American society. In 1641, for instance, three years after the founding of the colony of New Haven, a one-eyed servant was accused of "abominable filthynes" when a sow on the farm where he worked gave birth to a pig over whose single eye "a thing of flesh grew forth and hung downe, it was hollow, and like a man's instrum' of genration." After three years of trials, confessions, and recantations, he was executed; though not before his presumable offspring was stabbed through the belly as he watched. Ours has been from the start a land where lonely tenders of animals seek sexual solace with their charges, horrifying moralists still, though they have ceased believing that such unions are fertile or merit capital punishment.

The newer explanations of nineteenth-century teratologists have fared somewhat less well. Geoffroy Saint-Hilaire and his distinguished successor Dareste put their faith primarily in two: "amniotic adhesions" and "arrest of development." The first, which postulated a perfect fetus mutilated by its restraining bonds, owes much to the intensive embryological research of the age. And the second, which imagined malformations resulting from a failure of one part of the unborn organism to develop along with the rest, was similarly indebted, though more influenced, perhaps, by the post-Darwinian belief that "ontogeny recapitulates phylogeny," the intrauterine development of the individual following step by step the development of species. The first seems a better explanation for malformations with single limbs or none than the traditional theory of "too little seed," but modern researchers find it "mechanical." Valid as an explanation of a small number of cases, it provides no clue to the major problems they confront. The second represents an attempt to replace the hypothesis of "hybridization" with one more congenial to contemporary science. But it has failed to satisfy modern teratologists. "Arrested ontogenesis," Warkany writes, "does not give any hint as to the *causa causans* [the cause of causes]. Why is there arrest at all?"

A third, however, which has better stood the test of time, the so-called nosological theory, postulated that many monstrosities resulted from "diseases of the embryo." At first glance, this seems little more than a sophisticated updating of Paré's ninth cause, "hereditary and accidental illnesses." And, indeed, when it was first formulated, the role of bacteria and viruses in producing inflammation of uterine tissues was still unsuspected. Nonetheless, recent research identifying antenatal rubella, cytomegalic inclusion disease, and toxoplasmosis as teratogens has validated the surmise that "diseases of formed parts of the embryo may . . . possibly interfere with the formation of the other parts," and that "parts which have been developed monstrously in the embryonic epoch will be very liable to become the seat of disease in the foetal period."

Moreover, from the "nosological theory" there have been developed corollary hypotheses about the etiological role of vitamin deficiencies and therapeutic drugs. It has been demonstrated, for instance, that lack of iodine leads to goiter and cretinism, and lack of vitamin A to eye abnormalities, horseshoe kidney, and hydroenphrosis; while thalidomide can produce phocomelia, and typanum blue imperforate anuses and thymic absence. Moreover, the relative weight given to intrinsic factors as opposed to extrinsic agents has shifted in recent years. Though only 10 or 15 percent of observed malformations have been reliably traced to the former, chiefly in the area of the intersexes, this represents a much higher percentage than have been verified for the latter; and modern researchers assume that most of the remaining 85 percent will be proved to arise from genetic mutation. Indeed, since the discovery that DNA (deoxyribonucleic acid) in the cell nucleus carries "encoded" genetic information to the cytoplasm, the ancient theory of the "germ originally monstrous," contemptuously rejected by nineteenth-century science, has carried the day.

Some skeptical teratologists like Warkany warn their colleagues that "at present, the gaps between the biochemical concepts of mutation and the facts of congenital malformation are immense and bridged mostly by beliefs and speculations" not much different from Paré's "thirteen causes," but they tend not to be heeded. From my layman's vantage point, it seems, in fact, that reliable knowledge about the genesis of Freaks has not increased much since the time of Aristotle. To be sure, we have learned a great deal in the past century and a half about human reproduction and the "laws" which govern inheritance. It is, therefore, possible to state with certainty—as it was not before the human ovum was discovered in 1827 and its fertilization observed in 1877—not merely that some congenital malformations are genetically transmitted, but more specifically, that extra digits and lobster-claw hands are dominantly inherited, while diastrophic dwarfism and microcephaly are products of autosomal recessive genes, and imperforate anuses and testicular feminization of sex-linked inheritance.

Such discoveries, however, have left unsolved the problem of the biological function, as well as the essential nature, of malformation. As T. E. Glenister observed a few years ago, "It is thus obvious that progress is being made as regards the elucidation of how malformations occur, but why they should occur is still a question of philosophy." Or of religion, he might have added; though as a child of his time, he did not. In any event, it is clear that science—despite occasional references to a *causa causans*—is not interested in pursuing the question of "why" lest it be betrayed again into teleology, metaphysics, and theology. Similarly, most scientists, committed to the investigation of means rather than ends, try to avoid the question of value. Yet they proceed from value-laden assumptions: in the area of teratology, the axiomatic belief that, like all diseases, congenital malformations are bad and, therefore, whatever will cure or eliminate them is good.

Experiments with "monstrosities" were carried on as early as the seventeenth century, limited at first, however, to their production rather than their cure or prevention. They were, moreover, accidental in the very beginning, by-products of the attempt by enterprising chicken farmers to reinvent artificial incubation. Their experiments produced live chicks, but they tended to be "monsters"—

to the dismay of the farmers, but the subsequent delight of historians of teratology. The first deliberate attempt at creating terata did not occur until 1774, when Abraham Trembley (taking a cue from mythology) managed to produce multiheaded hydras by hacking through the upper part of their organisms. And the Saint-Hilaires followed his example in the next century by jarring, pricking, varnishing, and inverting chicken eggs, with, it would appear, inconclusive results. By the time of World War II the art of monster-making, though confined to oviparous fish, amphibians, and birds, had extended its arsenal to include anoxia, electric shock, and chemical injection. Moreover, it had discovered how to create specific Freaks by inflicting specific "insults" at particular points on the egg.

The scientific community has always contended that "understanding" and "control" were the ends to which its experiments were directed. But some reports evidence a relish in the callous procedures employed and the monstrous results achieved, or so at least many modern writers have felt. Before the end of the nineteenth century, H. G. Wells had tried in *The Island of Dr. Moreau* to imagine what would happen when the successors of Trembley and Geoffroy Saint-Hilaire adapted their techniques first to mammals, as they have in fact done since, and then to humans, as they still aspire to do. His negative view differs radically from that of his more utopian predecessors like Sir Francis Bacon, who foresaw in *The New Atlantis* a community of scientists able to produce new and useful species of animals by cross-breeding. In our own time, the Baconian view has prevailed among practicing teratologists and the Wellsian among science-fiction novelists, who by and large portray the "biological engineers" of the future not as Promethean heroes but as black magicians, whose methods are an assault on life and whose achievements are the creation of unforeseen horror. Typically, such misguided experimenters are destroyed by the monsters they create, like Dr. Frankenstein; but this has been by no means the fate of their actual counterparts.

Dr. Etienne Wolff, whose *La Science des monstres* I find more terrifying than Wells's tale of Dr. Moreau, is cited respectfully in current teratological works, though his experiments were carried on more than thirty years ago. First published in 1948, his major study was apparently written in 1941, then revised in 1945, while the author was in prison or forced exile—perhaps as a Nazi, though the cryptic note in the text leaves this unclear. The book opens, in any case, on a note of self-congratulation, observing that though it has been "scarcely a century since monsters ["monsters" or "monstrosities" is his preferred name for what his more circumspect successors call "congenital malformations"] entered science . . . decisive progress has been made." Nor are we left in doubt about the nature of that "progress," since he continues, "Once we began by describing monsters, today we know how to reproduce them; we can create new forms, hitherto unknown . . ." As he approaches his climax, the illusion of omnipotence overwhelms him and he boasts, "One can, in a sense, play [it is a verb he loves almost as much as he does the noun "monster"] with the forms of the embryo . . . construct at will and . . . 'in series' most monstrosities." The phrase "in series" prophetically suggests "cloning," that latest breakthrough of experimental biology, which has opened up the possibility of endlessly replicating from a single body cell identical life forms. To the science-fictionist, cloning represents the ultimate bad dream of the experimentalists: an ideal "normal" asexually and unvaryingly reproduced out of the conviction that individual difference can and should be rendered obsolete.

The experiments of Etienne Wolff, however, were all postconceptual, so that genuine "mutations," able to reproduce their deformities in the next generation, lay outside his scope. If he knew that the chromosomes of the drosophila were already being bombarded with radiation in the hope of achieving just such results, he does not confess it. Rather, he deplores the fact that he was not permitted to "play" with mammals, though that, too, had occurred by his time. Between 1933 and 1937, in fact, a teratologist called Hale had reported experiments in which sows deprived of vitamin A produced piglets "all of which were born without eyeballs," and some with accessory ears, cleft palates, and misplaced kidneys. Hale's results were greeted with skepticism, but similar experiments by Dr. Warkany and others eventually convinced the skeptical. And by now pregnant mammals are being subjected not just to traditional "insults" and deprivations, but to irradiation and forced feeding of hormones and drugs.

Pigs are still used along with dogs and monkeys; but the rat, the rabbit, the hamster, and the mouse are preferred, because they are relatively cheap, easy to maintain, highly fertile in captivity, and (in the words of a recent article) produce "pups sufficiently large to permit easy macroscopic examination . . . but small enough to permit easy maceration for skeletal examinations." Unfortunately, their response does not exactly parallel "the teratogenic response observed in humans . . . Thus, man must be the ultimate test species." But, the article concludes, "Moral and social factors, outside the province of this article, prevent the use of human subjects." Once more, we are confronted with problems of value before which science stands mute.

Yet human Freaks have, in fact, been manufactured for ritual aesthetic and commercial purposes ever since history began. We have already remarked how certain societies deliberately deform infants to meet standards of beauty which transcend or deny natural norms, most usually in the case of women. Examples are the binding of feet by the Chinese, the stretching of the lower lip among the Ubangis, the extension of the labia in Hottentot culture—and more mildly, the corseting and lacing common in the West during the later nineteenth and early twentieth centuries. But members of both sexes have been subjected to such malformation, the skulls of newborn babies being pressed between boards in many North American Indian tribes, the bodies of children stunted and twisted in late Renaissance Europe so that they could be used as props by beggars or peddled to exhibitors. It is a subject on which Victor Hugo grows impassioned:

> In order that a human toy should prove a success, he must be taken in hand early. The dwarf must be fashioned when young . . . a well-formed child is not very amusing; a hunchback is better fun.
>
> Hence grew an art. There were trainers who took a man and made him an abortion; they took a face and made a muzzle; they stunted growth; they distorted the features. The artificial production of teratological cases had its rules. It was quite a science; what one can imagine as the opposite of orthopedy . . .

But the goals of modern teratologists are quite different. It is knowledge they pursue, is it not? And they are, therefore, motivated not by sadism or greed but by disinterested curiosity and good will. Moreover, they are *accountable* to their fellow scientists, the society in which they live, and to the yet unborn. It is, however, precisely with the unborn that they "play," having at long last the means to create monsters *ab ovo*. No wonder that they hesitate before moving on from gravid sows to expectant mothers of their own species. But no wonder, too, that they are tempted to claim as their right what is now in their power, to experiment with unborn human beings, which is to say, with the future of us all. Especially after the great thalidomide scandal of 1961–62, in which an anti-depressant, anti-nausea drug given to pregnant women turned out to be a powerful teratogen, more than one doctor's voice was raised in defense of that right.

Had it been tested, they argued, on just twenty or thirty pregnant women "prior to therapeutic abortion," thousands of monstrosities need never have been born. But it was, in fact, tried, however inadvertently, on a much larger number, many of whom were persuaded to undergo precisely such "therapeutic abortions" by the same doctors who had earlier prescribed thalidomide. Yet some experimentalists manage to find occasion for rejoicing in the whole sorry event, pointing out that it "provided a tremendous impetus to teratological investigations." And Ian Leck, professor of social and preventive medicine at the Universities of Manchester and Birmingham, cites the reaction of his colleagues to the disaster they had themselves created as a model for future research. Never before, he insists, was an investigation so systematically conducted, proceeding from descriptive, correlative, and analytic studies to the indicated "experiment," which, ironically, consisted in withdrawing the chemical compound previously prescribed.

What he fails to explain, however, is why it was so hard, even by late 1962 when the evidence was overwhelming, not just for the companies that manufactured the drug (under the names Contergan, Softenon, Neurosedyn, and Distaval), but for the medical profession itself to acknowledge the teratogenic effects of thalidomide. At that point, particularly in West Germany, where it was first synthesized, the increase in atypical phocomelia among the newborn was generally blamed on atomic fallout or radiation from TV sets. Meanwhile, the managing director of Distillers Company (Biochemicals) Ltd. was still assuring physicians in the columns of *The Lancet* that "in response to a number of requests his firm would continue to make supplies available to hospitals." Dr. Lenz, the first researcher to call for the withdrawal of thalidomide, did so only after the birth of a monstrous baby to the wife of one of his colleagues, prefacing his appeal with an apology I find touching and significant. "From a scientific point of view," he wrote in 1961, "it seems premature to discuss it. But as a human being . . . I cannot remain silent."

How much easier it has been for teratologists to point the finger of blame at teratogenic agents for which they were not responsible, like the virus which produces rubella. Nor do they find difficulty in talking about malformations arising from the pollution of Minamata Bay with mercury wastes by Japanese industrialists, or the presumed aftereffects of the atomic bombing of Hiroshima by the United States Army. The latter case is particularly illuminating, since no doctor feels it impugns his scholarship to suggest a proliferation of anomalous births among the survivors of that catastrophe, though statistical research does *not* support the charge. But blowing the whistle on one's own colleagues is another matter, involving questions of value, with which "value-free" science is forced to deal even while denying they exist.

In the case of the thalidomide babies, analogous value problems were involved in the question of whether to "interrupt" pregnancies with a 15 or 20 percent chance of eventuating in abnormal births: a question especially difficult when the physician was himself speaking from a bad conscience. Obviously, parents had first to settle in their own minds questions even less amenable to scientific analysis: Did they believe in abortion under any circumstances? And if so, how great did the odds have to be in favor of disaster to justify such action? Were they really convinced that it is wrong to bring a malformed child into the world, in light of evidence that in terms of career, marriage, and family life, a large number of Freaks, including some notable phocomelics, have proved able to cope as well as anyone else? In any case, have parents the right to deny life to a child, merely because it will be a charge on its family and the state for as long as it lives?

Other problems present themselves once such a baby turns out to be phocomelic or amelic (lacking one or more limbs). Does one turn to prosthesis, or teach it to manage with the limbs it has, like the heroic Armless Wonders of the past? Similar questions are posed more sharply by more "repairable" malformations like Hermaphrodites and Siamese Twins, or by borderline cases like Giants and Dwarfs. Moreover, it seems to me that behind any personal decision to seek treatment for a malformed child is a more basic decision, typically unconscious because predetermined by society as a whole, to define that child as a "patient," whose deviation is something to be corrected, rather than as in other times and cultures, to be celebrated, exploited, or merely *lived*.

When we move from anomalies as individuals to anomalies as groups, which is to say, from pathology to epidemiology, the value problem is even more exacerbated. I have listened to bitter debates with doctors on both sides, often in private, once over public television, about whether or not "life supports should be removed from non-viable major terata." And on every occasion the argument has turned on who decides what child is "non-viable" and according to what standards. Nor do the difficulties disappear when the subject becomes how to prevent such births wholesale, rather than how to deal with them retail. Indeed, the former constitutes the present center of most teratologists' concern, since, as Dr. Warkany assures us, "there is general agreement" in such quarters "that prevention is the final goal."

Ironically, that was also the belief of Hitler, who left the identification of such "cases" to professionals: a board called euphemistically "The Reich Association, Hospital and Navy Establishment," consisting of "four doctors, plus a top medical authority." But by 1941 the public outcry in Germany against the excesses of that "Association" had grown so great that all "adult euthanasia" was officially called to a halt. It continued, however (according to Dr. Elie A. Cohen's *Human Behavior in the Concentration Camp*, which appeared in English in 1953), to be carried on secretly in the concentration camps under the code name "14f13."

The judgment of those willing to work for Hitler was, like that of all doctors, conditioned by the medical doctrine of their time and place. They proceeded, therefore, on the assumption that (a) all bisymmetrical malformations being hereditary, those suffering from them should be kept from reproducing themselves; and (b) certain ethnic groups, notably Jews and Gypsies, were by virtue of that fact monstrous and must be destroyed. But Dwarfs were favorite targets, too, for reasons harder to understand, and twins, in part because they provided opportunities for controlled experiments. A certain Dr. Mengele, for instance, describes an experiment in which twin brothers were simultaneously killed by injections of chloroform into the heart as "a unique thing in the history of medicine . . . Two twin brothers die together and at the same time under circumstances which make an immediate autopsy possible." It is like a bad dream of Dr. Wolff come true, or the good dream of Western teratology gone bad; which explains why, perhaps, Dr. Warkany, though himself an advocate of creating a malformation-proof genetic pool, was moved to warn his fellow physicians in 1964:

> During the Third Reich in Germany the Law for the Prevention of Heritable Diseases may have eliminated, by its crude and cruel methods, a number of defective genes, but the spirit that motivated this law led also to the elimination of twenty million healthy people with an inestimable treasure of sound and valuable genes.

On the other hand, he reports having learned from certain epidemiological studies that among the factors influencing the incidence of congenital malformations are not only birth order, seasonal and secular variations, and the socioeconomic status and chemical environments of the parents, but also maternal age at the time of conception. He accepts, in short (as doctors must in order to function, though aware of the way in which each generation of researchers denies the "facts" of the one before), the doctrine of *his* time that overripeness of the ova in women approaching the menopause is a factor in embryonic malformation. And he urges that it be offset, when possible, "by endouterine treatment of women of advanced age," or failing this, "*by prevention of fertilization of abnormal eggs by regulation of sexual intercourse.*" The italics are mine and represent the special resonance with which those words have continued to ring in my head. But the vision of Prophylactic Police patrolling motels and marriage beds which they evoke for me belongs not to the neutral realm of science but to the mythic and passionate world of art, in which the teratologist tends to be portrayed not as the benefactor of Freaks which he seems to himself, but as their ultimate exploiter.

10

Freaks and
the Literary Imagination

Frederick Treves, author of the essay on the Elephant Man, is the only doctor who ever made moving prose of the myth of the scientist as the Freak's friend. But many less gifted writers of his profession continue to try, one of them, for instance, sending me a letter which caught me just as I was finishing the last chapter. I had spoken of this book in an interview, locally headlined "Fiedler Surveys Role of 'Freaks' in Our Culture," and that headline rather than anything I was reported as saying moved him to protest:

> . . . As program coordinator of the Psychoendocrinology Clinic at Children's Hospital and as medical advisor to the Human Growth Foundation of Western New York, I have very much to do with the psychosocial management of dwarfed and over-tall patients. Of course, a major part of the problem is to cope with society's labels. How will they feel when they see a book that deals with part of their problems under the title "freaks"? Com-

> ing from a department of the same university where they re-
> ceive treatment in another department?
>
> For the sake of these people, I urge you to change the title
> of your forthcoming book to something less drastic and thereby
> less harmful . . .

Though he avoided the fairy-tale word "giant," my corre-
spondent was inconsistent enough to use the term "dwarf." Not so
his colleague, who wrote the next day to inform me "how fragile the
human spirit is when medical problems are discussed in uncompli-
mentary terms," and to advise me that "for this reason, we avoid the
use of the words midgit [*sic*], freak, dwarf and speak of growth
problems." Clearly, the difference between the "we" of such doctors
and any "we" with which I can identify begins with language. Their
community prefers words like "psychosocial management" and
"growth problems," which demystify and euphemize human anomaly, to those like "freak" and "midget," which keep faith with its
ambiguity and wonder so prized by poets.

Like many differences that begin at the level of vocabulary, this
difference ends in political action: the expurgation and censorship
of literature, and the closing down of the Ten-in-One. As early as
1908, a leading article in *The Nation* (London) announced that:

> . . . there was a reaction long ago against making public sport
> of what was merely pathological. The perception that . . .
> freakishness itself was generally a disease, has finished the work.
> The giant . . . when considered as a physical superman, or even
> as the villain of the nursery tales, was worth going to see. But
> we are taught now that . . . something at the base of his
> brain is responsible for the extraordinary and disproportionate
> growth . . .

Nonetheless, the decline in popularity of Freak shows, though real,
has been too slow (in the 1960s some 75 million Americans still attended them each year) to satisfy their "enlightened" enemies, who
have called on the law to complete what unaided medical science
could not.

At the beginning of that decade a Florida reporter, inspired by
the story of a fifteen-year-old girl crippled in all four limbs who had

been dragged screaming from a carnival side show, launched a crusade against "the business of exhibiting human and animal oddities," and reminded his readers of a long-unenforced statute providing for imprisonment or a fine for "Whoever shall exhibit for pay or compensation any crippled or physically distorted, malformed or disfigured man, woman or child in any circus, show or similar place to which an admission fee is charged."

But when an attempt was made to enforce that law, it was challenged by Selo the Seal Boy and Poobah the Pygmy ("Where are they gonna send me? Back on the farm? No, thanks, I'd rather be dead!"), who insisted on their right to earn a living as their kind had for centuries. In October 1972 the Supreme Court of Florida found in their favor by a vote of six to one. As far as I know, no painters, writers, or film makers were called as expert witnesses, though they have been testifying for a long while in behalf of those they insist on calling "Freaks." Such artists have created in the process the Congress of Human Oddities, immune to banning, which in variety and scope puts to shame the best efforts of the "American Collective Amusement Industry." Yet it was not until the nineteenth century that human anomalies moved to the center of fiction and drama, as writers learned how to restore to them the mythic aura of which they had been stripped by the coming of Christianity and the rise of Science.

Dwarfs may have been favorite subjects of Renaissance court painters and have acted out in court masques travesties of their own condition, but they did not appear in plays written for the public stage, even in the role of Fools, which they acted in real life. Though Thersites is listed in the Dramatis Personae of Shakespeare's *Troilus and Cressida* as "a deformed and scurrilous Grecian," he represents not so much the occasional Freak whose birth calls into question our notions of the normal, as the primordial element which persists in us all, giving the lie to the codes of civility by which we pretend to live. He derives, in short, not from the actual deformities shown at fairs, but from a nightmare projection of the savage self as old as English literature. Called Grendel in the Anglo-Saxon epic *Beowulf*, he is described as "monster," "demon," and "fiend," though he seems more a shaggy protohuman out of a cave than an evil spirit out of Hell. When John Gardner re-creates him and attempts to redeem him from infamy in a 1971 novel called by his name, he is, therefore, redefined as "a brute existent," a surrogate for our unsubdued animal inheritance; but he is also dubbed affectionately a "freak."

In the centuries between he was not forgotten, but appears in the unsympathetic guise of a "savage man," his troglodyte origins overlaid with characteristics borrowed from the satyrs of classical legend and the "Wodewose" (wild man) of English folk tradition. An eater of his fellow men and a rapist of women, he is recognizable by his hairy hide, his girdle of leaves, and especially the rude club or uprooted tree he uses for a weapon, as in Book III of Spenser's *The Faerie Queene:*

> . . . With huge great teeth, like to a tusked Bore:
> For he liv'd all on rauin and on rape
> Of men and beasts; and fed on fleshy gore . . .
>
> His wast was with a wreath of yuie greene
> Engirt about, ne other garment wore;
> For all his haire was like a garment seene;
> And in his hand a tall young oake he bore . . .

Further transformed, he reappears as Caliban in Shakespeare's *Tempest,* where he no longer eats human flesh but still lusts for the daughters of men. When Prospero makes the accusation, "In mine own cell . . . thou didst seek to violate/ The honour of my child . . ." he answers, like a proper monster, "Oh ho! Oh ho!—would it had been done . . . I had peopled else/ This isle with Calibans." He is therefore referred to generically throughout as a "monster," when not more specifically labeled "moon-calf," "hog-seed," or "A freckled whelp hag-horn,—not honour'd with/ A human shape." And seeing him for the first time, one character is reminded of show Freaks at the fair, musing: "Were I in England now,—as once I was,—and had but this fish painted, not a holiday fool there but would give a piece of silver . . ."

But Caliban is also an aboriginal, much like the Indians whom explorers were just then discovering in the New World and bringing home to exhibit for profit, side by side with English oddities. Shakespeare suggests that he was native to Algiers rather than the "stormy Bermoothes," but that makes little difference, since for poets of the

Caliban confronting Prospero and Miranda. Illustration by Henry Fuseli for Shakespeare's *The Tempest*. Engraved by P. Simon. Executed for John Boydell's Shakespeare Gallery. Late eighteenth century.

Renaissance monstrosities are associated with all non-European lands, Africa as well as America. Even Shakespeare's courtliest African, Othello, tells stories of having met in his own country the Anthropophagi and Blemmyae; while the Moor Aaron is described in *Titus Andronicus* as a "wall-eyed" villain with a "fiend-like face," whose half-white child is "loathesome as a toad." For Shakespeare, in short, the exotic and the freakish remain synonymous, as they had been from the time of Pliny. Yet, like his contemporaries, he found exotics more amenable to mytholicizing than home-grown human monsters.

The latter were excluded even from Ben Jonson's *Bartholomew Fair*, though it is set in Smithfield, where such "monsters" had been shown for five centuries. Jonson represents or alludes to other famous attractions of the fair, including the woman who sold roast pig, a horse courser, a clothes peddler, an exhibitor of puppets, the rabbit who played a drum, and a five-legged calf. But he draws the line at human oddities, who did not come fully into their own perhaps until the end of the seventeenth century but were surely present in his time. Even after they had become so fashionable that men of letters like John Evelyn and Samuel Pepys rushed to see the latest two-headed girl or Hermaphrodite, they remained absent from dramatic and satiric poetry. Moreover, though popular artists of the eighteenth century like George Cruikshank produced pictures of show Freaks, popular novelists like Defoe, Richardson, and Smollett scarcely noticed them.

They were dealt with, as they had been for many centuries, chiefly in nonfiction: encyclopedias, cosmographies, medical treatises, and handbooks of the occult, in which they were treated not as fantasies but explicable facts of nature. There were also pamphlets and leaflets distributed to advertise the latest wondrous birth for commercial or pious purposes. A Hermaphrodite might be publicized to help pay for its upkeep, or a child born with a "ruff" of flesh below the ears described with appropriate scriptural quotations as an instance of God's wrath against newfangled fashions.

If such treatises and broadsheets strike us as disconcertingly naïve in their failure to discriminate between a genuine two-headed child seen by the authors themselves and a fabulous winged monster with an eye where his kneecap should have been, we must remember that the latter was attested not only by the Church but by the protoscience of the time. Where faith did not skew judgment, mature readers from the Renaissance on had no trouble distinguishing between real monsters and fantastic ones. Fairies, Elves, and Sylphs, for instance, were considered the province of writers of Romance like Spenser and Bunyan, or poets like Alexander Pope, in whose works they flourish side by side with Giants, dragons, and the hybrids of classical mythology.

Only children and the simplest country folk failed to realize that such creatures belong to a world of charming "make-believe," best evoked, perhaps, by Shakespeare in *A Midsummer Night's Dream* and Mercutio's Queen Mab speech in *Romeo and Juliet*:

> She is the fairies' midwife, and she comes
> In shape no bigger than an agate stone . . .
> Drawn by a team of little atomies
> Athwart men's noses as they lie asleep:
> Her waggon-spokes made of longspinners' legs;
> The cover, of the wings of grasshoppers;
> The traces, of the smallest spider's webs;
> The collars, of the moonshine's watery beams . . .

It was apparently Shakespeare who first reduced the substantial though dwarfish fairy folk of tradition (originally perhaps the native Celts as they had appeared to the much taller Teutonic invaders of England) to infinitesimal size and dreamy-moon-beamy consistency.

Though later showmen sought to identify the stunted creatures they exhibited with this elfin crew ("The *Little-Woman*, not 3 foot high, and 30 years of age . . . which is commonly called the *Fairy Queen* . . ."), playing on the tendency of "normals" to see abnormal others through mythological grids, actual show Freaks were considered out of bounds in the world of "let's pretend," which is to say, in imaginative literature. When Cervantes launched a full-scale attack against Romance in *Don Quixote*, he tried not to substitute "real" Giants for mythic ones, but to suggest that they had never existed at all. His half-mad hero refused to believe him, aware that without fantasy the world would be intolerable, but those who took up the genre he had helped invent used it to continue his war against the fantastic. Samuel Richardson, for instance, was still boasting a hundred years later that his "new species of writing" differed "from the pomp and parade of Romance writing" in "dismissing the improbable and marvelous with which novels generally abound."

Even when the "improbable and marvelous" reappeared in tales of terror written toward the end of the eighteenth century by alienated rebels like William Beckford, M. G. Lewis, and the Marquis de Sade, or best-selling women novelists like Clara Reeve and Ann Radcliffe, they were embodied not in Freaks but grotesques: vestiges of medieval superstition which their authors only played at believing, like children scaring themselves to allay boredom. Everywhere in the genre, psychological abnormalities like sado-masochism, incest, fratricide, and parricide were exploited to titillate the reader.

But physiological abnormalities appear nowhere except in the underground pornography of de Sade, in which genital monsters of both sexes assault "normal" innocence in a nightmare of terrifying monotony.

It was a woman, or rather a girl of seventeen, who broke through the ban, by introducing a new kind of Freak into the new genre. Mary Shelley may have believed that she was only trying to write a better "ghost story" than her husband or his friends Lord Byron and Polidori, but her *Frankenstein* turned out to be an account of modern technology creating a monster unknown in nature. Though she was more familiar with the ancient myths of Prometheus and Dr. Faustus than the scientific experiments of her age, she had listened just before her tale came to her in a waking dream to a discussion about revivifying dead matter with electric shock. Small wonder, then, that there appeared to her before she could close her eyes in sleep "the hideous phantasm of a man stretched out and then, on the working of some powerful engine show signs of life."

Frankenstein's Monster. Boris Karloff as the Monster. Still from *Frankenstein,* directed by James Whale, 1931.
The Museum of Modern Art/Film Stills Archive

That her "tiresome ghost story" was the beginning of the genre we have since come to call "science fiction" she seems never to have suspected, using traditional terms like "specter," "fiend," "demon," and "monster" to describe a creature who, though a human/non-human hybrid like many Freaks of the past, was a hybrid of man and machine rather than man and beast. Later writers have created for its descendants new names like "humanoid," "android," "robot," "cyborg," and "bionic man," projecting them into the future Mrs. Shelley invented without knowing it. And we who inhabit that future never tire of retelling her tale in print, in comic books, and on film. We have, moreover, gone further, imagining scientists who, unlike her doctor, deliberately make hideous metahumans, or—reversing the archetype—strive to eliminate all chance of their appearance by "biological engineering."

But all that lay far ahead when *Frankenstein* appeared in 1818. The century was almost over before Jules Verne and H. G. Wells gave science fiction its second start; so that Mrs. Shelley's immediate successors in the Gothic mode looked backward rather than forward in quest of models for monsters. Edgar Allan Poe, for instance, writing "Hop-Frog" in 1847, sets his story in the Renaissance, when "professing jesters had not altogether gone out of fashion at court" and "Dwarfs were as common . . . as Fools." His crippled hero is both a Dwarf and a Fool: a "triplicate treasure," who "could only get along by a sort of interjectional gait—something between a leap and a wiggle . . ." yet wins the love of a beautiful Midget girl and destroys the king who abuses them both.

The tale is gratuitously sadistic and somewhat less than convincing, but clearly Poe identifies with Hop-Frog and wants us to sympathize with his successful vendetta against "normals" much like ourselves. As children we learned to love kindly little people like the Shoemaker's Elves, Snow White's Seven Dwarfs, and St. Nicholas, who in Clement Moore's classic poem is portrayed as "a right jolly old elf." But Hop-Frog is malevolent as well as dwarfed and hideously deformed. Indeed, Poe seems to have been incapable of imagining a male dwarf who was not grotesquely ugly, though in Dirk Peters of *The Narrative of A. Gordon Pym* he created one who was at least more benefactor than destroyer. Described as "not more than four feet eight inches high," with bowed legs, a hairless mis-

shapen skull, and protruding teeth, fixed in a grin "indicative of . . .
the merriment . . . of a demon," Peters enters the novel a mur-
derer, but exits as the savior of its disaster-prone hero.

Peters, however, is portrayed as a contemporary American, a
half-breed Indian who had presumably set sail from Nantucket only
a few years before Poe's novel was published in 1837. More typically, Poe preferred to set his monsters in the European past, like
his equally Freak-obsessed French contemporary, Victor Hugo.
Though Hugo's favorite human oddities were full-sized uglies rather
than Dwarfs, he, too, moves them back in history, telling us that his
"Laughing Man" had been bought and turned into a Freak by the
comprachicos, "a hideous and nondescript association of wanderers
famous in the seventeenth century, forgotten in the eighteenth, un-
heard of in the nineteenth."

The *comprachicos* are, according to historians, fictional, but no
more so than the late Renaissance England which Hugo creates
around his hero. Kidnapped, mutilated, exhibited at a side show,
erotically exploited by the decadent aristocracy, he becomes, improbably, a Member of Parliament, but is howled down by the Peers
of the Realm, whom he addresses on behalf of the oppressed and
exploited. They respond not to his words, but to the comic mask of
his countenance: "a hiatus for a mouth, a snout with two holes for
nostrils; for a face, a mangled pulp."

Yet this figure compounded of fantasy, social allegory, and personal nightmare was modeled on actual Freaks: Perkeo, the hideous
Dwarf of Heidelberg, and Triboulet, most famous of the court
Dwarfs of France. Similarly, Habira, the slave of the Governor of
Jamaica in Hugo's first novel, *Bug-Jargal*, is portrayed as a big-
bellied achondroplastic, with legs like a spider's and an enormous
head covered with kinky red fur. Between him and the "Laughing
Man," however, intervenes the most famous of Hugo's uglies, Quasimodo, the Hunchback of Notre Dame.

We first see Quasimodo at the Carnival of Fools, competing in a
contest to determine who can make the most monstrous grimace
and become thereby the "Pope of Fools." He wins hands down, since
"his whole person was a grimace. His large head, all bristling with
red hair, between his shoulders an enormous hump, to which he had
a corresponding projection in front, a framework of thighs and legs

LEFT: Quasimodo, the Hunchback of Notre Dame. Lon Chaney in a still from the film, 1923.
The Museum of Modern Art/Film Stills Archive
RIGHT: Perkeo, the Hideous Dwarf of Heidelberg. Painting by Adriaen van der Werff, early eighteenth century.
Kurpfalziesches Museum, Heidelberg

so strangely gone astray that they could touch one another only at the knees." He seems, moreover, a kind of Cyclops, his "small left eye overshadowed by a red bushy brow, while the right eye disappeared entirely under an enormous wart," and by the same token more "a giant that had been broken and awkwardly mended" than a Dwarf. In any case, like the "Laughing Man," Quasimodo reveals the horror behind the painted faces and pious façades of the seventeenth century. And though both go down to defeat, they foreshadow a day of vengeance in which the oppressed will, out of baffled love or sheer hatred, bring down a regime which, defining them as ugly, condemns them to darkness.

They represent, in short, what Friedrich Engels and Karl Marx were calling at almost the same moment the "specter" haunting Europe. The specter of the *Communist Manifesto*, however, was a

ghost not out of the past but a future already embodied in the ex-
propriated proletariat dreaming of expropriating its expropriators,
for whom the court Fools and pet Dwarfs of the Renaissance are
symbols almost as inappropriate as spooks out of medieval folklore.
If Freaks of any kind could figure forth the revolutionary terror below the surface of Victorian optimism, it was those living human
"curiosities" whose exploitation was being challenged by humani-
tarians even as their popularity increased.

No notable author dealt with them directly, however, before
Charles Dickens. Like Queen Victoria herself, Dickens was a Freak
fancier, who on his first trip to America insisted on being taken to
Barnum's American Museum. It is not surprising, then, that one of
the *Sketches by Boz* by which he first became known is devoted to
the show Freaks at Greenwich Fair. At that three-day springtime
festival, he saw for the price of a penny a Dwarf, a Giantess, "a
young lady of singular beauty, with perfectly white hair" and a genuine "Wild Indian." He was most fascinated by the Dwarf, who was
crammed into a little box painted like a six-room house, out of one
of whose windows he rang a bell and fired a pistol. When he came to
write *The Old Curiosity Shop* a few years later, therefore, he remembered that carnival world and its performers, whom he, like
Barnum, called "curiosities"—a name used also for old furniture,
suits of armor, and assorted bric-a-brac.

Having imagined a small orphan girl in the midst of such mold-
ering antiques, he moved on to envision her surrounded by card
sharks, pickpockets, racetrack touts, prostitutes, performing dogs, a
pair of mountebanks on stilts, the operators of a Punch and Judy
Show, the proprietress of a traveling wax works—and finally a Giant
and "a little lady without arms and legs." His book constitutes, in
fact, a guide to the popular culture of the period, of which it is itself
as much a part as the Freak show at Greenwich. But when it first appeared, critics were too entranced with the pathetic flight of little
Nell and her little old grandfather, and especially her tearful demise,
to notice.

The Old Curiosity Shop was, however, also comic-horrific, as its
earliest admirers acknowledged, laughing through their tears at
Quilp, Nell's implacable pursuer. He is a character who owes as
much to burlesque as to Grand Guignol: a caricature of the author

The Marchioness: The Midget as heroine. From an illustration by Phiz for Charles Dickens' *Old Curiosity Shop* (1841).

as a bad husband, worse son-in-law, and luster after barely nubile girls. Moreover, though he appears solely in domestic or business settings, Quilp is a link between the novel's sentimental foreground and its Freak show background, being described at one point as "an uglier dwarf than could be seen anywhere for a penny." He is, in fact, the only leading character actually called a "dwarf," despite the fact that at least half the dramatis personae are freakishly small, especially the women—from Nell herself, through "pretty, little mild-spoken" Mrs. Quilp to "soft-hearted, foolish little Barbara," a lower-class girl who serves as a consolation prize for Kit, and the three-foot-high, mysterious "Marchioness," who may be Quilp's bastard child.

Though Dickens sought in the Shakespearian climax of his book to emulate the pathos of Cordelia's untimely death, the final effect is of *King Lear* seen through the wrong end of a telescope, or acted out by Midgets. I sympathize, therefore, with Henry James, who having (like me) wept over Little Nell, felt free to laugh at her and such later versions of the Dwarf heroine as Jenny Wren, of whom he remarked: "Like all of Mr. Dickens's pathetic characters, she is a little monster . . . she belongs to the troop of hunchbacks, imbeciles, and precocious children, who have carried on the sentimental business in all Mr. Dickens's novels." James was himself not immune to the lure of the grotesque, but—no fan of the side show—he preferred imaginary specters to actual "monsters," ghosts to Freaks, like his contemporaries Sheridan Le Fanu, Bram Stoker, and (except in the case of *Dr. Jekyll and Mr. Hyde*) Robert Louis Stevenson.

Edward Lear and Lewis Carroll, on the other hand, indulged their taste for the freakish by creating "for children only" a world in which the boundaries between animal and human, large and small, self and other, blur and dissolve. It is "all nonsense" both insist, and Carroll is not above telling his nursery readers that it is "only a dream," from which presumably they will permanently awaken with the coming of adulthood. At that point, too, they will leave behind the fairy tales, which, despite some effort at censorship, continued to be written by eminent Victorians like Hans Christian Andersen, Christina Rossetti, William Morris, John Ruskin, and Dickens himself. In such stories, as in pop horror fiction and "nonsense," Goblins, Mermaids, Giants, and Dwarfs were kept alive for the imagination, but at the price of enduring the "make-believe" status to which they had been demoted in the Renaissance.

Even when he drew on fairy-tale sources, however, Dickens managed to transform fabulous monsters into creatures as real as ourselves or the side show Freaks about whom he also wrote, unlike any of his contemporaries except for Mark Twain. Yet Twain always spoke deprecatingly of Dickens' work, confessing a fondness only for *A Tale of Two Cities*, which treats his own favorite theme of indistinguishable doubles. Nonetheless, along with tens of thousands of other Americans, he went to hear Dickens during his lecture tour of 1867, when he was within three years of his death. Twain himself lived to 1910, when Halley's Comet, which had last appeared in his birth year of 1835, reappeared—bringing to his mind a metaphor out of the side show.

"Here are those unaccountable freaks," he imagined a scarcely-believed-in God saying of him and that returning meteor. "They came in together, they must go out together." But Freaks thus joined for life are Siamese Twins, which of all human oddities most possessed his imagination. The only other human oddity to whom he devotes a story is a "shrivelled, shabby dwarf" covered with "a fuzzy green mold," a "vile bit of human rubbish," who pops up in "The Facts Concerning the Recent Carnival of Crime in Connecticut," published in the *Atlantic* for June 1876. Even that Dwarf, however, turns out to be an alter ego, whom the narrator ends by murdering and burning for revealing guilts of which he had hitherto been unaware; which is to say, yet another version of what Twain called "my double, my partner in duality, the other and wholly independent personage who lives in me."

From the moment he gave himself the telltale pseudonym Mark Twain, Samuel L. Clemens was haunted by that second self, and his last words were inchoate murmurings about Jekyll and Hyde and dual personality. In between, he created fictional look-alikes, ranging from Tom Canty and the heir to the British throne in *The Prince and the Pauper* to Tom X and Jeff in the unpublished manuscript "Which Was the Dream?" Even Tom Sawyer and Huck Finn are utterly confused with each other toward the end of *Huckleberry Finn*, and the series culminates in the slave Valet de Chambre and the "free" Thomas à Becket Driscoll of *Pudd'nhead Wilson*. In each, one of the paired characters is called Tom for reasons nobody has ever convincingly explained, and in each a main theme is usurpation: a servant passing as a master, a commoner as a king, an outcast as a favored son, a Negro as white.

Not until he encountered real conjoined twins, first *the* Siamese Twins, Chang and Eng, and then the Tocci Brothers or the Two-headed Boy, did Twain find the right metaphor for his inseparable other. But having found it, he could not quite make it work, though he tried three times with a pair of joined Italian aristocrats, Luigi and Angelo, modeled after the Toccis: first in a short farcical piece devoted almost entirely to milking their plight for laughs; then in a long novel, in which their intrusion into a small American town was intended to reveal not only the comic implications of their deformity, but the limited moral sensibility of the society around them; finally, as an episode in *Tom Sawyer Abroad*, in which he planned to call on Huck's voice once more in order to tell what seemed otherwise an untellable tale.

Mark Twain contemplating a poster advertising the Tocci Brothers. Frontispiece to *Those Extraordinary Twins*, by Mark Twain (1894).

The short farce refused to stay short; the novel moved off in directions that turned Luigi and Angelo into comic supernumeraries whom Twain was able to save only by cutting them in half; Huck wearied of his new assignment before getting to their episode. What remains is *Pudd'nhead Wilson,* in which Luigi and Angelo are no longer joined, and the remaining jokes about them were therefore incomprehensible; plus a group of fragments called "Those Extraordinary Twins," which preserves Twain's original title and a few of the incidents he began with, including their death by hanging. The former is, on its own terms, a successful work of art, and the latter little more than a record of a failure; but in neither does he really come to terms with the mystery of duality and identity to which the Siamese Twins had seemed to provide so tantalizing a clue. Perhaps for this reason such Freaks continue to tantalize writers in our own time, who keep trying, as Twain did not, to present them on show and from within.

Except for Victor Hugo, no writer before the twentieth century had attempted thus to portray from within *any* Freak, so that when

Those Marvelous Siamese
Twins. Illustrations by F. M.
Senior for *Those Extraordinary Twins*, by Mark Twain
(1894).

Walter de la Mare's *Memoirs of a Midget* appeared in 1922 it seemed unprecedented and baffling. His heroine, a fairy-like Victorian gentlewoman called Midgetina, unable to cope either with her sexuality or the responses to her size, decides to display herself in a traveling circus as an "amazing prodigy of nature." Dressed first in a costume which emphasizes her blond innocence and childish frailty, she ends by painting and padding herself into the semblance of "abject evil," which is to say, flagrant erotic allure. She enjoys both roles, eliciting awe and shame in one guise, and lust in the other. But her double masquerade ends in disaster: the death of a male Dwarf who loves her and tries to carry her off on horseback, and her own failed attempt to commit suicide.

The show world which de la Mare evokes seems spectral and distorted, a Gothic grotesque rather than a slice of low life. The Elephant Man, the Fat Lady, and the Spotted Boy who are Midgetina's co-performers remain shadowy background figures, while the showman and his Gypsy mistress, who equally repel and attract her, are falsified by a genteel vocabulary and a condescension of which she and her author seem equally unaware. Yet in that world she learns a truth which makes what remains of her life livable: "Aren't we all of us on show? And aren't nine out of ten of us striving to be more on show than we are entitled to be?" And we leave her asking of the novel in which she appears, "And this tale itself? . . . what is it but once more to have drifted into being on show again—in a book?"

The real world of show Freaks is, however, no better captured here than in the other fictions which, from the time of Poe, have turned human prodigies into metaphors for something else: the plight of the artist, the oppression of the poor, the terror of sexuality, or the illusory nature of social life. They provide us, therefore, with no satisfactory clue to what it is like to be a performer of one's own anomalous and inescapable fate.

11

The Silence of Freaks and
the Message of the Side Show

Not even Freaks have left reliable records of what it *feels* like to be what they are, avoiding publication as if words were an inappropriate medium for what their bodies so eloquently express. Official "autobiographies" have always been circulated by their exhibitors, but these are invariably ghost-written, a part of the act rather than a way of seeing beyond it. Consequently, fictions like *Memoirs of a Midget*, whatever their limitations, come closer to breaking the stubborn silence of Freaks. The real meaning of their plight, however, remains implicit in the popular art form which developed in Victorian times out of the break-up of the seasonal religious fairs and has descended to us as the circus side show and the dime museum.

A key figure in that development was P. T. Barnum, a nineteenth-century creator as important in his own medium as Dickens in his. It is surely more than coincidence that both of them, along with Hugo, Poe, and Walt Whitman, who all helped mold the imagination of the first mass audience, were born within a single dec-

Other sketches of seventeenth-century show freaks. From *A Short History of Human Prodigies and Monstrous Births* . . . , by James Paris du Plessis. Unpublished manuscript, seventeenth century. RIGHT: "A Man with a Head Growing out of his Belly." BELOW: "Two Children Born United Together." BOTTOM LEFT: "A Monstrous Child with Two Heads." BELOW RIGHT: "A Child Born with a Pair of Horns."

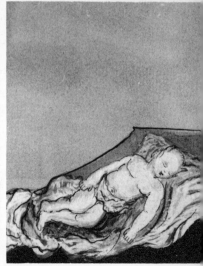

P. T. Barnum instructing General Tom Thumb. From *Struggles and Triumphs: or The Life of P. T. Barnum,* by P. T. Barnum (1927).

ade. Theirs was a time of unprecedented social mobility and rapidly expanding literacy, in which successful men in all fields recorded their lives in books intended for that new audience. Barnum was no exception, writing and rewriting throughout his career an autobiography called at one point *The Life of P. T. Barnum, Written by Himself,* at another *Struggles and Triumphs; or, Forty Years' Recollections of P. T. Barnum.* It is a work as naïvely sophisticated, fictionally true, egregiously arrogant, and resolutely American as Walt Whitman's *Leaves of Grass,* whose first edition also appeared in 1855, and whose final revision coincides with Barnum's last version of his life.

In it he recalls along with his rise to fame and fortune, the "curiosities" he provided for an American public whose tastes he both shared and made: his two favorite hoaxes, Joice Heth and the "Feejee Mermaid"; his three favorite performers, Tom Thumb, Jenny Lind, and Jumbo the Elephant; and the two beloved edifices he lived to see destroyed by fire, "Iranistan" and the American Museum. The former was an absurdity, an American country home modeled on the Prince Regent's pseudo-Oriental palace in Brighton; but the latter became an institution as unique to our culture as its name suggests. Originally a storehouse of curios and Freaks bought from a man called Scudder and stuffed to the bursting point with the leftovers of other defunct "museums," it became what Barnum described as "a vast National Gallery . . . a million of things in every brand of Nature and Art, comprehending a cyclopaediacal synopsis of everything worth seeing and knowing in this curious world's curious economy." When it was gutted by flames, he rebuilt it, decorating its façade with paintings of the replenished wonders within, and making it so famous a landmark that a band of Confederate arsonists attempted to burn it down again.

Their firebombs failed, but in 1865 a faulty heating system started a blaze which totally destroyed the last total museum in America. The first had been established in 1790 by John Peale, more famous for his portrait of George Washington. Barnum's two American Museums, however, dwarfed earlier attempts at creating a commercial, all-inclusive, multi-media showplace. Yet during his lifetime such institutions were on the way to obsolescence, as government agencies and private foundations began to take over, breaking up their giant grab-bag collections into smaller, more specialized ones, supervised by "professionals" and open without charge to the public. Sensing this, Barnum left the streets of lower Manhattan and took to the road, displaying under canvas what came to be known as "The Greatest Show on Earth." Whatever he could not manage to transport he contributed to the newly founded Museum of Natural History in New York and the Smithsonian Institution in Washington.

For the rest of his life, he continued to give them his surplus "curiosities," which they gratefully accepted, as well as his advice, which they rejected with polite contempt. It is an attitude for which an occasional acknowledgment of "Barnum's stimulus to the Museum movement and popularizations of natural history" does not really make amends. In his heyday he "packed them in" as his successors, despite their boasts of having substituted "scholarly work" and "educational services" for ballyhoo and humbug, did not, confessing less than a decade after his death that the new museums "had failed by and large . . . to capture the sustained interest of

ABOVE: Barnum's American
Museum after the great fire.
RIGHT: Barnum's "Genuine
Mermaid" as actually shown.
BELOW: Publicity picture for
Barnum's "Genuine Mer-
maid." Illustrations from
*Struggles and Triumphs: or
The Life of P. T. Barnum,* by
P. T. Barnum (1927).

the majority of the people. They were public but not popular." Yet it is not primarily as a pioneer in the museum movement that we remember Barnum, since his major contribution is elsewhere.

But *where?* Surely it is not as a grand tycoon, like J. P. Morgan or John D. Rockefeller. He died a millionaire, and even after his last bankruptcy lay far behind continued to make new investments, but he seems never to have enjoyed business for its own sake—moving on to politics, social reform (he almost ran for President on the Prohibition ticket), and even the pleasures of retirement. Nor can it be as a literary artist, since scarcely any critic (before me, at any rate) has taken him seriously. Even as a founding father of the American circus, he fares little better, for he was never, true aficionados tell us, "a circus man by choice," turning to that business as a second best when the heyday of the pop museum had passed. In the mass mind, he lives on primarily as a "humbug" and hustler, crying out to the delight of the suckers themselves, each of whom thinks the phrase applies to his neighbor, "There's one born every minute!" And this is surely a piece of the truth, though by no means the whole truth.

Nor will "showman" suffice to describe him, though this was his description of himself; for he was a mass educator as well as a mass entertainer, and finally a magician able—long after science thought it had neutralized nature—to remythify it by reviving in adults the awe children feel before its variety and abundance. And at the center of his vision of the World as Wonder are the Freaks. Almost everything else he took for his province has been preempted by others, ranging from anthropologists to zoo keepers, and curators to theatrical managers. But despite efforts by teratologists and psychoendocrinologists, when we think of human oddities most of us still think of Tom Thumb and Anna Swann, Jo-Jo and Lionel the Lion-faced Man, and especially, perhaps, Chang and Eng: those prototypical figures who stand unchanging on the platform at Baraboo, Wisconsin—as if the dream Barnum taught us to dream has been, like Sleeping Beauty, charmed out of time.

The exhibition of Freaks has, of course, existed from antiquity, and like other pagan practices, was revived in Europe during the Middle Ages. For a while, however, human oddities were shown in their family homes or at the courts of local princes. When they began to be exhibited in groups to the general populace, it was under the auspices of the Church, which insisted they be displayed only on feast days and on holy ground. How early "monsters" appeared at the great fairs which celebrated such occasions is hard to say. They were preceded by display booths of merchants, stalls offering food and drink, mountebanks who walked on stilts or balanced themselves on the points of swords. Even live plays, ostensibly religious in theme however ribald in tone, came before them, and perhaps puppet shows as well.

It was not until Elizabethan times, at any rate, that their appearance is recorded, and not until the Restoration that they became stellar attractions. Writing in 1858 about Bartholomew Fair, the largest, liveliest, and most long-lived of all such "yearly concentrations on one spot of entertainments that at other times were scattered over town and city," Henry Morley observes that "the tone of society was degraded by the Court of Charles the Second . . . the taste for monsters became a disease." Then he assures his contemporaries that "Bartholomew Fair is gone and there are few English boys who would now care to see the Giant, under whose arm it pleased Charles the Second to walk." He is being, however, a little disingenuous, since his book—adorned with initial letters out of old manuscripts and illustrations from Renaissance and eighteenth-century handbills—was produced to satisfy the nostalgia for "curiosities" which he deplores.

Even his account of the riots which led to the dissolution of the fair in 1840—the drunken fistfights and stripping of female spectators—betrays a sneaking fondness for the carnival spirit which Victorian morality sought to ban from English life. And he ends with an elegy for that annual bout of gluttony and misrule, first chartered in the year 1133 by Henry I at the behest of Rayer, a court jester-turned-monk, who drew visitors to the fairgrounds at Smithfield by faking a series of miracles with all the shameless aplomb of P. T. Barnum.

I have told from first to last the story of a Festival which was maintained for seven centuries in England. Of the few popular Festivals that occasion yearly gatherings of strangers in the open streets of one of our great cities, this was the chief. In

ABOVE LEFT: The monk
Rayer, founder of Bartholo-
mew Fair.
ABOVE RIGHT: Miss Buffin;
LEFT: Mr. Simon Paap; BE-
LOW LEFT: the Spotted Boy;
BELOW RIGHT: Kelham White-
law, as exhibited at Bartholo-
mew Fair. From *Memoirs of
Bartholomew Fair*, by Henry
Morley (1859).

its humours, we have seen the humour of the nation blended with the riot of its mob. Yet when the nation had outgrown it, a Municipal Court with the help of but a few policemen put it quietly away.

If Bartholomew Fair died, however, it was only to be reborn. At the moment Freak shows were being banned in Smithfield, a new Rayer was exhibiting the Feejee Mermaid; and in 1849, when that fair, shrunk to a little more than a dozen gingerbread stalls, was declared open for the last time, the American Museum was beginning to draw crowds which would eventually include Dickens, Thackeray, and the Prince of Wales.

But nothing is immortal, and like Bartholomew Fair, the American Museum died, along with the traveling circus in its original form. The Freak show itself has not died, however, persisting as the "dime museum" in shoddy city storefronts and booths along the boardwalks of seaside resorts, and on the midways of carnivals built overnight in vacant lots on the edges of smaller towns, where beside the Ferris wheel, the kootch show, the hot-dog stand, and the games of chance, the talker spiels and the "marks" file into the seedy wonderland of the Ten-in-One. It is a kind of drama they behold once they are inside: the silence of Freaks translated into an iconic-verbal form as fixed and conventional as a Byzantine mosaic. Even the number of performers is set at no more nor less than the magic ten; though all of them do not have to be congenital malformations. Permissible alternates include sword-swallowers, flame-eaters, and otherwise normal humans able to thrust spikes up their noses or hammer nails into their flesh. And there are self-made Freaks as well, like tattooed men and women, along with such out-and-out fakes as Mermaids, the Headless Woman, and the girl who turns into a gorilla: "illusions," as they have come to be called. And for a little while, the surviving relatives of notorious criminals were also displayed, like John Dillinger's father or the mother of Bonnie Parker.

But it is the standard Freaks who embody the message of the Ten-in-One: Armless and Legless Wonders, Giants, Dwarfs, Fat Ladies, Living Skeletons, and Bearded Women, along with an occasional Pinhead or Siamese Twins or Half Man/Half Woman—nothing unexpected or unforeseen. Nor can there be anything novel about the mode of presentation, so that after a minute or two we do

not know in what town we are, or at what point in our lives. The human oddities on show are never displayed on our level—the level of
reality and the street outside. Most often they stand against a cur-
tain on a draped platform, to which we have to look up; though
sometimes, especially in the "blow-off," a last super-attraction for
which there is an extra charge, they are placed in a railed "pit," into
which we have to look down. Moreover, the Freaks do not just
stand there, but do something, visibly perform: pound nails into
their bodies, when that is their sole excuse for being on show, or
light cigarettes with a match held between their toes or between
chin and neck, if they are Armless Wonders or Seal Boys.

At the very least, they move about, gimping, hopping, wad-
dling, as they tell some half-legendary version of their origin and
fate. And meanwhile the voice of the speaker goes on and on—sometimes against a background of recorded music, sometimes these days
itself on tape, telling us what we are seeing; even as coming in, we
were told what we were going to see by painted banners on which
the role each performer perfunctorily enacts was portrayed by artists dead perhaps before he was born. In Barnum's time, the Freaks
on display sold pamphlets illustrated with line engravings flagrantly
misrepresenting their actual malformations. And after a while, they
were also selling those black-and-white photographs which look out
at us still from the pages of nostalgic histories and albums, the focus
blurred so that they seem like figures in a dream.

Even now if the spell works, if we are lucky or stoned or drunk
or blessedly simple, we see what we are supposed to see: not some
poor unfortunate approximately embodying the myth after which
his affliction is named, but the myth itself—the animal hybrid skulk-
ing at the edge of the jungle, the Giant taller than the Ogre whom
Jack cheated of his harp and hen, the Midget smaller than a mustard
seed. If, however, the spell does not work or is broken, we awake to
the moldy stench of old canvas and the squish of filthy sawdust under our feet. And looking up, we see the hostility and boredom in
the eyes of those we thought were there to be looked at, not to look
back. It is at this point that we hear behind the camouflage of words
and music the silence of the Freaks. And we cry out "hoax" or "fake,"
though we mean it is all only too real; or we laugh, as we do at all
failed magic, and at ourselves for having dared believe in it.

The Ten-in-One has, in any case, become not just a part of

American popular culture, but a stock symbol for the interdependence of illusion and reality, pleasure and pain, revulsion and awe,
available to the simplest and most sophisticated alike. As it has re-
treated, therefore, from the center of our culture to its periphery,
from the metropolis to the small town, from Broadway to Skid Row,
artists have attempted to assimilate its meanings to other media:
words on the page, images on the screen. Beginning, that is to say,
as a form of naïve or pop art, the side show has become the subject
matter of more self-conscious high art or more up-to-date mass art.

We have already noticed the role of the Freak show in Carson
McCullers' *Member of the Wedding* and in Eudora Welty's stories
"The Petrified Man" and "Keela, the Outcast Indian Maiden," both
of which have become standard anthology pieces. Such female
Gothicists intrigue critics more and more these days, Ellen Moers,
for instance, speculating in the *New York Review* for April 4, 1974,
about McCullers' *Reflections in a Golden Eye*, which she describes
as a study of a "normal" woman's love for "a gifted, sensitive, ridiculous, mad, dwarfish creature, as diminutive as a monkey or a child."
From there she moves on to the work of other Freak-obsessed female
artists from Isak Dinesen to that ill-fated photographer Diane Arbus, lingering over Djuna Barnes, of whose *Nightwood* she uses the
phrase, which T. S. Eliot once wrote he hoped would never be applied to it, "a horrid sideshow of freaks."

But the phrase in this context remains a metaphor, because
Nightwood, like the other literature (Arbus is another matter) Ellen
Moers especially notices, deals not with Freaks *on show* but in society—or rather with "Freaks" more like their authors than Barnum's
performers. From the start, the Gothic novel has been chiefly produced by writers who considered themselves, or were aware that
others more secure than they looked on them, as "freakish." Certainly, it is members of psychologically stigmatized groups who are
remembered as masters of the genre: not just the women, straight or
gay, whom Ellen Moers evokes, but Irishmen, like Charles Maturin,
Bram Stoker, and Sheridan Le Fanu; homosexual males, more often
than not adolescent, like William Beckford, M. G. Lewis, and the
early Truman Capote; Americans in general, that "nation of escaped
slavery," most of whom D. H. Lawrence thought had turned into
monstrous Calibans, and, especially since the defeat of the Confed-

eracy, Southern Americans in particular—most notably, perhaps, Flannery O'Connor.

In all of them, self-hatred is at work, so that it is not surprising also to find in their ranks troubled members of despised ethnic minorities, like Nathanael West and Jean Toomer. The single full-fledged abnormality at the center of West's fiction is the hideous Dwarf Abe Kusich, in *Day of the Locust*, one of the few characters whom West specifically labeled, as he did not like to label himself, a Jew. Similarly, Jean Toomer, the first notable black novelist of our century, who spent the latter part of his life passing as white, introduces in a nightmarish scene in *Cane* a stage full of grotesque black Midgets wearing boxing gloves on their heads. And finally, after World War II, Freaks of various kinds come to obsess German writers like Günter Grass and Jakov Lind, symbolizing the residual guilt felt by all Germans when the Nazi dream of a monster-pure race had collapsed.

Other twentieth-century writers, however, "realists" more interested in debunking the side show than in finding images for their secret selves, have dealt head-on with the circus and carnival, where some of them have in fact worked, typically as spielers. I have read scores of such novels, most of them so inept and unconvincing that little from them remains in my memory: a few scenes, for instance, from Herbert Gold's *The Man Who Was Not with It*, and the section of Robert Heinlein's *Stranger in a Strange Land* in which his Martian super-hero works briefly in a Freak show. "The ten-in-one," Heinlein writes, "did not have a mentalist, it had a magician [the Martian himself in fact]; it had no bearded lady, it had a half-man-half-woman; no sword-swallower but a fire-eater, no tattooed man but a tattooed lady who was also a snake charmer, and for the blow-off she appeared 'absolutely *nude*!'"

For some reason, I remember best Jim Tully's *Circus Parade*, published by that hobo-novelist in the year Lindbergh flew the Atlantic and Sacco and Vanzetti were executed. It recounts in a style alternately sentimental and brutal a tale through which the Moss-haired Girl, the Fat Lady, the Strong Woman, and the Little Pygmies move not as mythic figures but as victims and losers, more exotic perhaps than mill hands and sharecroppers, but just as depressing. Yet novels involving Pinheads and 790-pound ladies provided for middle-class readers, to whom they are as alien as Tahitian princesses, not a sense of life as it is lived, but of wonder and awe. And certain later novelists have deliberately exploited that fact, like Lindsay Gresham, who evokes the marvelous in the title of his 1946 novel *Nightmare Alley*, and raises the symbolic ante throughout with allusions to the tarot pack, used from ancient times for magical purposes.

Nonetheless, the performers in his Ten-in-One are realistically described, from the Midget, Major Mosquito, through the fake Electrified Woman and a Tattooed Man called Sailor Martin, right down to the wino Geek. There is, moreover, lust and larceny in the heart of every one of them, so that contemporary taste was offended. The 1947 film version, starring Tyrone Power and Joan Blondell, moved *The New York Times* reviewer to speak of "shock and revulsion" and to protest that the movie "traverses distasteful dramatic ground."

A later critic, however, has listed it as one of "the thousand best films" on the grounds that it provided Tyrone Power "with the most satisfying role of his career" and was "the most accomplished film of Edmund Goulding's later career." But Goulding was an odd choice for director, having made his reputation with "women's films" like *Grand Hotel, The Constant Nymph*, and that smash hit *The Razor's Edge*. He did not know what to do with what was hardest and most brutal, which is to say, truest in Gresham's novel, euphemizing and sentimentalizing where he did not cut with an eye to the censor. Yet somehow the magic survived, thanks perhaps to the scrupulously constructed set: a carnival "with a hundred sideshow attractions spread over ten acres," to which, if the publicity releases are to be believed, half of Hollywood came:

> Joan Crawford pitched rings to win a Kewpie doll. Lana Turner brought her daughter Cheryl, to see the Fat Lady and the Thin Man. Gregory Peck tried out his muscle and rang the bell when he brought the sledgehammer down on the "Test-Your-Strength" machine. Rex Harrison got the Fire-Eater to give him a couple of lessons. Dana Andrews tried his hand at shooting ducks.

It was the Geek, however, that remained in the minds of the mass audience—surviving the script, the production, even the publicity, by achieving a pitch of horror which the new medium had seemed for a while too slick and conventional to portray.

Nonetheless, moved by the sense that it was they who must now provide the public with what they had formerly found in the Freak show, film makers determined not just to "make 'em laugh and make 'em cry," but to "make 'em shudder," too. In the beginning they were not very successful, since their movies were without color or sound, except for the tinkling of the piano in the pit. And though black-and-white worked well enough, not until the screen learned to speak could it appropriate a form dependent for part of its appeal on the ballyhoo of the leather-lunged spieler. Indeed, one of the earliest successful uses of Vitaphone audio techniques is to be found in the "talking scenes" of an otherwise silent film of 1928, *The Barker*. Certain newspaper reviewers complained that "the sound device did not add one whit to the effect last evening. In fact, it was a relief when the scenes were silent, accompanied by the now much despised titles." But they must have been aficianados of the silents rather than lovers of the Freak show.

Long before the division of movies into pop and elite, Freaks had come to seem as much at home on the screen as on the circus platform, though they continued to be regarded with distrust by moralists determined to keep the new medium "family entertainment." The mass audience, however, has always been ambivalently fascinated, because film Freaks are somehow more *real* than show Freaks—and therefore both the attraction and repulsion we feel in their presence rises closer to the lintel of consciousness: a fact which has made them favorites ever since, not only of directors looking for success at the box office, but of those seeking critical esteem, like Ingmar Bergman, Luis Buñuel, and Federico Fellini.

Bergman's Freaks, however, are more allegorical than actual, like much else in his black Lutheran mystery plays; and Buñuel is concerned less with true human oddities than *mutilés*, physical and sexual cripples. Only Fellini, whose most moving films deal with pre-cinematic popular culture, has evoked authentic images of the circus and the fair. Even when his Freaks are not actual performers as in *La Strada* and *The Clowns*, but a part of the ongoing stream of life like the malformations of his *Satyricon*, or the Fat Ladies who appear throughout his works, or the Dwarf nun climbing a ladder to

Freaks and normals viewing Hermaphrodite. Still from Federico Fellini's *Satyricon.*
The Museum of Modern Art/Film Stills Archive

deliver a madman from the top of a tree in *Amarcord,* they are spot-lighted in our memories like stars of the side show.

But the greatest of all Freak movies, which is also the greatest of all Freak shows—exploiting the expansible space–time continuum of film to create what a hundred thousand actual Ten-in-Ones had only imperfectly suggested—was the creation of Todd Browning, a hack film maker who thought of himself not as an "artist" but as a collaborator in "the Industry." He is credited with having directed some twenty-five full-length films, a good many of which he wrote himself; and doubtless there were others now lost. But he was nearly forty before he turned to directing, having been a film actor and stunt man, as well as a contortionist, a burlesque "top banana," and a black-face comedian in vaudeville, where he appeared in an act called "The Lizard and the Coon." His first experience in show business, however, came with a traveling circus, to which he ran away at age sixteen, abandoning forever Louisville, Kentucky, where he was born in 1882.

In all of his peregrinations, he never left the circus behind, returning over and over in fantasy to the Ten-in-One, where he had worked as a talker. For many of us, in fact, born after the movie-house had replaced the tanbark as the dream place of the Freak fancier, his celluloid side show was the first we ever knew. Yet for nearly a decade after his discovery by D. W. Griffith, who used him as an assistant director on *Intolerance* (1916), he had to work on movies which gave him no chance to evoke the presence of the Freaks. Almost from the start he was a box office success, but under the aegis of Universal he was called on to produce vehicles for Priscilla Dean, an actress associated with "program pictures," which is to say, exotic melodramas like *The Virgin of Stamboul* (1920) and *Under Two Flags* (1922).

From 1923 to 1925, baffled perhaps by having to fantasize in such uncongenial modes, he suffered a total breakdown. But even while trying "to drink up all the bad liquor in the world," he became obsessed with the notion of filming "a magazine story written by C. A. Robbins called 'The Unholy Three,'" and starring in it Lon Chaney, whom he had discovered while directing Priscilla Dean. He had a hard time, however, persuading producers that he was capable of drying out, and that the public would pay to see a film about "a crook dressed up as an old woman and a dwarf disguised as a baby." Nor were they particularly impressed when Browning informed them that the "crook" would double as a ventriloquist in a Ten-in-One, side by side with the Dwarf and a Strong Man.

He had, in fact, hit upon the figures and themes that would inform his most authentic work, as Irving Thalberg seems finally to have guessed, producing a movie with Lon Chaney as the drifter-ventriloquist, Harry Earles as the "Baby," and Victor McLaglen as Hercules, which grossed more than $2 million. Even critics like Mordaunt Hall, often skeptical about Browning, hailed it as "a startling original achievement which takes its place with the very best productions that have ever been made." And Chaney was so fond of his role in it that he remade it under another director in 1930 as his first and last "talkie." Meanwhile, he worked with Browning between 1926 and 1929 on seven other films, six of which Browning wrote as well as directed.

It was a strange moment in our history, a time of prosperity and rising expectations, bounded on the one side by a terrible war, and on the other by our worst depression. But the terror which haunted it remained for the mass audience without a name or shape, until the drive of an actor to assume ever more monstrous forms gave it the one, and the need of a director to move those forms through nightmare sequences without sound gave it the other. For Browning, Chaney represented personal salvation, delivering him, he was to say later, from the burden of inventing "plausible plots," and thus releasing from his deep psyche images of "revolting hideousness" in a dream scenario best realized, perhaps, in his Freak-within-a-Freak drama, *The Unknown*.

In that 1927 movie, Chaney plays a counterfeit "Armless Wonder" who lights matches and throws knives with his feet. Only the Dwarf who helps him put on and take off the harness which conceals them knows that he has two good arms. Yet though not what he pretends, he is a genuine Freak, with two thumbs on his left hand: a deformity which the girl he loves spots as he angrily stabs her father to death. In the darkness and confusion of the scene, she sees nothing else by which he might be identified, and to keep his secret he has both his arms "really" cut off. But she jilts him for the Strong Man, whom he attempts to deprive of all four limbs by stopping with his toes the treadmill that keeps a team of horses from tearing him apart in another "illusion." The now genuine Armless Wonder is caught at the last moment, however, and the "truth" revealed in a climax which makes explicit what Freak shows always implicitly suggest: that we only make believe that horror is make-believe.

None of the films on which Browning and Chaney worked are much shown these days, when almost all silents except comedies are forgotten. Consequently even ardent moviegoers are more likely to remember Browning as the maker of *Dracula* and *Freaks*, which he directed after the death of his favorite actor and the coming of sound. Chaney was slated to appear in the first, which was released on Valentine's Day of 1931 and billed as "The Strangest Love Story of All"; but before shooting could begin, he had died of cancer.

The realization of Dracula on the American screen was therefore not, as it should have been, Chaney's crowning triumph, but the beginning of Bela Lugosi's career as Monster-in-Chief (along with Boris Karloff) to the age of the Great Depression. It is Lugosi's name, in fact, rather than Browning's which we are likely to associate with that horror classic, though Bram Stoker's Vampire Voivode possesses our imaginations more than any of the players who have incarnated him—from Max Schreck, the star of *Nosferatu*, which preceded Browning's version, to Christopher Lee, best-remembered of the actors in the hundred or so more recent reworkings of the theme.

And this seems to me just, since no film *Dracula* works as well as the book—not even Browning's, despite some effective scenes, particularly the opening sequences and the eerie gathering of Dracula's wives. It is too dependent on a hopelessly static stage version, and contains little of what is most characteristically his in terms of cinematography, tone, and theme. There is no Strong Man, no transvestite, no circus or carnival setting—and above all, no Freaks; only monsters, which are not quite the same thing. Even in these terms, it is not as effective as James Whales's *Frankenstein* and *The Bride of Frankenstein*, or Cooper and Shoedsack's *King Kong*, which followed it in the monster-obsessed thirties. Besides, it is overshadowed by *Freaks*, which Browning did two years later, and which represents his only film without a star, his unmediated vision. The plot was suggested to him, it is true, by "Spurs," a short story by Tod Robbins, published in *Munsey's Magazine* in 1923; but before he was through, he had profoundly altered the original sequence of events and their meaning.

Rereading old reviews, we remind ourselves that half-remembered actors called Wallace Ford, Leila Hyams, Henry Victor, and Olga Baclanova played the "normals" who keep its romantic action moving. But what really stays in our minds are the human oddities, whose careers we associate not with movies but with the carnival and circus: Daisy and Violet Hilton, the Siamese Twins; Prince Randian, the Hindu Living Torso; Olga Roderick, the Bearded Lady; Slitzie, the Pinhead; Johnny Eck, the Boy with Half a Torso; Joseph-Josephine, the Half Woman/Half Man, etc., etc. Somewhere between such side show performers playing themselves and the featured actors playing fictional roles come Harry Earles, who had earlier taken the part of the Dwarf baby in *The Unholy Three*, and his sister Daisy. They act Hans and Frieda, a pair of betrothed Dwarfs temporarily separated when an aerialist called Cleopatra marries Hans for his money and attempts with the aid of her Strong Man lover, Hercules, to poison him.

Hercules is the closest thing to a Giant in Browning's super Ten-in-One. But though stronger and taller than any of the Freaks or the sympathetic "normals" who befriend them, he is not monstrously large. As the plot develops, however, and the camera focuses more and more on the child-sized human oddities among whom he moves, he comes to seem the sole evil adult in a world of innocent children. "But they're like children and God loves them," Madame Tetrallini cries out early in the film to a grounds keeper horrified by the rabble of Dwarfs, Pinheads, Living Skeletons, and Half Men over whom she presides. Whether Browning's God loves anyone is a little unclear by the end; but the Freaks, who prove neither innocent nor harmless, are really like children in the sense of inhabiting a world whose values and scale are not their own. They are, however, ours if we are grown-up normals—as we are reminded in the film's two most memorable scenes.

In the wedding feast of Cleopatra and Hans, stunted oddities far outnumber the normals, who, except for the oversized bride, are kept on the shadowy periphery of the action. The camera is directed at the center of a long table, on which, as the noisy celebration peaks, a Pinhead does a faltering little girl's dance, and is succeeded by a hideous Dwarf, a classic Italian *bagonghi*, carrying an enormous crystal flagon filled with champagne. Staggering across the table on bowed legs, he offers a sip first to the assembled Freaks, then to Cleopatra. It is an initiation rite, an invitation to join herself in fellowship to them all, even as she is joining herself in matrimony to one of them. But as he places the cup to his lips and the whole group chants, "We accept her, one of us . . . *One of us, one of us . . . Gooble, gabble, one of us* . . ." she rises in terror and disgust, reducing them to scale by that simple act. And crying, "Freaks! *Freaks!*" she hurls the champagne into their grinning faces—scattering them, like Alice scattering the face cards who had seemed to her a threatening jury at the end of her *Adventures*. Then, in a final

ABOVE: The wedding feast of the Freaks. BELOW: The initiation of Cleopatra into the fraternity of Freaks. Stills from Todd Browning's film *Freaks* (1932).

From the MGM release Freaks, *copyright 1932 Loew's Inc. Copyright renewed 1959 by MGM Distribution Corporation*

shot—based, one gathers, on the single image in "Spurs" which had evoked for Browning his whole film—she picks up the drunken and abandoned Hans and carries him off piggy-back, like a sleeping baby.

It is the beginning of the end for her and her lover, though neither of them suspects it; and the action moves quickly to the second major scene, the finale, in which armless and legless Freaks creep, slither, and hop through a nighttime storm of incredible ferocity. The elements, however, seem less ferocious than they, as they crawl on their bellies, their heads barely lifted out of the mud, pursuing first under the smashed wagons, and then across sodden fields, the fleeing aerialist and Strong Man. They and their prey are lit only by occasional flashes of lightning, and the camera remains fixed at their level so that we can see what happens only intermittently and through their eyes. Prisoners of their point of view, we do not see what happens when they catch the fleeing normals, since darkness settles down, and only the sound track is heard—a meaningless and incoherent racket pierced by what may be human cries.

The plot I have summarized, which is to say, everything in *Freaks* which is cinema rather than side show, is framed by a talker's spiel, with which the movie opens and to which we return at the end, with a sense of having left the darkened theater for the sunlit fairgrounds. "We didn't lie to you," we hear the announcer saying in the first scene to a small carnival audience of which we somehow feel a part. "We told you we had living breathing monstrosities! . . . Their code is a law unto themselves. Offend one—and you offend them all." And we move with him toward a pit, into which we are, at that point, not permitted to look, though the spectators on the screen can, one of them screaming out in terror as the spieler continues, "She was once a beautiful woman. She was known as the peacock of the air . . ."

As the sound of his voice fades, the film dissolves to a shot of Cleopatra on the high wire, and then to a series of vignettes of domestic life among the Freaks; and watching them play, laugh, flirt, do their laundry, and give birth, we begin perhaps to forget the suspended horror of the opening. But that feeling returns during the nightmare chase, with its disconcerting Oedipal overtones; and it is increased when we are returned to the pit side and the end of the talker's pitch. "How she got that way will never be known. Some say a jealous lover. Others . . . the code of the freaks . . ." Then looking down, we see at last what the carnival audience has presumably watched throughout: the Chicken Woman, a creature reduced in height to scarcely more than two feet, but with the face of Cleopatra, a feathered breast, no visible legs, and claws in the place of hands.

It is a finale so atrocious and contrived that it risks breaking the illusion completely. And I have sat in audiences which, not believing it for a moment, have laughed aloud, as if in relief at a welcome anticlimax; while others, absolutely convinced, have screamed or sat so silently that every intake and release of breath was audible, before the scuffle of feet and the rush toward daylight began. Critics, on the other hand, even after they had begun to take *Freaks* seriously, have been driven to reflect on the moral and metaphysical implications of the ending. Either they have argued that the spiel which frames the story, like most side show ballyhoo, is a hoax, and the whole enclosed plot therefore a lie; or they have decided that it is true, and that, therefore, despite Browning's editorial assurances that Freaks are no different from any of us, in action they prove to be "creatures of darkness and practitioners of black magic." To believe this, however, we must accept the patently manufactured Chicken Woman in the pit as "real" in the same sense as Johnny Eck or Prince Randian or the Hilton Sisters, though, unlike them, she exists as a Freak only on the screen.

The image of the human/barnyard fowl hybrid had haunted Browning for a long time, appearing in *West of Zanzibar* in 1928; but it is presented in that film as an "illusion," created on screen by a crippled stage magician played by Lon Chaney. Using it for the second time, however, in a movie where all other human oddities are "genuine," and refusing to identify it in that context as a "hoax," Browning has made an egregious error. Or perhaps he is only making an attempt to alert us, as we prepare to exit, to the fact that he, too, is a magician, rather than the realist we may have been tempted to believe him to be. But whether we are to assume that all magic is merely illusion, or sometimes, at least, something more terrible and potent, he does not tell us for sure either in this film or in the five or six he made after it. Yet the last of them is about a group of stage illusionists meeting in convention, while another returns to the subject of Vampires; and the best of the lot, *The Devil's Doll*, deals with a criminal in old woman's drag, who shrinks human beings so small that beside them an ordinary side show Midget would seem a Giant.

The formula which he uses in that movie comes not out of the arsenal of black magic but from the latest discoveries of science, involving some vaguely specified use of atomic radiation. At the end of his career Browning was flirting with science fiction, actually drawing on a novel called *Burn, Witch, Burn* by A. Merritt, who is recognized these days as one of the pioneers of the new genre. But by this time he had clearly lost the popular audience, and apparently his own nerve as well—undone by the failure at the box office of *Freaks*, which he must have known represented his supreme achievement. His producers and distributors did not give up easily; yet even when they had retitled his film *Nature's Mistakes* and launched a new advertising campaign centering on a favorable blurb by Louella Parsons, it drew no audiences. They added an apologetic foreword as well, which began with a hilarious piece of pop mythology explaining that "misshapen misfits have altered the world's course. Goliath, Caliban, Frankenstein, Gloucester, Tom Thumb and Kaiser Wilhelm are just a few . . ." and ending with the assurance that "never again will such a story be filmed, as modern science and teratology is rapidly eliminating such blunders of nature from the world."

It proved impossible, however, to stop the attack which had begun with mild demurrers like those in *The New York Times*: "The difficulty is in telling whether it should be shown at the Rialto . . . or in, say, the Medical Center . . . The only thing that can be said definitely for 'Freaks' is that it is not for children," and had climaxed in reviews describing it as "so loathesome I am nauseated thinking about it . . . It is not fit to be shown anywhere." Both theater owners and parents agreed, the former canceling bookings and the latter joining in protests through the PTAs and other organizations specializing in moral indignation. Even some of the Freaks who had played in it, most notably the Bearded Lady, were convinced in retrospect that Browning had vilified their kind, and said so in public. And though he went through the motions of film making for five or six more years, he himself seems to have been persuaded that the world had grown uncongenial to his kind of fantasy, and retired in 1939, spending the last twenty years of his life in relative obscurity.

Perhaps he went back to heavy drinking, though the record is not clear on this score. The accounts of his retirement inform us only that he never entered a movie theater again. "When I quit a thing, I quit," he told a friend. "I wouldn't walk across the street now to see a movie." But he apparently continued to read popular fiction as avidly as ever, selecting stories he thought would make good films, and casting them in the privacy of his own head with actors and actresses he had known, many of them already dead. The coming of television, however, made it possible for him to catch up on all he had missed, and he settled down to a routine of sleeping all day and staying up all night to watch the replays on the Late Late Show, perhaps even seeing occasionally something of his own, most likely *Dracula,* which alone of his films was regularly revived.

When he died in 1962 at age eighty, his modest obituary in *The New York Times* was overshadowed by a tribute to Sylvia Beach, first publisher of Joyce's *Ulysses.* More space was devoted to *Dracula* than anything else he had done; and though it was reported that among his "scores of Hollywood movies" were "25 two-reelers for the Majestic picture organization," neither *Freaks* nor any of the films he had done with Chaney were mentioned. Yet the latter were not completely forgotten at that point, having been, in fact, highly praised in an Italian film lexicon published in 1958. But even that source, which includes *Freaks* in an appended list of his films, refers to it obliquely and disparagingly, observing "that with the death of Chaney the decline of Browning began."

There were almost everywhere in the Western world aficionados of the horror movie who kept alive in the years between 1939 and 1962 not only memories of *Dracula,* never completely abandoned by the mass audience in any case, but of *Freaks* as well. The small group who especially admired the latter were drawn almost exclusively from those for whom the cinema was art rather than entertainment. But Browning had addressed ordinary moviegoers rather than the elite audience who frequented the tiny moviehouses of the Latin Quarter, where I myself saw *Freaks* for the first time. It seems odd that I should have had to go abroad to find so American a movie. But it had long since ceased playing even at those all-night

porn and horror theaters on 42nd Street, where it had been shipped
after bombing at the Rialto. Moreover, as far as I know, no American
critic had up to the year of his death written such praise of Browning's *chef-d'oeuvre* as had appeared in 1951 in Paul Gilson's *Ciné
Magic*. Speaking of the "magic" which redeems "the black images
of this cruel film" and the "grandeur of its terror," Gilson is led to
evoke Edgar Allan Poe's *Tales of the Grotesque*, especially, of
course, "Hop-Frog."

The Poe to whom he compares Browning is that half-imaginary
author, the patron saint of dada, surrealism, pataphysics, and the
theater of cruelty, reinvented by Baudelaire and Mallarmé in contempt of reality and American critical opinion. And like Poe a century before, Browning therefore returned to the United States in the
1960s as an export of French avant-garde culture. Yet however
Freaks may have been misrepresented in the process, we must be
grateful. It might never have been revived at all if it had not been
selected to represent the horror category at the Cannes Film Festival
in the year of Browning's death. In the same year it was released in
England for the first time, and a couple of years later was hailed
in this country as a "minor masterpiece" and "a source for contemporary baroque cinema." Only the most naïve popular reviewers at that
point continued to celebrate Browning as the popular film maker he
was, one insisting that "he made great horror films because he believed horror is naturally cinematic."

Meanwhile, in more highbrow journals, critics were asserting
that "*Freaks* is not really a horror film at all," or "*Freaks* is an anti-
horror movie." For them, to establish its greatness meant to distinguish it from Browning's own *Dracula* and *The Mark of the Vampire*
and link it instead to o.k. films like *Sawdust and Tinsel*, *La Strada*,
and *Lola Montés*, "which depict life as a tragic circle or circus."
"*Freaks* will disappoint no one," one such critic wrote, "but the
mindless children who consume most horror films." Yet in our own
time, it is those to whom both "mindless" and "children" seem terms
of praise, though they prefer to call themselves "Freaks," whom that
film—along with *Dracula*—especially moves.

It has become part of the canon of the counterculture, the
mythology of the dissident young, who in the late sixties demonstrated in the universities and took to the streets, and whose tastes

in the popular arts have imposed themselves ten years later on the whole Western world. But to understand the importance of that new mythology and the way it has altered permanently our consciousness both of Freaks and our normal selves, we must first understand the Cultural Revolution which created it.

12

Freaking Out

Like all genuine cultural revolutions, that of the late sixties has changed the very language men speak, giving to the word "Freak," for instance, a whole range of new meanings. I was talking recently in the halls of my university about letters I had been receiving from psycho-endocrinologists protesting the title of this book, when a student just out of a mental institution, a "longhair" dedicated to dissidence and dope, interrupted to ask whether I intended to include *him*. I knew the sense in which he understood the word, as I know what it means to the protesting doctors. Nor do I have any difficulty figuring out which of those senses was in the minds of the writers of the graffiti in the men's room just down the hall:

I HATE FREAKS

WHAT THE FUCK DO YOU THINK <u>YOU</u> ARE?

I JUST LIKE TO FREAK

Yet I am child enough of an earlier time to feel confused when I pick up from some airport newsstand a Playboy publication about the current scene entitled *Freaks*, though it contains nothing about Midgets or Siamese Twins or Geeks, or a 1973 paperback novel with the same title, described on its cover as "A novel of today's drop-outs and their hang-ups." To allay such confusion, however, the first-person narrator quickly explains, "I'm not a freak in the circus sense, apart from being a Welsh gentile who's been circumcised . . . What I mean by a FREAK is somebody who—well, everyone knows what it means, don't they? Everyone who wants to know, that is . . ." That everyone apparently includes the readers of such underground publications as the *L.A. Free Press*, the *East Village Other*, *Yellow Dog*, *The Rag*, *Gothic Blimp Works*, *The Rat*, *Radical*

LEFT: "Freaking Out." The Furry Freak Brothers freaking out. RIGHT: "On the Run." The Furry Freak Brothers on the run.
From the contemporary comic book series by Gilbert Shelton

America Komiks, Zap Comics, and *Hydrogen Bomb Funnies,* in which episodes have appeared of Gilbert Shelton's *Those Fabulous Furry Freak Brothers,* one of the most long-lived and popular of the so-called head comics.

Pitted against the hostile forces of law and order, represented by cops, narcs, and straights (i.e., beer-drinking solid citizens with short haircuts and ties), the "hirsute trio," unredeemably filthy and happy, stumbles from misadventure to misadventure in pursuit of dope, chiefly marijuana. Sex and revolution are also possible goals for them, though secondary and elusive, unlike grass, which can be scored by anyone with money. And money, for reasons never made clear, is always available in a world where no one works and what comes to hand is immediately spent. "DOPE will get you through times of no MONEY better than MONEY will get you through times of no DOPE," the Brothers chant over and over in the reprints and collections in which they survive to this day.

But as the street people in San Francisco, Los Angeles, and New York, the hippies, who were their first audience as well as the models from whom they were drawn, grow older—which is to say, become totally crazy or approximately sane—images of the Furry Freak Brothers in zonked-out flight, a hubbly-bubbly tucked under one arm and Keystone Comedy cops in hot pursuit, begin to seem more myth than actuality. Moreover, as state after state decriminalizes pot, and long hair, beards, and unwashed blue jeans turn into the accouterments of one more permissible life style, such images stir nostalgia rather than passionate allegiance or rejection. We have all become a little freakified, and what has done the trick—along with rock music and the drug revolution—is precisely our long exposure to a new mythology of Freaks, which never took itself seriously enough to become just another drag, like Home, Mother, the Church, and Old Glory, against which the new Freaks defined themselves.

Some apologists for the Cultural Revolution have tried to make it seem serious and boring. Most of them, however, like Charles A. Reich in *The Greening of America,* Philip E. Slater in *The Pursuit of Loneliness,* Theodore Roszak in *The Making of a Counter Culture,* and Robert Hunter in *The Storming of the Mind,* avoid the ridiculous and colloquial word "Freaks" in favor of highfalutin terms like "Consciousness III," the "new Gnosticism," or, at their most preten-

tious, "holistic, existential, post-operational, phenomenological consciousness." But Daniel Foss, a sociologist at Rutgers University
who lists among his credentials charter membership in the Mous-
keteer Club, calls his study *Freak Culture*, using the name originally
directed as an insult against its extreme representatives, and
adopted by them as an honorific title in contempt of their detractors.
He begins by considering the ironies implicit in this choice, writing:

> It may disturb some Americans to discover that a number of
> youths (as of 1967–1968) have been referring to themselves with
> pride as "freaks," or that expressions such as "it's freaky, man" or
> "that really freaked me out" are used in a positive sense. But
> that is part of the whole point.

Then he moves on to a non-ironical definition of Freaks which
his more "serious" professional commitments demand:

> "Freaks"—as I use the term—are *visibly* members of middle-
> class youth subcultures which include a subcultural reality in
> complete discontinuity with the conventional reality. Freaks are
> walking counter-environments who . . . assert the right to total
> control over their physical appearance and outward behavior—
> to the total irrelevance of the culture and informal norms of those
> who dwell within conventional reality . . . except insofar as it
> is desired to stimulate *disorientation* among the cultural enemy
> . . . "Freak" devotes an ideal type which embraces the hippie
> (1965) and New Left (1967–?) subcultures . . .

Yet despite such lapses in tone, he proves himself the wariest
of all scholarly commentators on the new Freaks, pointing out that
even they—reflecting confusions in the general culture—use the word
"Freak" pejoratively as well as honorifically, calling, for instance,
the uptight tourists who came to gawk at them in the Haight-Ash-
bury and the East Village "uptown Freaks." Moreover, they sometimes speak contemptuously of their less trustworthy allies in the
demonstrations which were their chief political activity as "speed
Freaks," "violence Freaks," or "structure Freaks," while those who
joined them in urban or agricultural communes, but took time off
from sex and meditation to read books or write them, were put down
as "print Freaks."

"Speed Freaks," meaning users of amphetamines, and "violence Freaks," meaning those committed to "wasting pigs" rather than merely throwing Coke bottles and talking dirty in their direction, seem especially equivocal. Not just hallucinogens like marijuana and LSD, but all drugs forbidden by the aspirin-alcohol-tranquilizer society of their parents have been a part of the Freak scene from the start, as the *Furry Freak Brothers* and other head comics sufficiently attest; and the same publications have always featured violence and sado-masochistic sex as well. Indeed, "Freak" in street language signifies not just "heads" but anyone given to kinky sex, especially in its bloodier forms. Its use, therefore, betrays an undercurrent of self-hatred, natural enough in a group of rebels drawn from the least violent, most educated, and most self-deprecating segment of our society, the suburban bourgeoisie.

But of this Foss seems unaware—though he acknowledges that the subculture he describes was in the main created by young white males of middle-class origin, chiefly college drop-outs. And he notes that even as he wrote (his study was published in 1972), the movement was in danger of not surviving the prosperity which had bred it and the delayed maturity of its members. Many of them, he observes, had learned to accommodate to the straight life by becoming wage earners and "hippie capitalists," or by leaving good dope for bad, hallucinogens for heroin or "consciousness-contracting" religious sects. That one of the most successful among the latter, the Jesus Freaks, preserves in its name the metaphor with which the "new consciousness" began gives him no consolation. In fact, his last sentence reads, "The situation does not easily lend itself to optimism."

He does not pause to reflect on other survivors left "freaked out" totally by the wonder drug LSD and turning now to the shrinks they once derided or a counter-drug therapy they once despised. His book was written before Timothy Leary, apostle of that drug and creator of the slogan "Drop Out, Tune In, Turn On," had informed on his fellow Freaks, but not before it had become clear that the Freak subculture was born, flourished, and had begun to die in less than a decade. This much at least he, unlike Reich or Roszak, realizes, though he seems no more aware than they that studies like his and theirs are symptoms of the decline of that culture. Only a revo-

lution that has already succeeded and failed—succeeded in changing a little the consciousness of us all without radically changing the
society in which we live—can be so rationally interpreted and understood.

We know, for instance, that one thing it has irrevocably
changed is our way of responding to Freaks, the balance of revulsion
and attraction shifting toward the latter. And we can see, too, that in
its origins it owes less perhaps to pundits like Herbert Marcuse, Nor-
man O. Brown, and Wilhelm Reich, about whom its early apologists
liked to talk, than to the mass culture of the fifties, especially that
consumed by kids and hated by their parents: early rock-'n'-roll and
the horror comics. That these were harbingers of a Cultural Revolution no one seemed aware until, in reaction to the unforeseen hostility they engendered, they entered into an alliance with the equally
feared drug culture, developing in the process into hard or acid rock
and the underground or head comics. Forbidden drugs were never
mentioned before 1971 in mainstream comics, however bloody and
sadistic; but their enemies, ranging from spokeswomen for the PTAs
to psychiatrists like Frederić Wertham and cultural critics like Ger-
shon Legman and Geoffrey Wagner, recognized that they were
themselves a kind of dope, one indignant protester on the "Town
Meeting of the Air" in the early fifties labeling them "the marijuana
of the nursery . . . the curse of the kids."

By the time the Freaks-to-be of the late 1960s had reached the
age of eight or ten, it had become illegal in New York "to sell obscene, objectionable comics to minors, or to carry words like 'crime,'
'sex,' 'horror' or 'terror' in any title." It was a time of growing repression on all fronts, though no one then made the connection between
McCarthyism and the pressure which forced E. C. Comics, the
most splendidly drawn as well as the grossest of the horror "funnies,"
to cease publication. Others survived by adopting a "voluntary"
code, pledging that "all lurid, unsavory, gruesome illustrations shall
be eliminated"—and that correct spelling and grammar would be
observed in their written texts.

At one point, the Kefauver Crime Commission threatened to interrupt its crusade against gambling, prostitution, and murder in
order to protect the innocent from what Wertham had called "seduc-
tion" by the comics. A few valiant critics, it is true, protested the

curtailing of First Amendment rights, or sought to defend the medium by pointing out the high incidence of violence in the Bible, Shakespeare, Mark Twain, and fairy tales, works considered desirable reading for the young. But no one in authority listened at a moment when it seemed almost as "subversive" to say a good word for horror comics—one of which portrayed a baseball game played with the head of a murder victim, whose entrails had been used to mark the base lines—as to defend the Hollywood Ten. In the end, however, there was no Congressional investigation and no criminal charges were brought against anyone, though Legman continued to argue that "editors, artists and writers of comic books are degenerates and belong in jail."

The ones who suffered were kids in need of ready-made fantasies to project dreams of revenge on the adult world, and to immunize themselves against real loss and terror by frightening themselves with what they knew to be fictions. Even horror classics like *Grimm's Household Tales* were bowdlerized, the wolf no longer permitted to swallow down Little Red Riding Hood. Meanwhile, the over-zealous kept their children away from television and movie matinees lest they be corrupted by the "sadism" of Bugs Bunny or scared silly by *Snow White and the Seven Dwarfs*. But such children outwitted their censors, acquiring E. C. Comics on the sly and passing them from hand to hand, or gathering at the houses of the more laxly supervised to watch the Friday night fright film with the added thrill of transgressing a taboo. As they grew older, they came to experience that thrill also in listening to rock and smoking pot.

They could not think of themselves as heretics, since they espoused no religion, nor as rebels, since they had no cause; they knew only that they were *different* from those who had begotten and nurtured them. But they had neither a name nor a mythology for that difference, until they discovered and identified with Freaks, creating about them a fantasy world as different from that of their suburban homes and schools as possible. The images for that world they found in the rock-'n'-roll lyrics, television horror shows, Disney cartoons, and the super-hero comic books they had loved. But now they celebrated sex, bloodshed, and the flight from "reality" at their heart openly and without apology. The newer comics bore, therefore, in place of the stamp-shaped label reading "Approved by the Comic

Code Authority," such mock seals as: "Rated Z² by Americans secretly serving Higher Order, Law Enforcement and Subservience," or "Approved by the United Geeks of America."

It was not only head comics like *Zap*, written by Freaks for Freaks, which in the sixties and early seventies made everything the fifties had found monstrous the norm. The newsstands were being flooded with journals aimed at the youngest and most naïve readers which ignored the old censorship. Calling themselves *Creepie, Spirit, Eerie, Vamperella, Monster, Death Rattle,* they drew their bloody themes from Edgar Allan Poe, Bug-eyed Monster science fiction, and the classic horror films of the thirties. Even newly invented comics like *The Fantastic Four* and *The Hulk* (creations of Stan Lee and the Marvel Comics Group), which were given the seal of approval, would have dismayed Wertham or Legman. Terror is woven into the fabric of their fantasy, and their super-heroes are as often hideous Freaks as handsome defenders of the status quo. But

BELOW: The new monsters
from Marvel.
From Stan Lee's Marvel Comics
RIGHT: Martian monsters.
From Head Comix

those who had once risen up against the E. C. Comics were too busy going to *Deep Throat* or *Rosemary's Baby* or *The Exorcist* to protest; which is to say, their deep consciousness, too, had been altered by a new mythology in which Freaks and monsters represented no longer the Other, but the Secret Self.

Extraterrestrial beings with multiple limbs or heads, along with monsters created in the laboratory, and side show performers had appeared in comic books from the start. And the original superheroes were marginal Freaks, of course; but they differed from the norm, as their Nietzschean name indicates, in greater strength, beauty, intelligence, and invulnerability. Typically, it was the super-

LEFT: "Sy" Klopps and Merciful Percival.
By R. Crumb
RIGHT: The Pinhead as lover. From Real Pulp Comics, No. 1, by Bill Griffith.
Copyright 1976 by Bill Griffith

villains they confronted who were deformed, like (to take instances only from *Bat Man*) Zebra Man, Penguin Man, and the Joker.

Never before our time, however, have sub- and metahumans played so central and sympathetic a role in the comics, though only in the hard-core head comics do side show Freaks appear as often as fabulous monsters. In "The Lighter Than Air Boys," for instance, a more or less "normal" Merciful Percival appears side by side with the one-eyed "Sy" Klopps, speaking like him a fashionable jargon loaded with terms like "vibes," "Karma," and "lower Chakras." Both are equally obsessed with sex, though neither is as horny or sexually attractive as Bill Griffith's Pinhead Zip or Zippy, who makes his microcephalic way from bed to bed not only in his own series, but as an occasional "guest star" in others. "Of course he was *handicapped*," says one of his many women. "But in one way or another, aren't we *all?* He'd *suffered* so long . . ."

The Aesop Brothers, George and Alex, on the other hand, a pair of Siamese Twin schlemiels featured in the *National Lampoon*, never make it sexually at all. But the magazine in which they appear is both slick and snide, "camping" what true underground comics do straight. Nonetheless, the series exploits both the breakthrough to explicit porn and the obsession with Freaks which began in the youth underground, and still offends certain right-minded parents. Driven at one point, for instance, to present themselves as a brother–sister team at a carnival, George and Alex have to flee a threat of rape against their female half on the part of a Geek. Escaping him, they fall into the hands of a nymphomaniac ex-movie star, who longs to have both of them at once. When they prove unable to perform as she desires, she drugs them and manages to achieve erotic satisfaction by riding their connecting bond bareback.

It is significant, I think, that granted freedom from all taboos, the comics should end by confessing the kinky desire for deformity which has always constituted part of the appeal of the Freak show. In the heyday of Dr. Wertham, there was no explicit sexuality in comic books, though the jock straps of the super-heroes and the breastplates of the super-heroines may have bulged suggestively as G. Legman liked to point out. In their lives as cosmic avengers, however, such super-creatures had no time for love, and in their normal existence they were notably incapable of consummating anything.

What erotic overtones persisted beneath their impotence were largely homosexual, most notably, perhaps, in the long liaison of Batman and Robin. On the other hand, even in the times of tightest repression there were hard-core porno-comics, the black-and-white "eight-page bibles," but these never appeared on news racks, being sold only under the counter. Moreover, they were in general innocent of sado-masochism, and out of bounds to Freaks. The standard three ways of sexual penetration were practiced over and over in their sleazy pages by "normals" or characters out of the daily funnies, like Tillie the Toiler or Barney Google, whom kids loved to see in rut, precisely because in their ordinary adventures there was no hint of an erect penis or a wide-open beaver under the ritual garb they never removed.

After World War III.
By R. Crumb

After the Cultural Revolution, Freaks came to seem especially at home in the liberated erotic center of the comics, since sex with them is at the furthest possible remove from the idyllic, sentimentalized notion of romance against which the dissident young were then revolting; and in the case of Siamese Twins, even further from bourgeois notions of monogamous fidelity. When the orgy rather than the family became the key image of erotic bliss, and total transgression replaced fulfillment as an erotic ideal, human oddities came into their own—not just as desirable partners in the sack, but as role models.

It was the artists and writers associated with such underground "comix" who in large part created the mythology of the new Freaks. But the kind of pop music equally rejected by the adult world carried the New Gospel as well—not only in the lyrics of its songs, but in the spiels of the DJs who broadcast it over post-TV radio, in the jacket copy with which pop albums were adorned, and especially in the life style of the musicians whose pictures illustrated such copy. In his study of Freak culture, Daniel Foss quotes appropriately from the manifesto written by Frank Zappa and reproduced in very small print (as if only for the really initiate) inside the front cover of *Freak Out!*, the first album released by the Mothers of Invention in 1966:

> On a personal level, *Freaking Out* is a process whereby an individual casts off outmoded and restricting standards of thinking, dress and social etiquette in order to express CREATIVELY his relationship to his immediate environment and the social structure as a whole . . . We would like everyone who HEARS this music to join us . . . become a member of *The United Mutations* . . . FREAK OUT!

There is something grimly missionary about all this, as if Zappa thought of himself as a kind of Peter the Hermit about to launch a second Children's Crusade. But the curse is taken off by the music itself, in which parody and noise drown out the evangelical tone, as well as by a put-on text (in considerably larger print) on the back of the jacket, signed "sincerely, forever" by the mythological Suzy Creamcheese of Salt Lake City, Utah:

These Mothers is crazy. You can tell their clothes. One guy wears beads and they all smell bad. We were gonna get them for a dance after the basketball game but my best pal warned me you can never tell how many will show up . . . sometimes the guy in the fur coat doesn't show up and sometimes he does show up only he brings a big bunch of crazy people with him and they dance all over the place. None of the kids at my school like these Mothers . . . specially since my teacher told us what the words in their songs meant.

Underneath this letter, a hairy Frank Zappa, whose freaked-out state is indicated by his having turned purple, asks in a comic book balloon, "Suzy Creamcheese, what's got into you?" And on the front, an even hairier and purpler Zappa cries silently, FREAK OUT! The point is clear: if he can do it, anyone can—even Suzy; since freakiness is not a fate, a condition to which one is born, as the old-time

Speed Freaks.
From a comic book by S. Clay Wilson

Freak show seemed to assure us, but a goal, a state which one can attain with the aid of drugs and/or music.

The singers, instrumentalists, and especially the charismatic leaders of recent rock groups are living testimonials to that possibility: role models able in live performances—and particularly at monster festivals—to preside over mass freak-outs, whether benign orgies like Woodstock or ugly outbursts of hysteria like Altamont. Moreover, when such moments are over, and everyone else's high has collapsed (the momentary lovers in separate beds, the wounded in hospitals, the totally bibbled-out in psychiatric wards, and the promoters counting the take), the musicians must still perform their roles for TV cameras, newspaper interviewers, and talk shows. They are self-condemned to play the Freak full-time, never allowed to shed even their costumes and makeup when anyone is watching. And those roles become harder—more desperate, more excessive, more rigid—as the euphoria of the late sixties subsides and the off-beat clothing, the long hair, the taste for psychedelics and easy loving, once sufficient to make Good Bad Boys like the Beatles scary for parents and titillating for their children, become the standard accouterments of prole barflies and bourgeois swingers.

What can still shock enough to matter is sex-shifting and S-M violence, especially in the form of cannibalism; which is why Arlo Guthrie has been driven to chant, "I want to see blood and gore and guts and veins in my teeth. Eat dead burnt bodies . . ." and Grace Slick sings, "Where are the bodies for dinner?/ I want my food!" It is, however, Alice Cooper, that transvestite wrapped in a python, butchering live chickens and blood-filled dolls on stage, or Mick Jagger, painted to sexual ambiguity and suggestively nibbling the mike under the logo of a toothed, open mouth with a lolling tongue, who really give the game away. Spokesmen for the Rolling Stones like to explain the whole thing with high-tone references to Kali, the Hindu Destroying Mother (after all, Mick Jagger is a professor's son), while Vincent Damon Furnier, the preacher's son who calls himself Alice Cooper, blames it all on the audience: "People like to be scared . . . Offstage I'm Ozzie Nelson. It's like Jekyll and Hyde to me."

But neither allusions to Indian mythology or evocations of late Victorian thrillers can conceal the fact that the rock stars of the mo-

Mick Jagger. Still from the Rolling Stones movie *Gimme Shelter*.
Museum of Modern Art/Film Stills Archive

ment have taken on the personage of two classic side show Freaks:
the Geek and the morphodite. Or rather they have improbably combined the two to create a new Single O: the androgyne as cannibal,
a zoophilous Half Man/Half Woman, who for the blow-off screams
over the electronically magnified rhythms of what has come to be
called "freak rock," "You could learn to dine on your friends."

The new view of human oddities formulated by self-identifying
Freaks has proved as salable as faded and patched blue jeans, tie-
dyed T-shirts, Day-Glo posters, and records made by musicians
high on hallucinogenic drugs. The renewed interest in side show
Freaks had, however, appeared everywhere in our society even before the counterculture had become a byword, and it has therefore
survived its dissolution: the flight of its aging acolytes into hard-core
drugs, mysticism, Satanism, terrorism or insanity, or their accommodation to bourgeois life. Moreover, the most thoroughly "co-opted"
of the former Freaks cannot forget that their brothers and sisters in
the side show represent not some absolute Other but a Secret Self,

denied in the business of daily living but glimpsed occasionally on acid or in drugs. And they are pleased, therefore, when they find their kids wolfing down a bowl of "Freakies" for breakfast, or playing—like other kids in the neighborhood, no matter how "straight" their parents—with one of the "free Freakies" tucked away inside the box.

Looking over the shoulders of those children as they move on from the material on the cereal containers to comic books of the 1970s like *The Fantastic Four,* such ex-Freaks recognize the mythic figures of their own childhood, rebaptized and mutated, but still alive and well. Even TV commercials, which they may affect to despise, those sixty-second fantasies in which Giants and Dwarfs appear and disappear as quickly as "normal" faces are wiped clean of features and restored, are, as they taught us to say, "psychedelic," too. In order to realize that Disney's *Fantasia,* the *Looney Tunes,* or fantasies with live actors playing cartoon-like hybrids like *The Wizard of Oz* were "psychedelic," their generation had to watch them stoned out of their minds. But the second-generation Freaks whom they begot *begin* freaked out, which is to say, retribalized, reunited with their remotest ancestors, for whom distinctions between the real and the imagined did not yet exist.

By the mid-twentieth century, however, fantasy, once a staple in art of all kinds, had been relegated to dime museums, carnival side shows, pulp fiction, and Grade B films. It was here Freaks lived on, especially in "genre movies," horror films of which Browning's *Freaks* came to seem the prototype. Shown again and again for the benefit of those unborn when it was first released, it was reimagined in 1974 in *Mutations,* which shamelessly rips off its two most compelling scenes, as if Browning's human oddities had become public property; which is to say, true myths, communal dreams as widely shared as were David and Goliath or Theseus and the Minotaur between the fall of Constantinople and the end of World War II.

But so, too, are King Kong, Frankenstein's Monster, Dracula, and Dr. Jekyll, which inspire not just remakes of the works in which they first appeared, but original film scripts, ostensibly responding to new concerns, and as different from each other as *Beyond the Valley of the Dolls* and *The Night of the Living Dead.* The former, written and directed by Russ Meyer in order to outdo not just

Jacqueline Susann but his own early "nudies," moves from cliché to cliché toward a climax in which a teen-age rock producer dressed as Wonder Woman commits a series of sadistic murders with the aid of an ex-Nazi in full Hitlerian regalia. He himself is killed, but only after he has been stripped of his costume and revealed as a woman rather than a transvestite male. We see no more than a pair of rather skimpy female breasts, however (Meyer never shows nudity below the waist), so that some viewers leave the theater convinced that he/she is really an androgyne.

In any case, the film, which cost $90,000, almost nothing by Hollywood standards, brought in $9 million, attracting the new audience for porn created by the Cultural Revolution, which is to say, "almost everyone who was under thirty, and went to movies." To appeal to them, Russ Meyer provided not just (as his collaborator Roger Ebert points out) "rock music, mod clothes, black characters . . . lesbians, orgies, drugs," but (as Ebert does not) comic book mythology and a total S-M freak-out. The latter won for it many of the viewers who made *The Night of the Living Dead* first a cult success among the young and then a box office smash, despite the fact that it was produced by unknowns, and it cost less than a tenth as much as *Beyond the Valley of the Dolls*. Released in 1968, it was living an underground life in college film series and small specialty houses between health food stores and head shops when Meyer's film was packing them in in first-run theaters.

But it promises to live a longer life, in part perhaps because its most ardent fans averaged closer to twenty than thirty in age and included eight- to ten-year-olds, for whom its fashionable politics—anti-cop and pro-black—seemed totally irrelevant. What moved them were images of cannibalism, all the more effective because so amateurishly rendered: the old rising from the grave to eat the young and retreating with entrails between their teeth, a child gnawing at the body of her mother who bends over to protect her. Of all Freak archetypes the most universally appealing surely is that of the cannibal or the Geek, which is based on fantasies that begin with suckling and weaning; while that of the androgyne or morphodite, upon which *Beyond the Valley of the Dolls* depends, arises only with the sexual uncertainty of early adolescence. Both films, however, possess a kind of blessed naïveté; and both, like fairy tales and classic myths, can be experienced visually by those incapable of understanding their more cerebral "meanings."

In this respect, they resemble more recent successful schlock movies like *Jaws* or *The Exorcist*, though these present the monstrous as sub- or superhuman, sharks or demons rather than mutants or Freaks. But by the same token, they differ radically from films of limited audience appeal like Fellini's *Satyricon*, which draws on the same pop mythology, as one of its early critics felt it necessary to point out: "One does not think of Goya . . . but of Todd Browning . . . It is a Space Odyssey among the Freaks." Fellini's declared source is a Latin novel by Petronius, but he did not need to consult that text any more than Meyer and Ebert did Susann's to create a film script whose basic images are bisexual, plurisexual, and androgynous.

Both movies appear at the same cultural moment, by-products of the porno-politics practiced by the dissident young at the end of the sixties, and though the Fellini film purports to deal with an irrecoverable pre-Christian past, it obviously comments on the post-Christian present. Writing of his two protagonists who move unmoved through the orgies and murders and hallucinations endemic to a world in which all traditional definitions of the human have been superseded, Fellini comments:

> . . . two students, half beatnik, half-*vitellone*, like those . . . we can see today on the Piazza d'Espagna, or in Paris, or London . . . Their revolt has nothing in common with traditional revolutions, not faith nor despair nor the will to modify or destroy, but it seems a revolt all the same, translating itself in terms of absolute ignorance and detachment from the society which surrounds them . . .

It is, however, precisely his self-consciousness which alienates Fellini a little from those with whom he is concerned—making his film, unlike *Beyond the Valley of the Dolls*, more *about* a movement pledged to "absolute ignorance" than of it. It is finally art rather than myth, interpretation rather than primordial image (though such images take over the screen whenever its director is content to see rather than think), and it belongs, therefore, to the critics rather than the kids. So, too, do the still photographs of Diane Arbus,

Myths and Images of the Secret Self

whose Dwarfs and Giants and transvestites remain fixed forever in melancholy black and white on the walls of galleries and in the catalog made of a retrospective show organized in 1972 after her death by suicide.

Feeling herself hopelessly separated from such unfortunates by the accident of having been born "normal" and privileged, she sought over and over to penetrate their mystery with the third eye of her camera. "One of the things I felt I suffered from as a kid," she once publicly confessed, "was I never felt adversity . . . And the sense of being immune was . . . a painful one." Meditating further, she tried to explain why of all the less fortunate it was the Freaks who especially obsessed her:

> Freaks was a thing I photographed a lot. It was one of the first things I photographed. I just used to adore them . . . There's a quality of legend about freaks. Like a person in a fairy tale who stops you and demands that you answer a riddle. Most people go through life dreading they'll have a traumatic experience. Freaks were born with their traumas. They've already passed their test in life. They're aristocrats.

But her photographs say all of this better for the relatively few who know them, though even they seem somehow too intellectual, an attempt to solve a riddle, rather than the presentation of our last taboo in the guise of an entertainment. In any case, she is cut off by her medium from the mass audience which Browning and Meyer and even Fellini reach. How many moviegoers ever pass through the turnstiles of a museum to see one of her shows, or pick up the elegant monograph which preserves her words on the subject along with her pictures? Perhaps any bound and printed book, however profusely illustrated, inevitably betrays the mystery of Freaks. It is a disconcerting thought for one in the process of writing such a book; but certainly most normals in the dying twentieth century are more likely to experience them vicariously in comics or movies, where words are subordinate to images.

Some hardback volumes on the subject, replete with pictures and disreputable enough not to seem "literature," succeed in the mass market still. Indeed, at least one mail-order book club exists largely to distribute them to readers who never enter a bookstore.

All of them, if the flyer which lies open before me can be believed, deal with creatures describable only in terms of superlatives which once stirred our disgust, but now presumably titillate us: the Ugliest, the Crookedest, the Deadliest, the Sickest, the Porniest, the Weirdest, the Whackiest, the Strangest. Many of them turn out to be classic Freaks: the Ugliest, the Elephant Man and the Mule Lady; the Strangest, Big Foot—that imaginary blend of Giant and Missing Link; the Sickest, a kind of Geek who eats little girls; the Crookedest, a Fat Man weighing seven hundred pounds.

The two books given top billing are Frederick Drimmer's *Very Special People* ("What makes these people *very special* is that they were all born 'freaks'") and Carmichael's *Incredible Collectors*, the blurb for which shows the Elastic Man under the caption "From a photographic collection of the greatest freaks of all time." As a kind of "blow-off," there is an ad for Gould and Pyle's *Anomalies and Curiosities of Medicine*, headed in large caps: IF YOU'RE BIG ON SIDE-SHOWS, YOU'LL JUST LOVE THIS BOOK, and in smaller red letters: WARNING: THIS BOOK IS NOT FOR THE SQUEAMISH. Even the *Guinness Book of World Records* is presented as essentially about Freaks, with a photograph of Robert Earle Hughes under the banner THE HEAVIEST HUMAN ON RECORD WEIGHED 1,069 POUNDS AND WAS BURIED IN A PIANO CASE. In every instance, the primary appeal is to the eye, and words —like the spieler's ballyhoo—come second to tell us the wonder of what we are seeing, and to assure us that it is fact not fiction.

13

The Myth of the Mutant
and the Image of the Freak

Contemporary fiction about Freaks is read by a much smaller audience than nonfiction, except for certain novels based on the notion of an evolutionary leap which in a single generation produces children as different from their parents as *Homo sapiens* was from Neanderthal man. It is a hyperbole, a myth or metaphor better able to illuminate the family crisis of the late sixties than clichés like the "generation gap." Taken literally, it leads to portentous assertions about how "many of the kids who . . . call themselves 'freaks' are in reality *mental mutants*. They have mutated through an auto-evolutionary process triggered by technology . . . and further stimulated by the use of psychedelic drugs." But it makes for good science fiction, especially in the work of Isaac Asimov, A. E. Van Vogt, Arthur C. Clarke, and Robert A. Heinlein, four writers recognized—now that critics have deigned to take the form seriously—as the modern masters of the genre.

The self-styled "Freaks," however, were there first. Children of

Jacket from *I, Robot,* by
Isaac Asimov.
By permission of the publisher,
Fawcett World Library

advanced technology, whose first mirror was the flicker of light on
the TV screen, they responded to the stories written by Asimov in
the 1940s and reissued in book form in 1968 as *I, Robot.* In these
tales of robots striving to be accepted as persons and competing
against men, he gave classic form to the new kind of Freak prefig-
ured in the monster of Mary Shelley's *Frankenstein.* Hybrids which
challenge the boundary between humans and machines, as the Elephant Man and the Dog-faced Boy once challenged that between
humans and beasts, they stir similar feelings of sacrilege and terror.
"It has no soul," cries a jealous mother of Asimov's Robbie, the com-
puterized humanoid who has apparently alienated her child's affection, "and no one knows what it may be thinking."

It is, however, an image of man manufacturing rather than mu-
tating into the metahuman which Asimov evokes, and none of his
books, therefore, has ever achieved scriptural status among the
young like Van Vogt's *Slan,* Clarke's *Childhood's End,* and Hein-

lein's *A Stranger in a Strange Land.* Dealing with the transmogrified children of men, all three are still to be found among the cult books preserved in communes where the hard-core survivors of '68 await the Second Coming. Part of a standard list which includes also Tolkien's *Lord of the Rings,* the *Tibetan Book of the Dead,* the *Whole Earth Catalog,* the *I Ching,* Carlos Castaneda's *The Teachings of Don Juan,* and Robert Pirsig's *Zen and the Art of Motorcycle Maintenance,* they are read—whatever the intent of their authors—as guides to freaking out.

Slan is the hardest of such books for literary critics to accept, banally written, clumsily constructed, and based on "scientific" theories which are pure mumbo-jumbo. Yet Van Vogt's raw mythopoeic power finally prevails, and his tale has for nearly forty years compelled the interest and assent of those who long for the occult but insist that it be rendered in the language of science. Even large numbers of otherwise skeptical readers, like me, find it after frequent rereadings not only moving but convincing, while aging Freaks continue to read it as a parable of what they would like to believe is still their plight. "Why was he feared?" reads the jacket copy describing its mutant hero. ". . . to all appearances he was human and harmless. But the slim tendrils half-concealed in his hair identified him as a SLAN. And to the men who ruled the world, naturally all SLANS were freaks."

It is also central to the vision of futurologists like Louis Pauwels and Jacques Bergier. In *The Morning of the Magicians,* they claim Van Vogt as a fellow prophet—along with Julian Huxley, J. Robert Oppenheimer, Henry Miller, Jean Cocteau, Aurobindo Ghose, and Adolf Hitler, whom they quote more often than the others: "The New Man is living among us. He is there! What more do you want? I will tell you a secret: I have seen the New Man. He is intrepid and cruel! I was afraid in his presence!" But their sanguine view of the coming of the metahumans seems less like Hitler's than Van Vogt's: "Intelligent and rational mutants, endowed with an infallible memory, a constantly lucid intelligence are perhaps working beside us disguised as country schoolmasters or insurance agents . . . there is every reason to believe that they are working and communicating with one another in a society superimposed on our own . . ."

In Europe, we are assured, their work "has shaken the conviction of hundreds of thousands of people . . . Fourteen volumes of a new encyclopedia have appeared . . . as a direct consequence of this one book." In this country, however, it has not had a similar impact, perhaps because its views were in 1960 already old hat to American readers not just of *Slan* but of *Childhood's End*, first published in 1953. The continuing influence of the latter is attested by the fact that in 1971 Robert Hunter borrowed its title for the first chapter of his panegyric to the "Consciousness Revolution," calling it "probably the most important science-fiction work of our time." It was known, however, to only a small coterie of s-f fans, until in 1968 the self-identifying Freaks began to identify themselves with the mutated young who at its conclusion are about to abandon planet Earth. Up to that year, it had been reprinted eight times, an average of once every two years; in the following five, reprints appeared at the rate of three a year. And why not? Clarke had projected his final catastrophe far into the future, but by 1968 there were many to whom the prophecy which he put in the mouth of the Overlord Karellen seemed already a fact, or at least a lived myth, which for them was all the fact there was:

> All the earlier changes your race has known took countless ages.
> But this is a transformation of the mind, not the body. By the
> standards of evolution, it will be cataclysmic—instantaneous. It
> has already begun. You must face the fact that yours is the last
> generation of *Homo sapiens*.

For historians of science fiction like Cory and Alexei Panshin, its publication (along with Theodore Sturgeon's *More Than Human*) represented something radically new in the genre. "Previous representations of superior man in s-f pictured the odd sport or mutant who was just like us, only stronger and gifted with a higher I.Q.," they write; whereas Clarke's mutated children portray "the species on the brink of a general evolutionary leap." *Slan*, however, had already done something similar, and there are hints of the myth of the mutant in Jerome Bixby's all-time favorite science-fiction story, "It's a Good Life," as well as Olaf Stapledon's classic, *Odd John*, which appeared in 1935. Nonetheless, there is a sense in which Clarke functions for his youngest readers as a contemporary in a way in which Stapledon, Van Vogt, and Asimov do not. His late novel *2001: A Space Odyssey*, both as a book and a movie co-authored by Stanley Kubrick, has come, therefore, to seem not just a mythological source for the new sensibility, but one of its major achievements. The film is experienced by young audiences as an actual freak-out, a "trip" in itself rather than one more version of the myth of the mutant, though it begins by portraying the evolutionary leap from subhuman and ends, however ambiguously, by projecting a further leap to the metahuman.

Dealing in primordial images, science fiction seems ideally suited for iconic or semi-iconic forms. Indeed, in its heyday, it was almost invariably published first in illustrated pulp magazines; but in book form, whether paper or hardback, it was detached from pictures, except perhaps for a garish cover or jacket. Movies, therefore, and TV, along with comic books, would appear to be more appropriate media, though only a very few directors have done justice visually to the archetypal elements in s-f. Chief of these is Kubrick, who has also adapted the genre in *A Clockwork Orange* from Anthony Burgess' novel of the same name, and *Dr. Strangelove* from Peter George's *Red Alert*. Indeed, he has been so successful in these attempts that Brian Aldiss has suggested he "should perhaps be acknowledged as the great s-f writer of the age." Of his three films, however, only *2001* is concerned with the myth of the mutant, and for reasons I find hard to understand, no other s-f novel of this kind has been successfully filmed by anyone, though the theme becomes ever more popular with writers young and old.

There is, for instance, *A Canticle for Leibowitz* (1960) by Walter Miller Jr., which opens with a terrifying view of a Freak-infested world after the Last Nuclear War: "The two-headed woman and her six-legged dog waited with an empty vegetable basket by the new gate . . . one head was as useless as the extra legs of the dog . . . It lolled uselessly on one shoulder, blind, deaf, mute, and only vegetatively alive . . ."; and closes with a priest blessing that second head, whose eyes open as the first one dies. And more recently, there have been the novels of Samuel Delany, a member of the so-called New Wave young enough to have had his consciousness altered by psychedelic drugs and the pop mythology of the comics. He finds, therefore, joy rather than terror in the possibility of worlds swarm-

The best-selling underground novel
by the dean of American science fiction writers

STRANGER IN A STRANGE LAND
ROBERT A. HEINLEIN

Jacket from *Stranger in a
Strange Land,* by Robert
Heinlein. The mutant as
savior.
*By permission of the publisher,
Berkeley Publishing Corporation*

ing with "madmen and mind readers, dwarves and duchesses, giants
and geniuses . . . and a gallery of aliens who fly, crawl, burrow, or
swim."

It is strange that Heinlein's *Stranger in a Strange Land* has
never been adapted for the screen. Published in a hard-cover edition
in 1961, it had already begun to sell widely before its paperback
appearance in 1968. It is, in fact, the first hard-core s-f novel ever
to have broken through the relatively small circle of science-fiction
buffs to the total youth audience, not just students in college, high
school, and even grade school, but those between twelve and thirty
whose only libraries are the bookracks in supermarkets and bus sta-
tions. Nor did it stop there, reaching finally the parents and teachers of its first readers, then all adults who at a troubled time sought
to emulate or simply to understand the new life styles. It was, however, the young—and particularly the self-declared Freaks at their
leading edge—who most deeply responded to what they took to be

Legion of the Charlies: The mutant as monster.
Copyright 1971, Veitch, Irons, Sheridan

Manson, by R. Crumb. The mutant as home breaker.
By permission of the artist

the essential myth of Heinlein's novel: learning to speak its special language (for a little while "grok" became a verb and "water brother" a noun in common use) and adopting the rituals of the underground cult founded by its hero, Valentine Michael Smith.

Most notorious of Smith's extraliterary disciples was Charles Manson, who, though he had banned all books to his own followers, had a copy of *Stranger in a Strange Land* in his possession when he was arrested, and called his only child Valentine Michael. It was doubtless Smith's ability to murder his enemies without compunction, along with his espousal of ritual cannibalism and communal sex, which led Manson to identify with him. But what seems to have impressed him even more was the fact that Smith was science fiction's first mutant-turned-guru: a proselytizer, who though he himself had become what he was ("Smith . . . is . . . not . . . a . . . man") through the accident of having been born on Mars and brought up by Martians, taught that anyone could, simply by learning to freak out, become more than human.

Heinlein seems on the face of it an improbable writer to have imagined such a blending of the myth of the mutant and the notion of freaking out. A right-wing militarist hack, many of whose earlier books had been placed on the recommended reading lists of American neo-fascist organizations, he was nearing sixty when he wrote the only novel which seemed to the young to speak directly to them. It can, in fact, be interpreted also as the daydream of an aging Goldwaterite, in which a lifelong bully who has come to feel impotent erotically and politically suddenly makes it with a bevy of sexy young girls, even as Big Government is getting its long overdue comeuppance by an invader from outer space. No wonder that Heinlein was uncomfortable about his odd success. "I hate all of my readers," he is reported to have said, "even the grown-ups." And he must have been made especially uncomfortable by the leftist politics of V. M. Smith's ardent admirers, whether young or old.

But the Cultural Revolution has made even stranger bedfellows: not just Abbie Hoffman and Jerry Rubin, Heinlein and Manson, but Adolf Hitler, who though he condemned human oddities to the gas chambers, himself shared the tastes of many self-declared Freaks. A vegetarian food Freak, who preferred dope to booze, he created an anti-family without bourgeois marriage in which a pet dog took the place of a child, and spurned high culture in favor of pop, his favorite song being "Who's Afraid of the Big Bad Wolf," his favorite film *King Kong*. Moreover, he knew that the mutants were already among us.

He was honored only by the maddest fringe of the Rebels of '68, bikers with black leather jackets and dangling swastikas. But the movement as a whole, right down to the dewiest flower child, found no difficulty in identifying with the fantasies of other oldsters more like the parents they distrusted than themselves: the super-patriotic Christian Scientist Walt Disney, for example, or the High Church Oxford don J. R. R. Tolkien. No matter what reactionary doctrines such men preached from the tops of their heads, they were accepted for having dreamed Other Worlds in which the boundaries between child and adult, male and female, the self and other, hallucination and reality, were challenged as they had long been at the side show.

Bilbo and Gollum: Freaks in Fairyland.
Illustration by Tim Kirk for his Master's Thesis project based on J. R. R. Tolkien's The Lord of the Rings, *reproduced in the 1975 J. R. R. Tolkien Calendar from Ballantine Books*

Between World War I and World War II, the image of the Freak and the myth of the mutant haunted the imagination of a world which was losing faith in Renaissance definitions of the human and of standards of normality. For a while, indeed, it seemed as if everyone was trying to get into the side show. Attempting to distinguish himself from other Jewish-American writers like Saul Bellow and Bernard Malamud, Philip Roth explained, "They're Jewish Sages. I'm a Jew Freak, like Tiny Tim." Then he wrote a tale (more reminiscent of Kafka than Tiny Tim) about a Freak who turned from a man into a female breast. In early 1975, moreover, an eighty-five-year-old, newly knighted Charlie Chaplin announced that he was about to start shooting a film about a South American girl with wings, starring two of his daughters, and called, of course, "The Freak."

Even the dead are not immune to posthumous freakification, especially when they seem to the living prototypes for the mutant life style. A recent biography of James Dean, thought of in his own lifetime as a "rebel without a cause," calls him in retrospect a "mutant hero." And Lenny Bruce, who talked dirtier than anyone else and died in 1965 of an O.D. after long harassment by the police, has recently been mythologized as the Freak *par excellence*. That word, however, was apparently not in Bruce's vocabulary. Certainly he never uses it of himself in the autobiography compiled out of his comic routines and published just before his death by the Playboy Press under the title *How to Talk Dirty and Influence People*. He thought of himself as a "hipster," and the myth to which he aspired was not the mutant but the Super-Jew—as the Crucified Christ or Shylock, it scarcely mattered to him which.

It is true he loved actual show Freaks, however, especially those in Hubert's Dime Museum and Flea Circus. His mother had first led him there by the hand as a child, and he returned again and again, featuring that sleazy 42nd Street joint in a TV film he once made about life in New York. Appropriately enough, we are taken there at the beginning of *Ladies and Gentlemen—LENNY BRUCE!!*, a biography published in 1974 by Albert Goldman, whose prose describing it becomes the spiel of a freaked-out talker:

It's like tumbling down a coal chute into another world. The whole Alice-in-Wonderland thing turned sordid and sick. A Pla-

tonic underworld of freakiness . . . elevated like statues on their
tiny spotlit stages, are all your archetypal freaks. Sealo, the Seal
Boy. Andy Potato Chips, the Midget . . . Congo, the Jungle
Creep . . . Jim Hailey, the Strong Man . . . Albertus Alberta,
half man and half woman.

And though we soon leave the Ten-in-One, we never really escape
the nightmare world it typifies. Freak . . . freaky . . . freakiness
. . . the words occur over and over until Lenny, bloated, bedridden,
drug-dazed and in pain, has himself turned into a side show monster.
We see him, as the book ends, through the eyes of an imaginary
friend come to call:

> *The bearded lady from the circus is rising to greet him!* It's
> Lenny—I guess!—but he's so freaky-looking that you're almost
> afraid to take his hand. This giant fat person dressed in a denim
> muumuu with a head on him—*a pinhead!* Bearded like a Trappist
> monk, his head is so much smaller than the rest of his body that
> it comes to a point on top!

This is the sensibility of the seventies: Goldman, the time traveler, come back some ten or a dozen years to gawk and free-associ-
ate. An actual visitor during Lenny's last days would not, I suspect,
have perceived him in these terms at all, since the heyday of the
head comix still lay in the future, and Frank Zappa was just preparing to issue his freak-out manifesto. Science-fiction fans had long
been identifying with mutants, but that was not quite the same
thing. Moreover, though more highbrow makers of fiction continued
to deal with traditional Freaks as they always had, the role and
status they attributed to such creatures were beginning to alter. Not
only were they abandoning old favorites like the Dwarfs, but their
symbolic use of all human oddities was changing in response to two
new possibilities opened up by science: "normalizing" the freakish
by endocrine treatment or surgery, and freakifying normals with
psychedelic drugs.

It would take a while, however, before such changes became
apparent. Dwarfs are so deeply rooted in children's literature, as
Tolkien and Disney reminded those who had forgotten, and so central to American fiction that they will probably never disappear

from the "mainstream" novel. Leafing through a pile of recently arrived books, I discover, for instance, a paperback edition of Edward Whittemore's *Quin's Shanghai Circus* (1974), in which a Giant, a Fat Man, and a Dwarf shuttle confusingly back and forth between the side show and history, nightmare and waking reality. And just below it another novel, still in galleys, which a publicity release assures me is about "a city, a dog, a dwarf, a child, a homosexual, a corpse . . ."

But the celebrated Dwarfs of history seem to have disappeared from literature, even Tom Thumb except for an occasional TV appearance in, say, a life of Abraham Lincoln. The only show Freaks associated with P. T. Barnum who have survived are Chang and Eng. It is their picture, complete with wives and kids, which dominates a recent ad for the Broadway Bookfinders captioned: CAN SIAMESE TWINS HAVE CHILDREN? Moreover, we are currently promised two new biographies, one, aimed primarily at children, by a young science-fiction writer called Lawrence Yep, and the other, aimed at everyone, by Irving Wallace, who always knows what everyone is ready to buy. Two of the most esteemed experimental novelists, Vladimir Nabokov and John Barth, have produced short fictions about joined twins, referring specifically to Chang and Eng. Nabokov's "Scenes from the Life of a Double Monster," which first appeared in 1950, alludes to those legendary prototypes with typical indirection, speaking in its first paragraph of "the fleshy cartilage-nous band uniting us—*omphalopagous disaphragomo-xiphodidymus*, as Pancoast has dubbed a similar case . . ."

Only those already in the know, perhaps, recall the famous Philadelphia autopsy presided over in 1874 by that eminent surgeon. But it is such readers to whom Nabokov addresses this tale about the degradation of the mythical in a commercial age, which ends with two Middle Eastern innocents about to be snatched from the pastoral world into which they were born and placed in that of the carnival, where clearly they will die:

> If at that moment some adventurous stranger had stepped onto the shore from his boat in the bay, he would surely have experienced a thrill of ancient enchantment to find himself confronted by a gentle mythological monster in a landscape of cypresses

and white stones. He would have worshipped it, he would have
shed sweet tears. But, alas, there was nobody to greet us there
save that worried crook, our nervous kidnapper . . .

A quarter of a century later, there seems something unredeemably
old-fashioned about Nabokov's treatment of the theme. He is not
afraid of pathos or so embarrassed by monstrosity that he seeks refuge in farce, as Mark Twain did. But unable to imagine the final
stage of development in the attitude of "normals" to Freaks, he looks
nostalgically to what is forever lost, rather than hopefully to what in
fact lay just ahead.

Even Nigel Dennis' cautionary tale "A Bicycle Built for Two,"
published in 1960, is more relevant to our present situation, since it
addresses those who have already persuaded themselves by "reading painful books, written by damned people . . . with no legs, or
only grown to a few feet, or with hermaphrodite parts . . . that
these creatures were on to a good thing." He attempts ironically to
undercut such attitudes, and at the story's close, his hitherto unhappy
joined twins are contentedly appearing in a circus act designed to
"show monstrosity struggling to behave normally—the very opposite
of what is going on outside." It is an improbable happy ending, since
like Twain, Dennis has until then evoked the bitter plight of two
humans yoked for life, though utterly different in temperament and
taste. One of his pair is an amiable and mindless golf pro and the
other a university don, intolerably theoretical and abstract; so that
only the sustained burlesque tone keeps their final acceptance of the
unendurable from seeming more painful than comic: a bad marriage
in a world without divorce.

Their author never lets them consider such an option, perhaps
because the first surgical separation of joined twins lay still a year
or two ahead. But such an option is central to John Barth's "Petition," which appeared in 1968, when the sundered Cleveland sisters
had survived some five or six years, so that a condition like theirs
no longer seemed a fate to be endured, but one to be accepted or rejected. Barth's story is, however, anachronistic. Though set in 1931,
it consists of a long plea to the King of Siam, who had come to the
United States for major surgery, to arrange for the separation of a
pair of American Siamese Twins. Presumably that monarch is quali-

Chang and Eng with wives and children. Contemporary publicity photograph.
Circus World Museum, Baraboo, Wisconsin

fied to commission such a still unperformable operation because
Chang and Eng had been blessed and sent forth by one of his dy-
nasty. We learn a great deal about those earlier twins in the course
of the story, including their difficulties in living at peace with each
other. But what the petitioner emphasizes throughout are the differences between his case and theirs:

> Only consider: whereas Chang and Eng were bound breast to
> breast by a good long band that allowed them to walk, sit, and
> sleep side by side, my brother and I are fastened front to rear—
> my belly to the small of his back—by a leash of flesh heartbreak-
> ingly short. In consequence he never lays eyes on the wretch he
> forever drags about . . . while I see nothing else the day long
> . . . but his stupid neck-nape, which I know better than my
> name.

The Persistence of Siamese
Twins.

LEFT: Four illustrations from
Pierre Boaistuau, *Histoires
prodigieuses* (1560).

BOTTOM LEFT: Prosopthoraco-
pagus and BOTTOW RIGHT:
Dispropus. From *Anomalies
and Curiosities of Medicine*,
by George M. Gould and
Walter L. Pyle (1896).

Unreal, surreal to the point of making the whole tale seem more parable than history, that improbable juncture also opens up possibilities for the grossest scatological and sexual humor:

> What I suffer in the bathroom is too disgusting for Your Majesty's ears . . . he belches up gases, farts in my lap; not content that I must ride atop him, as on a rutting stallion, while he humps his whores, he will torment me in the shower bath by bending over to draw me against him and pinching at me with his hairy cheeks.

In a time of kinky sex and compulsory candor, it is precisely such revelations about Freaks that we demand of those who reimagine them. What do they do on the stool? in bed? in all those private moments once considered out of bounds to public curiosity? There have always been some who suspected that the appeal of the Freak show was not unlike that of pornography, and in the age of the explicit, the secret is out. Nabokov and Nigel Dennis may still be as circumspect about the sex life of Siamese Twins as Mark Twain; but Barth, more like the creators of the Aesop Brothers in the *National Lampoon*, lingers over the coupling, or rather tripling, of natural prodigies, for whom any act of intercourse is by necessity an orgy. The two brothers in "Petition" after much difficulty find a suitable mate, "a pretty young contortionist of good family," called Thalia. And with Thalia they perform for nightclub audiences "a repertoire of unnatural combinations and obscene gymnastics," while an orchestra plays "Me and My Shadow" and "When We're Alone."

The basic conceit opens up endless opportunities for farce, which turns to terror when both fall in love with their partner. Or rather the embodiment of carnal grossness lusts for all in Thalia which responds to his needs, even as his "monkey on the back" brother longs for all in her which he would like to believe is left unsatisfied by that lust. The story ends, therefore, on a note of pathos, as the petitioner's plea for total separation blends with a lover's prayer for total union:

> . . . I dare this final hope: that at your bidding the world's most accomplished surgeons may divide my brother from myself . . . Or if a bond to *something* is necessary . . . graft my brother's Thalia in my place, and fasten me . . . to my own navel, to any-

thing but him, if the Thalia I love can't be freed to join me . . .
To be one: paradise! To be two: bliss! But to be both and neither
is unspeakable.

Yet the final resonances of the tale suggest that we are all of us
always "both and neither," and doomed therefore to long for both
division and copulation from cradle to grave.

Barth seems finally a writer whose sensibility was made in the
early sixties, too concerned with history and too prone to allegory,
perhaps, to render the image of the Freak that possesses the late
twentieth century. In Donald Newlove's *Leo & Theodore* (1972)
and *The Drunks* (1974), however, a pair of Siamese Twins appear who resist being turned into metaphors for anything, and have,
as far as we can discover, no awareness that Chang and Eng ever
existed. It is through a mythological grid derived from the monster
movies of the thirties that they see themselves and are perceived by
their author: *Dracula, Frankenstein* ("How the monster first got
sewn together!"), *Dr. Jekyll and Mr. Hyde*, and the *Bride of Frankenstein*. Of the last, Leo says, "This is the best story I ever saw,"
while Teddy responds, "I love it"; moreover, they address each other
jocularly throughout as "Jekyll" and "Hyde," knowing that what
they live is a monster feature, too, but refusing either to allegorize
it or take it too seriously.

Even more than the explicit sex scenes ("Put your leg over our
band, Teddy says. Beverly gasps."), which, unlike Barth, Newlove
renders without any suggestion of queasiness or moral disapproval,
it is the new mythological context which makes this pair of novels
different from all that have come before. By the second volume of
what promises to be a continuing series, moreover, Leo and Teddy,
born Freaks in the traditional sense of the word, have become Freaks
also in the contemporary sense; which is to say, they live in the East
Village, pop pills, and generally cultivate a life style as different as
possible from the small-town mores to which they were educated.
They have, in short, *chosen* a fate of which their unwilled condition
is a symbol. Like many "heads," however, they are also old-fashioned
alcoholics, though like all Siamese Twins—at least according to legend—they differ radically even in their double addiction. One of
them is also on "uppers," while the other prefers "downers"; and one

is a member of Alcoholics Anonymous, while the other is reasonably content to remain a drunk.

Despite his exploitation of the ambiguities of freakiness as defined in the seventies and his use of certain up-to-date narrative techniques, there is, in another sense, something hopelessly dated about Newlove's treatment of Siamese Twins. His consciousness of their plight seems to have been set before the first successful operations had occurred, and he refuses, therefore, to let the possibility of surgical separation haunt his joined pair, as it *must* all such twins in our time. Perhaps, as Brian de Palma suggests in the extraordinary film *Sisters* (1974), that possibility is finally a delusion on any level deeper than the physical; but de Palma begins at least with already separated siblings, as no novelist has yet done. And he ends by evoking the mystery long sensed in the presence of such prodigies—as a reporter-voyeur, seeking to discover which divided sister is guilty of murder, discovers not only that they are still one, but that she in the act of beholding has become one with them.

Still, Siamese Twins fail somehow to seem as central to the deepest obsessions of this age as they apparently did over a period which began just before the Civil War and ended with the Great Depression. All classic denizens of the Ten-in-One, which is to say, all Freaks with true mythological resonance, are able to move some normals always. But from time to time, one or another of them assumes special importance, symbolizing the deepest concerns of an era, like Dwarfs in the seventeenth century, Giants in the eighteenth, uglies and beast/humans in the nineteenth. In our own time Hermaphrodites and Geeks seem chiefly to fill that role. The former have a special pathos at the moment because, like Siamese Twins, they have become repairable, and the Half Man/Half Woman begins to pass from the realm of unalterable destiny to that of problematic choice.

The situation, however, of a parent asked, "Would you prefer to have this child go through life as a boy or a girl?" is radically different from that of one asked, "Would you prefer to have these children grow up joined or separated?" No matter how deeply traditional distinctions between self and other have been challenged by modern psychological, philosophical, or religious speculation, our basic notions of identity have not appreciably altered. Theories about sex roles and gender distinction, on the other hand, have been so rapidly changing that for not a few contemporaries androgyny has come to seem a desirable goal. Nonetheless, physiological intersexuality remains entangled in the minds of most ordinary men and women with homosexuality and transsexuality, both of which stir in them distrust, if not downright loathing. They are likely, therefore, to respond with horror as well as begrudged fascination to pop musicians who act out the mystery of sex-shifting on the stage, or to images of androgynous superstars in films like *Performance* (starring Mick Jagger) or Brian de Palma's *Phantom of the Paradise*. Indeed, such ambivalence is built into those movies by their makers.

Writers of science fiction, most notably Philip José Farmer and Ursula Le Guin, have imagined worlds in which physiological bisexuality is a viable norm. But in both his *The Lovers* (1952) and her *The Left Hand of Darkness* (1965), those worlds are remote and alien places, experienced more like dreams than everyday reality by genitally "normal" earth creatures, for whom they represent absolute otherness. Certainly, no major work about mutants born to humans has presented them in the guise of sexually active Hermaphrodites. Often, they are portrayed as pre-pubescent children, as if to avoid confronting that problem. And when they are permitted to attain genital maturity, like Heinlein's Valentine Michael Smith, they are likely to be "straight" heterosexuals, extraordinarily endowed, perhaps, but not with the equipment of both sexes.

Similarly, androgynes when they appear in the "mainstream" fiction of our century before 1967 tend to be located elsewhere, though in inner space rather than outer, as required by a tradition that denies itself the myth of intergalactic travel along with that of the mutant. In Virginia Woolf's *Orlando* (1928), which comes closer to s-f techniques than she could have been aware, her eponymous hero, who is to live five hundred years, turns overnight from male ephebe, English Renaissance style, to a "ravishing" female, who "combined in one the strength of a man and a woman's grace."

> He stretched himself. He rose. He stood upright in complete nakedness before us, and while the trumpets pealed Truth! Truth! Truth! we have no choice left but to confess—he was a woman.

The tone is confusing—ironic, mock-mythological. But one thing is clear: his/her sex-shifting has nothing to do with the eight or ten or twelve actual human intersexes but much with the AC/DC sex life of contemporary Bloomsbury, and especially with the bisexual longings of a well-born rich and scholarly lady who felt at home in Sodom as long as she could convince herself that it was continuous with the lovely and even more erotically ambiguous past she had first read about in her father's library.

James Joyce, born on the ragged edges of the Irish petite bourgeoisie, clearly was not at all at home with sexual ambiguity. Whatever impulse he recognized in himself toward transvestism or even assuming a passive role in the act of love, he found an occasion for guilt—though also for bitter amusement. And he projected such guilts onto Leopold Bloom, voyeur, masturbator, and sniffer of ladies' underwear, who in the midst of the Night-Town episode in *Ulysses* is turned into a woman, even as Bella Cohen, the madam of the whorehouse he is visiting, becomes a man.

> BLOOM
> (*A sweat breaking out over him*) Not man. (*He sniffs*) Woman.
>
> BELLO
> (*Stands up*) No more blow hot and cold. What you longed for has come to pass. Henceforth you are unmanned and mine in earnest, a thing under yoke.

Obviously, we are here not in the realm of revelation, but of drunken hallucination, where androgyny, though secretly lusted for, represents an ultimate horror rather than an idyllic vision. And the scene is rendered with queasiness and disgust, which reaches its climax when Bella/Bello, bemustached and bemuscled, thrusts his/her naked arm "elbow deep in Bloom's vulva," crying out like an auctioneer to the male bystanders:

> There's a fine depth for you! That give you a hardon? (*He shoves his arm in a bidder's face.*) Here wet the deck and wipe it round!

Bids are forthcoming, as Bella/Bello instructs Bloom on how to behave in order to increase his sexual allure. "Bring all your power of fascination to bear on them," she whispers in his ear; and when he

Bella/Bello and Bloom. Contemporary prints by Saul Field.
Courtesy the artist, Willowdale, Ontario

blushes and simpers, she adds, "What else are you good for, an impotent thing like you?" We have been watching a travesty of the myth of androgyny: a revelation of the sado-masochism, buggery, and impotence which Joyce believed lay behind all of its elegant mythologizing. We are, in any event, at a maximum distance from the advocacy of bisexual behavior, or the suggestion that actual sex Freaks might be models for possibilities of total satisfaction denied to most of us by our unambiguous genitalia.

It is not until 1974 that such a suggestion was made explicit in fiction with the publication of Alan Friedman's *Hermaphrodeity*. His heroine/hero, called eventually Millie/Willie, is born an intersex, chooses to remain one, begets a daughter on herself by himself, and at the end is about to beget a grandchild on her. But Millie is not aware that she has a viable penis as well as a penetrable vulva until she reaches puberty, when the decision on what to do with her doubleness is in her own power. The doctors, of course, urge surgery, and her parents give advice from the sidelines. "It's elementary logic!" her father argues. "Either! Or!"; to which her mother responds, "Neither," and she decides, "Both."

Not that she is untroubled by her monstrous status. Indeed, long after she ("Yes," Friedman writes at one point, " 'he' + 'she' = 'she' ") has made it with both sexes and has become an immensely successful business tycoon, poet, archeologist, and fertility goddess, she is still reminding herself that she "had always proposed to avoid becoming a hooting bleating walking talking Believe-It-Or-Not circus sideshow curio and freak." It is not until—by participating in surviving primitive rites, excavating to paleolithic depths to uncover ancient icons of androgyny, and releasing herself from ego consciousness with a long-buried psychedelic seed—that she is able to believe herself an avatar of the Hermaphrodite rather than a joke of nature. Before that, she had assimilated the lore of the rabbis about the bisexual primal Adam, the teaching of the alchemists about the hermaphroditic prime matter, and the speculations of evolutionists about the "obscure creature" at the beginnings of the human phylogenetic line, "who possessed both sexes *in the same individual.*" But not until, in the spirit of '68, she has "freaked out" on the Ur-drug does she realize in her mutant flesh what that flesh has peculiarly prepared her to know: "that images of sex had nothing to do with anything that was now happening or had ever happened. Nor did anyone's genitalia, never."

In many ways, *Hermaphrodeity* seems the book the age demanded, combining mysticism, biology, and psycho-chemistry, as well as blending the myth of the mutant with the image of the Freak. It is, moreover, skillfully written, learned but not ponderous, witty but not finally flip; but it did not win either old-fashioned "serious" readers of literature or the new youth audience. I tried in vain to persuade my fellow judges to give it the National Book Award, or even to consider it a real contender in the year of its appearance. And it has failed to become an underground favorite among those who prefer images to print but from time to time buy (or rip off) and read pop theology like Carlos Castaneda's and Robert Pirsig's or whimsical fantasy like Richard Adams' *Watership Down.*

Part of the problem arises surely from the fact that actual inter-

sexes have not yet been assimilated to the mythology of mass culture, like Siamese Twins and Pinheads, or even transsexuals who
have been surgically altered in gender. Typically, Hermaphrodites
by choice rather than biological fate move contemporary onlookers,
who rush home from the rock concert to seek assurance in fan magazines that Mick Jagger really balls girls and Alice Cooper offstage
is as straight as any of his bourgeois neighbors. It is androgyny as
sham or make-believe to which contemporary audiences respond: a
deliberately assumed condition which can be reversed when fashion
changes. Actual Klinefelters or Turners are too unequivocally *for
real*, and tend, therefore, to be surrendered to the doctors for repair
and "normalization."

The Geek, on the other hand, seems these days to be coming
into his own, precisely because he is a fictional Freak, not merely
perceived through a pre-existent mythological grid like Giants and
Dwarfs and the Lion-faced Man, but invented to satisfy psychic
needs bred by infantile traumas or unquiet ancestral memories.
He fits into the traditional category of Wild Men, like Zip before
him; or more specifically into that of the cannibal, associated by
Europeans from earliest times with other wonders of barbarian lands
like men "whose heads do grow between their shoulders." What he
eats raw, however, are not fellow humans but repulsive forms of
lower animal life, chiefly chickens and rats—biting off their heads
before they are dead and slobbering his chin with their fetid blood.
Nonetheless, he has been included recently in a vision of the primitive and archaic which stirs admiration and nostalgia, and includes
such contemporary heroes and beautiful anti-heroes as Kaspar Hauser, the Wild Boy of Aveyron, King Kong, Dracula, and Tarzan.
Burroughs' accounts of the latter, for instance, provide over and over
images of him gorging himself on raw flesh:

> The ape-man had no knife, but nature had equipped him
> with the means of tearing his food from the quivering flank of his
> prey . . . Ah, but it had been delicious! . . . in the bottom of
> his heart there had constantly been the craving for the warm
> meat of the fresh kill, and the rich, red blood.

Actually, it is nobler prey than rodents on which the immortal
Lord of the Jungle feasts, and he has first tracked them down and

killed them. But Bram Stoker's Vampire Voivode, who also has triumphed over death, prefers living victims; though it is not he who,
in a legend which has proved even more long-lived than himself,
seems the prototype of the side show Geek, since, belonging not to
the realm of pathology but of the occult, he is in the end more monster than Freak. It is, rather, Renfield, a mortal and weak human
like us, diagnosed as a "zoophagous maniac" and confined to an
insane asylum because he likes to eat flies, snatched living from the
air. Straitjacketed and chained to a wall, he still dreams zoophagy
even as he is tempted toward the ultimate horror of cannibalism by
Dracula:

> Then he began to whisper: "Rats, rats, rats! Hundreds, thou-
> sands, millions of them, and every one a life; and dogs to eat
> them, and cats too. All lives! all red blood, with years of life in it;
> and not merely buzzing flies! . . . All these lives will I give you,
> ay, and many more and greater, through countless ages, if you
> fall down and worship me!"

Moreover, a few pages later we are shown the wife of the tale's
first narrator, Jonathan Harker, actually performing the unspeakable
act in the presence of her husband, with the Count this time playing
the role of rapist rather than seducer:

> With his left hand he held both Mrs. Harker's hands, keeping
> them away with his, her arms at full tension; his right hand
> gripped her by the back of her neck, forcing her face down on
> his bosom. Her white nightdress was smeared with blood, and a
> thin stream trickled down the man's bare breast . . . The atti-
> tude of the two had a terrible resemblance to a child forcing a
> kitten's nose into a saucer of milk to compel it to drink.

At long last the ill-kept secret is out. The analogue always implicit
in vampirism becomes manifest as Mina Harker wipes from her chin
the vital fluids she has just sucked "in a half swoon" from the naked
body of one who we must assume had also drunk hers. "Unclean!
Unclean!" she cries, looking down on her unconscious husband afterward. "I must touch him or kiss him no more." Clearly she knows
that henceforth she will be betrayed by the chastest marital em-

brace to the ultimate sexual transgression she has learned in an adulterous union more intimate than mere copulation.

But the Victorian era is dead, is it not, and with it the odd conviction that God intended us to pleasure each other in one position only. We live in an age, in fact, in which medical authorities urge oral-genital sex on us all, and Linda Lovelace has demonstrated how to do it properly in *Deep Throat*, the most popular X-rated film ever made. It is not merely that fellatio and cunnilingus are permitted these days, but—in an age which has chosen orality over full genitality on all fronts—they have come to occupy the center of love-making; or so at least contemporary erotic literature would seem to indicate. Small wonder, then, that mythological Vampires and real-life Geeks appeal to us so deeply, symbolizing as they do both the desire to eat and be eaten by the other, and the self-punishing fantasy that the mouth which opens to receive our genitals may clamp down to maim and destroy us. "Eat me, baby," cries the rigid lover to the woman kneeling before him, theoretically as eager as he, but often as troubled as Mina Harker with a sense of being subjugated if not soiled, and a consequent desire for revenge. Repressed as unworthy in the heyday of sexual emancipation, such reactions have recently been legitimized by the rise of radical feminism, whose implicit slogan is MAKE WAR NOT LOVE. And they are expressed with characteristic lack of subtlety in a postcard published by the Berkeley Print Mart, which shows a young woman grinning triumphantly down on a skeleton and saying, "He asked me to eat him. And I did."

In any case, the image of the Geek begins to reappear everywhere in our culture, from the *National Lampoon* to the TV cop show "Starsky and Hutch" and the kind of experimental novel described on the flyleaf as "not in the tradition of psychological fiction which has dominated the twentieth century." To be sure, that image has never been entirely absent from our literature since Eudora Welty evoked it in "Keela, the Outcast Indian Maiden." But not until the publication of Craig Nova's *The Geek* in 1975 was such a Freak preferred as a model, or geeking as a way of life preferable to that which most of us lead. Earlier Geeks were portrayed as absolute victims, driven to the black abyss of debasement by alcoholism or the accident of being born black, deformed, and not very bright. Nowhere is it suggested that some human beings enter on such a career because they crave warm blood and the savor of still-living flesh, like the sober, churchgoing Veronica Shant, whose departure from the world of the Ten-in-One old carnies still deplore. Interestingly, too, no literary Geek is portrayed as a woman, though Eudora Welty's Keela was exhibited as one and painted red as well, in an attempt perhaps to indicate that such performers belong entirely to the world of illusion. Welty suggests, moreover, and in this, too, her point of view is shared by no one else, that the horror of being cast in such a role may exist only for the sensitive beholder. Her "little crippled nigger," at any rate, though he may have whimpered and gratefully clutched the hand of the man who delivered him from the side show, turns out to remember his experience only as "de old times when I use to be wid de circus—"

In Lindsay Gresham's *Nightmare Alley*, which appeared a decade later, the situation is less equivocal, since the first Geek we meet, an abject drunk who does his act wearing grease paint, a ratty wig, and dirty underwear, is presented as a creature disgusting even to his own sodden self. We see him through the eyes of Stanton Carlisle, a monster of ambition, who beginning as a talker, becomes at the expense of everyone who trusts him, including that Geek, an immensely successful "Mind Reader," only to wind up an alcoholic gnawing off the heads of chickens for a drink. On the last page, in fact, we overhear the carnie boss giving him the traditional con with which we have earlier learned such performers are always recruited. "Hey, wait a minute . . ." he begins, "I got one job you might take a crack at. It ain't much, and I ain't begging you to take it; but it's a job . . . What do you say? Of course, it's only temporary—just until we get a real geek." What the answer will be we know, as we leave Stan clutching with trembling hands the soiled canvas of the tent, though the book closes before he speaks. But the movie version, more explicit here as elsewhere, actually gives him a line. "Mister, I was made for it," he says in a final spasm of self-deprecation, and despite the perfunctory scenes which follow hinting at the possibility of redemption, it is these words we remember as the story's real ending.

In Craig Nova's *The Geek*, an equally driven protagonist called Boot meets a similar fate, leaving a no longer endurable world of drug smuggling and murder for a seedy side show on a Greek island.

But this time it is another Geek who issues the invitation: a filthy monster with scabs on his face and bugs in his hair, who eats human shit as well as live chickens. Moreover, that Geek represents not degradation but a mystery which transcends the very possibility of degradation:

> The geek was so far beyond self as to be more than fascinating. The men and women who watched him did so in silence . . . as though the geek were the animated remains of a saint, something more holy than abasement. It was beyond the understanding of those who watched because it violated the basis on which the islanders turned both hatred and love: an unbreakable sense of self.

And when Boot chooses that lot in full consciousness, it is, therefore, peace which he finds, and a detachment not unlike that purportedly achieved in the disintegration of the ego by drugs. But first he must learn to eat what he has always considered abomination:

> Boot kneeled in the pen and the geek sat at its side and someone gave Boot a chicken . . . Boot bit the head off, tasted blood, felt his teeth severing tendons, breaking bones, the skull, tasted the bitter brains, broke the palsied beak, felt an eye burst . . . His gaze was distant and steady, since he was now safe, in league with everything he had despised, having found immunity by relinquishing all that had made struggle necessary: honor, character, word, anger . . .

Here is the final freak-out, the assumption of a monstrous role which, precisely because it has long been associated with sham, can be carried off not just in metaphor or at the rock concert or on the TV talk show, but in the Ten-in-One itself, where marks pay to see only what they believe is real. No normal can become a Giant, a Dwarf, a Siamese Twin, even an intersex. But anyone, merely by altering consciousness, can become a Geek, become for others the Freak he has always felt himself to be.

Not everyone, however, even in the dying twentieth century chooses to play such dangerous games. Most congenital malformations, in fact, seek with hormones, surgery, and psycho-endocrinology to become for others the normals they suspect they are. And most of us most of the time consider theirs to be the better part—except when at the side show and not sure whether we wake or sleep, we experience for a moment out of time the normality of Freaks, the freakishness of the normal, the precariousness and absurdity of being, however we define it, fully human.

The Geek. Drawing by Brad Holland for *The Geek,* by Craig Nova (1975).
Brad Holland

Bibliography

FICTION

Barth, John. "Petition," *Lost in the Funhouse*. Garden City, N.Y.: Doubleday, 1968.

Carroll, Lewis. *Alice's Adventures in Wonderland* and *Through the Looking-Glass*. New York: Macmillan, 1925.

Dante Alighieri. *The Divine Comedy*. New York: Pantheon Books, 1948.

de la Mare, Walter. *Memoirs of a Midget*. New York: Alfred A. Knopf, 1922.

Dickens, Charles. *The Old Curiosity Shop*. London: Chapman & Hall; and Henry Frowde, n.d.

Egan, Pierce (the Elder), *Sketches from Sporting Life*. London: Albion Press, n.d.

Fowler, Gene. *The Great Mouthpiece*. New York: Covici, 1931.

Friedman, Alan, *Hermaphrodeity: The Autobiography of a Poet*. New York: Alfred A. Knopf, 1972.

Goldman, Albert. *Ladies and Gentlemen—LENNY BRUCE!!* New York: Random House, 1971.

Gresham, William L. *Monster Midway*. New York: Rinehart, 1953.

Hugo, Victor. *The Laughing Man*. London: Routledge, 1887.

———. *Notre-Dame de Paris*. London: J. M. Dent & Sons, 1910.

Jacobs, Joseph. *English Fairy Tales*. New York: Dover Publications, 1967.

Lagerkvist, Pär. *The Dwarf*. Trans. by Alexandra Dick. New York: A. A. Wyn, 1945.

Lang, Doug. *Freaks*. London: New English Library, 1973.

Mitchell, Joseph. *McSorley's Wonderful Saloon*. New York: Grosset, 1959.

Montaigne, Michel. "Of the Cannibals" and "Of a Monstrous Child," in *The Essays of Montaigne*. Trans. by John Florio; Intro. by J. I. M. Stewart. New York: Modern Library, 1933.

Nabokov, Vladimir. "Scenes from the Life of a Double Monster," *Nabokov's Dozen*. Freeport, N.Y.: Books for Libraries Press, 1969.

Newlove, Donald. *The Drunks*. New York: Saturday Review Press, E. P. Dutton, 1974.

———. *Leo & Theodore*. New York: Saturday Review Press, 1972.

Nova, Craig. *The Geek*. New York: Harper & Row, 1975.

Poe, Edgar Allan. "Hop-Frog," in *The Complete Works of Edgar Allan Poe*. Vol. VI. New York and London: G. P. Putnam's Sons, 1902.

———. "Narrative of A. Gordon Pym," in *The Complete Works of Edgar Allan Poe*. Vol. II. New York and London: G. P. Putnam's Sons, 1902.

Swift, Jonathan. *Gulliver's Travels*. New York and London: Macmillan, 1894.

Twain, Mark. *Pudd'nhead Wilson*. New York: Century Company, 1893–94.

———. "Personal Habits of the Siamese Twins," in *Sketches New and Old*. New York and London: Harper & Brothers, 1903.

Whittemore, Edward. *Quin's Shanghai Circus*. New York: Popular Library, 1974.

NONFICTION

Ambrosinus, B. Ulisse Aldrovandi's *Monstrorum historia*. Bologna: Tebaldini, 1642.

Anon. *An Account of the Life, Personal Appearance, Character and Manners of Charles S. Stratton, the American Dwarf, known as General Tom Thumb . . .* London, 1844.

———. *Biography of Madame Fortune Clofullia, the Bearded Lady*. New York: Baker, Godwin, 1854.

———. *Julia Pastrana*. London: C. Housefield, 1857.

———. *Life of the Celebrated Bearded Lady, Madame Clofullia*. New York: 1854.

———. *Life of the Siamese Twins*. New York: T. W. Strong, 1853.

———. *Millie-Christine, History and Medical Description of the Two-Headed Girl*. Buffalo, N.Y.: Warren, Johnson, 1869.

Aristotle. *Generation of Animals*. Trans. by A. L. Peck. Cambridge: Harvard University Press, 1953.

Baring-Gould, Sabine. *Curious Myths of the Middle Ages*. London: Rivingtons, 1886.

Barnum, P. T. *Struggles and Triumphs: or, The Life of P. T. Barnum*. New York and London: Alfred A. Knopf, 1927.

Bernheimer, Richard. *Wild Men in the Middle Ages*. Cambridge: Harvard University Press, 1952.

Betts, J. R. "P. T. Barnum and the Popularization of Natural History," *Journal of the History of Ideas*, 1959.

Boaistuau (or Boistuau, Boaystuau), Pierre. *Histoires prodigieuses les plus mémorables qui ayent este obseruées, depuis la Natiuité de Jesus Christ, iusques à notre siècle . . . A Paris, pour Vincent Serteras, etc. . . . ,* 1560.

Boruwlaski, Josef. *Life and Love Letters of a Dwarf.* London: Ibisher, 1902.

————. *Memoirs of the Celebrated Dwarf.* London, 1788.

Buffon, C. L. L. de. *Sur les monstres. In histoire naturelle de l'Homme.* Paris, 1749.

Buffon, G. L. le Clerc. *Histoire naturelle générale et particulière.* Paris: L'Imprimerie Royale, 1777.

Calvin, Lee. "There Were Giants on the Earth," *Seville Chronicle,* Seville, Ohio, 1959.

Carmichael, Bill. *Incredible Collectors, Weird Antiques, and Odd Hobbies.* Englewood Cliffs, N.J.: Prentice-Hall, 1971.

Cervellati, Alessandro. *Questa sera grande spettacolo.* Collezione "Mondo Poplare," Milan, 1961.

Chang. *Autobiography of Chang.* London: Arless, 1866.

Charpentier, Louis. *Les Géants et le mystère des origines.* Paris: R. Laffont, 1969.

Clair, Colin. *Strong Man Egyptologist.* London: Oldbourne, 1957.

Comas, Juan. *Dos Microcéfalos "Aztecas."* Mexico City: Instituto de Investigaciones Históricas, 1968.

Cuvier, G. L. C. F. D. de. *Discours sur les révolutions du globe. Etudes sur l'ibis et mémoire sur la Venus hottentote.* Paris: Passard, 1864.

Davenport, John. *Curiositatis eroticae physioligiae.* London, 1875.

Dawkes, Thomas. *Prodigium Willinghamense.* London, 1747.

Delcourt, Marie. *Hermaphrodite.* London: Studio Books, 1961.

Disher, M. Willson. *Pharaoh's Fool.* London: Heinemann, 1957.

Drimmer, Frederick. *Very Special People.* New York: Amjon Publishers, 1973.

Duhamel, Bernard, in collaboration with Pierre Haegel and Robert Pagès. *Morphogenèse pathologique: Des monstruosités aux malformations.* Paris: Masson, 1966.

Durant, John, and Alice. *Pictorial History of the American Circus.* New York: A. S. Barnes, 1957.

Edwards, Frank. *Strange People.* New York: Lyle Stuart, 1961.

Foss, Daniel. *Freak Culture: Life-Style and Politics.* New York: E. P. Dutton, 1972.

Futcher, Palmer Howard. *Giants and Dwarfs.* Cambridge: Harvard University Press, 1933.

Geoffroy Saint-Hilaire, Isidore. *Histoire générale et particulière des anomalies de l'organisation chez l'homme et les animaux; . . . ou traite de teratologie.* Paris: J. B. Balliere, 1832.

Gould, George M., and Walter L. Pyle. *Anomalies and Curiosities of Medicine.* New York: Bell Publishing Co., 1896.

Hodge, Margaret. *Early Anthropology in the Sixteenth and Seventeenth Centuries.* Philadelphia: University of Pennsylvania Press, 1964.

Hughes, Eileen Lanouette. *On the Set of Fellini Satyricon.* New York: Morrow, 1971.

Hunter, J. *On Monsters . . .* London: Van Voorst, 1775.

Hunter, Kay. *Duet for a Lifetime: The Story of the Original Siamese Twins.* New York: Coward-McCann, 1964.

Hunter, Robert. *The Storming of the Mind.* Garden City, N.Y.: Doubleday, 1971.

Janson, H. W. *Apes and Ape Lore.* University of London, the Warburg Institute, 1952.

Jones, Howard, Jr., and William Wallace Scott. *Hermaphroditism, Genital Anomalies and Related Endocrine Disorders.* Baltimore: Williams and Wilkins, 1958.

Jones, W. H. S. *Hippocrates Translation.* Cambridge: Harvard University Press, 1957.

Lee, Polly Jae. *Giant: Pictorial History of the Human Colossus.* New York: A. S. Barnes, 1970.

Lewis, Arthur H. *Carnival.* New York: Trident Press, 1970.

Ley-Deutsch, Maria. *Le Gueux Chez Victor Hugo.* Paris: Librairie E. Droz, 1936.

Leydi, Roberto (ed.). *La Piazza.* Milano Collano del "Gallo Grarde," 1959.

Licetus, Fortunis. *De monstrorum causis, natura, et differentiis libro duo, in quibus . . .* Patavii: Apud Gas Parum Criuellarium, 1616.

M'Crindle, J. W. (trans.). *Ancient India as Described in Classical Literature.* Westminster: Archibald Constable, 1901.

McKennon, Joe. *A Pictorial History of the American Carnival.* Sarasota, Fla.: Carnival Publishers, 1971.

McWhirter, Norris, and Ross. *Guinness Book of World Records.* New York: Sterling, 1976.

Mall, Franklin P. *A Study of the Causes Underlying the Origin of Human Monsters.* Philadelphia: Wistar Institute of Anatomy and Biology, 1908.

Malson, Lucien. *Wolf Children and the Problem of Human Nature.* With the complete text of *The Wild Boy of Aveyron,* by Jean-Marc-Gaspard Itard. New York and London: Monthly Review Press, 1972.

Martin, E. *Histoire des monstres depuis l'antiquité.* Paris: C. Reinwald, 1880.

May, Earl Chapin. *The Circus from Rome to Ringling.* New York: Duffield and Green, 1932.

Milligen, J. G. *Curiosities of Medical Experience.* London: Michael Bartley, 1838.

Mittwoch, Ursula. *Genetics of Sex Differentiation.* New York and London: Academic Press, 1973.

Money, John. *Sex Errors of the Body.* Baltimore: Johns Hopkins Press, 1968.

Montagu, Ashley. *The Elephant Man: A Study in Human Dignity.* New York: Ballantine Books, 1971.

Moreau, Paul. *Fous et bouffons.* Paris: Balliere et fils, 1885.

Moreno Villa, José. *Locos, enanos, negros y niños palaciegos.* Mexico City: Editorial Presencia, 1939.

Obsequens, Julius. *Des Prodiges.* Lyon, 1555.

Pancoast, W. H. "Report of the Autopsy of the Siamese Twins, Together with other interesting information concerning their Life." Reprinted from the *Philadelphia Medical Times.* Philadelphia: J. B. Lippincott, 1874.

Paracelsus. *De animalibus natis ex sodomia.* 1493.

Paré, Ambroise. *Animaux, monstres et prodiges.* Paris: Le Club Français du Livre, 1954.

Pauwels, Louis, and Jacques Bergier. *The Morning of the Magicians.* Trans. by Rollo Myers. New York: Stein and Day, 1964.

Plessis, James Paris du. "A Short History of Human Prodigies and Monstrous Births, of Dwarfs, Sleepers, Giants, Strong Men, Hermaphrodites, Numerous Births and Extreme Old Age." London: The British Library, unpublished.

Rueff, Jacob. *De conceptu et generatione hominis.* Francofurti ad Moenum: Book 5, item 7, p. 41, 1587.

Rund, Max. *Photo Album of Human Oddities.* Side Show Publications, 1975.

Saltarino, Signor (pseud. H. W. Otto), with M. Behrend. *Fahrend Volk.* Leipzig: 1895.

Stratton, Lavinia Warren. *Memoirs.* Library of the New York Historical Society, unpublished.

Thompson, C. J. S. *The Mystery and Lore of Monsters.* London: Williams and Norgate, 1930.

Tietze-Conrat, Erika. *Dwarfs and Jesters in Art.* New York: Phaidon Publishers, 1957.

Toole-Stott, R. *Circus and Allied Arts World Bibliography.* Derby, England: Harpur & Sons, 1967.

Treves, Frederick. *The Elephant Man and Other Reminiscences.* London: Cassell, 1923.

————. "A Case of Congenital Deformity." *Transactions of the Pathological Society.* London: Pathological Society, 1885.

Velasquez, Pedro. *Illustrated Memoir* . . . London, 1853.

Walff, C. F. *Theoria Generations.* Halle, 1759.

Wallace, Irving. *The Fabulous Showman: The Life and Times of P. T. Barnum.* New York: Alfred A. Knopf, 1959.

Warkany, Joseph. *Congenital Malformations.* Year Book Medical Publishers, 1971.

Wittkower, Rudolf. "Marvels of the East: A Study in the History of Monsters." London: *Journal of the Warburg and Courtauld Institutes,* 1942.

Wolff, Etienne. *La Science des monstres.* Paris: Gallimard, 1948.

Wood, E. J. *Giants and Dwarfs.* London: Richard Bentley, 1868.

Index